Sandra McCosh was born in the United States in 1950. She attended the University of California at Berkeley and graduated in 1973. She spent the following year in England, studying at Leeds University for her M.A. degree in Folk Life Studies, and it was during this time that she collected much of the material now included in *Children's Humour*. Since her return to the United States, she has been living and working in California.

Sandra McCosh

Children's Humour

A Joke for Every Occasion

With an Introduction by G. Legman

PANTHER
GRANADA PUBLISHING
London Toronto Sydney New York

Published by Granada Publishing Limited
in Panther Books 1979
in association with Hanau Publications Ltd

ISBN 0 586 04876 6

A Panther UK Original
Copyright © Sandra McCosh 1976
Introduction Copyright © G. Legman 1976

Granada Publishing Limited
Frogmore, St Albans, Herts AL2 2NF
and
3 Upper James Street, London W1R 4BP
866 United Nations Plaza, New York, NY 10017, USA
117 York Street, Sydney, NSW 2000, Australia
100 Skyway Avenue, Rexdale, Ontario, M9W 3A6, Canada
PO Box 84165, Greenside, 2034 Johannesburg, South Africa
CML Centre, Queen & Wyndham, Auckland 1, New Zealand

Reproduced, printed and bound in Great Britain by
Cox & Wyman Ltd, Reading
Set in Monotype Bembo

Granada ®
Granada Publishing ®

CONTENTS

INTRODUCTION

I. CHILDREN, FOLKLORE & SEX

CHILDREN are the last frontier. Beyond them there is nothing, and
when they are destroyed everything is destroyed. Friedrich Froebel,
who introduced the first kindergartens, said it forever: '*Our children
will be our judges.*' Until now, most of the judging has been done by
adults, with children as the objects and generally the victims. This is
very ancient, as witness the incredible chapter of perverted gloating
on the subject of punishing children, two thousand years ago, in the
Apocrypha to the Old Testament, *Ecclesiasticus,* chapter XXX,
beginning: 'He that loveth his son causeth him oft to feel the rod.' It
is not by any means a thing of the past, as the Societies for the
Prevention of Cruelty to Children in all countries can testify.

We have been present and assisting, for over two hundred and
fifty years in the West, at a process of purposeful perversion of the
character, the life and lore of children from almost their earliest infancy. In this process, the rather mild and normal expressions of the
sexual and scatological interests and explorations of the children
themselves, in rhymes, games, jokes, puns, and stories common
among them throughout childhood and adolescence, are turned – or
are attempted to be turned – by helpful adults, springing up with
prefabricated expurgations and imitations, into violently cruel and
sadistic *fakelore,* with which it is intended to block out and replace
all authentic expressions of the child's nascent sexuality. The whole
literature of 'nursery rhymes,' as they are called, and all of the
children's formal literature and even games since the mid-eighteenth
century in the West, are the complete course in this attempted
retraining of normally sexual and scatological children into nasty
and neurotic adults, seething with the demanded sexual repression
that is matched by the openly inculcated anal compulsions and
aggressions. This is the 'official' contour of all children's folklore in
the West, and of much of the folklore of adults as well, and has been

the entire content of the wholly faked children's literature and the study of their folklore until very recently.

The earliest attack on the immorality of children's folk-rhymes in English seems to have been made by the Puritan poet and satirist, George Wither, in his collection of pious exercises and political diatribes, *Halelujah, or Britain's Second Remembrancer* (1641), the last firing-up of the strain of his *Abuses Stript and Whipt* (1613) in which, among many other things, Wither had castigated the smoking of tobacco as bestial, sinful and foolish. It took nearly a century for Puritan repressiveness of this type to become the ideal of all middle-class morality in England, keyed as this was to the open and yet somehow tacit political goal of wresting power from the hereditary nobility in and after the English Revolution.

Literary sin having been condemned as the culpable prerogative of courts and Royalists, flowering up rankly in one last unashamed burst after the Restoration in the 1660's, the British middle class backed up its slow-burning revolutionary powder-train in the early eighteenth century with a fiercely Puritan morality, at least in what concerned language and literature. The whipmasters-general of this movement were, as is well known, Pope, Addison, Johnson, Richardson, and all the rest of the Augustan and Della Cruscan would-be 'purifiers' of English. This intense sexual restraint also absurdly attacked most of the early folksong collectors of the period, from Allan Ramsay in his *Tea-Table Miscellany* in the 1730's – note the title – and onward, as I have shown in *The Horn Book* (1964) p. 343–44. A glacial veneer of literary morality and tergiversating prose, combined with a violent censorship both sexual and political, became the rule and stayed the rule in English (and American) letters for a full two centuries, until the first cracks broke open in the censorship structure in Europe during the 1890's, leading to its virtual collapse at the present time.

Here is a striking example, to start with, of how the literary censorship has operated on the body of children's folklore and folk-rhyme, to substitute sadism and violence for harmless sexual allusions. One of the most charming folk-poems of known authorship in the English language is "There Was a Little Man," attributed in the 1764 edition to the Restoration wit, Sir Charles Sedley, who died in 1701. It begins:

There was a little man,
And he woo'd a little maid,
And he said, Little maid, will you wed, wed, wed?
I have little more to say,
Than will you, yea or nay?
For the least said is soonest mendèd, ded, ded.

Then this little maid she said,
Little sir, you've little said
To induce a little maid for to wed, wed, wed.
You must say a little more,
And produce a little ore,
E're I make a little print in your bed, bed, bed.

The first improvement later wreaked on this delightful piece, with its infectious, stamping rhythm, which stands first in *Mother Goose's Melody* entitled "A Love Song," was in the final line, expurgating the maid's *'little print in your bed, bed, bed'* to the religio-moral *'Ere I to the church will be led, led, led.'* But even that was not enough: the whole thing was evidently too amorous to suit. And so we find it wholly rewritten in the earliest extant nursery-rhyme book in English, *Tom Thumb's Pretty Song Book,* Vol. II (*ca.* 1744), into the gloatingly sadistic version still current today:

There was a little man,
And he had a little gun,
And his bullets they were made of lead, lead, lead.
He went to the brook,
And he shot a little duck,
Right through the middle of the head, head, head!

(*Sometimes:* 'And he left the little birdie dead, dead, dead!')

Whatever else might be said about this, one thing is sure: this nasty little revision of Sedley's charmingly sexual love song, from mild erotism into crude sadism, is not the work of any child. We have here, instead, the intrusive hand − not to say foot − of some helpful adult, throwing out the little man and maid in their little bed-bed-bed, to replace all these with the more edifying combination of the little man and his little gun-gun-gun, and the little duck whom he shoots dead-dead-dead. It would probably be too Freudian to suggest that perhaps this gun and shooting are still sexually symbolic, under their 'pure' sadistic disguise, and I will not insist. Let us agree that it is all *perfectly pure* sadism. And that is how children's nursery songs and rhymes, and the matching charms and stories, have been purified since the early eighteenth century to satisfy the moral exigencies, not of children but of adults.

A dozen further examples could be given of the method just demonstrated, but actually this one, "There Was a Little Man," typifies and subsumes all of them, on the principle involved in reconstructing dinosaurs' skeletons to scale from one single discovered bone: *Ab uno disce omnes.* But here is one other. In the first serious English folkloristic collection, John Aubrey's curiously superstitious *Remaines of Gentilisme and Judaisme* (MS. 1686/7, edited by James Britten, 1881, Folk-Lore Society, Vol. IV), a work about which I have said a good deal more in *The Horn Book* (1964), Aubrey gives among numerous other bawdy folk-rhymes and charms of the children of his century the following homely little item, probably referring actually to inguinal pinworms in children, which he calls 'An old filthy Rhyme used by base people, *viz.*:

> When I was a young Maid, and
>   wash't my Mothers dishes,
> I putt my finger in my — and
>   pluck't-out little Fishes.'

Compare Mercutio's description of Queen Mab's waggoner, in Shakespeare's *Romeo & Juliet* (about 1595) I. iv. 65–66, as being 'Not half so big as a round little worm, Prick'd from the lazy finger of a maid.' This unseemly reference to the child's genitals or rectum, recorded by Aubrey, immediately disappears in the purified nursery collections, and even in Will Penkethman's late-seventeenth century play, *Love without Interest, or The Man too hard for the Master* (1699), where the inquisitive finger is instead put 'in the pail,' as, in the later nursery-rhyme books, 'in my ear,' and even 'in my eye'! In a mid-nineteenth century American collection, *The Only True Mother Goose Melodies* (Boston, *ca.* 1843), the whole situation is expurgated edifyingly into:

When I was a little boy
I washed my mammy's dishes,
Now I am a great big boy
I roll in golden riches.

The identical process modified into 'pure nonsense' – another important type of disguise – an openly phallic folk-rhyme first quoted by the mad Edgar in Shakespeare's *King Lear* (1608) III. iv. 78, as 'Pillicock sat on Pillicock-hill,' and still in circulation in its complete form two centuries later, as recorded in Joseph Ritson's *Gammer Gurton's Garland, or The Nursery Parnassus* (ed. 1810):

Pillycock, pillycock, sate on a hill,
If he's not gone – he sits there still.

As first in print, however, even in the bawdy songbooks of the early eighteenth century, for example *The Academy of Complements* (ed. 1714), 'pillicock' disappears, and the rhyme is given only as part of an old catch in 'pure nonsense' form:

There was an old woman liv'd under a hill,
And if she's not gone she lives there still.

One final example, and this more significant than might appear. In the earliest extant collection of English nursery rhymes, *Tommy Thumb's Pretty Song Book*, Vol. II (London: Mary Cooper, 1744), here is the second little rhyme innocently given:

Little Robin red breast
Sitting on a pole,
Niddle, Noddle, went his head,
And Poop went his Hole.

By the end of the century this mildly scatological last line had dived into almost total obscurity, with a record number of expurgations. In their magistral *Oxford Dictionary of Nursery Rhymes* (1951, rev. 1973) No. 452, p. 372, Iona & Peter Opie observe its being originally a 'rude little jest.' This remark is improved upon in William & Ceil Baring-Gould's heavily derivative – though chronological rather than alphabetical – *Annotated Mother Goose*

(1962) p. 26, note 4, as 'a crude little jest which later editors were quick to refine.' Actually, they were not so quick, since it is only in the 1790's that Robin Red-breast is generally found sitting instead on a *rail*, so that whatever his head might do, 'Wag went his tail.' The Opies also interestingly give a lightly-expurgated survival of the original version into our own century, as 'learnt from a nanny' in 1950:

> Little Robin Redbreast sat upon a pole,
> Wiggle waggle went his tail, pop! through the hole.

Note again that these are by no means all the old nursery rhymes which have been expurgated. Some have entirely disappeared, *spurlos versenkt,* from the usual collections, such as two also appearing in *Tommy Thumb's Pretty Song Book*, about 1744: one beginning 'Blackamoor, Taunymoor,' which shocked the Baring-Goulds so much that they would not quote it complete, though on the same page 35 they do give the other:

> Piss a Bed, Piss a Bed,
> Barley Butt,
> Your Bum is so heavy
> You can't get up.

By the late eighteenth century, children's folklore had completely capitulated, at least in its public appearances in print. Big literary guns were shooting at the nursery rhymes as immoral, in particular Mrs. Sarah Trimmer (who died in 1810), a Sunday-school teacher and early author of properly educational children's books. So also her later American counterpart, Samuel Goodrich, the first real tycoon of the children's book industry, who, under the name of 'Peter Parley,' beginning in 1827, produced over a hundred volumes of instructive tales for children, actually written for him by a staff of hacks. As, later, Alexandre Dumas began the modern best-seller mill, with his string of historical novels in the style of Sir Walter Scott, using a whole corps of 'collaborators' and ghost-writers. William Holmes McGuffey's famous *McGuffey's Eclectic Readers* (1836–37), of which over 120,000,000 copies were sold – principally in the nineteenth century, you understand – hardly more than pressed down on the profitable groove that Mrs. Trimmer and 'Peter Parley' had already discovered, of depriving children of their folklore, so far as possible, and substituting for this the didactic little volumelets preferred by parents and eventual employers, and also very profitable to their authors and publishers.

One last work gave some of the authentic old rhymes, before the ultimate blackout under the crushing influence of the then-new children's book industry and the concomitant censorship of early Victorianism, which in fact settled down upon England long before Victoria's time, during the powerfully reactionary period following upon the French Revolution in the 1790's. This last farewell to children's folklore in its unabashed entirety was a humorous work called *Infant Institutes, or A Nurserical Essay on the Poetry, Lyric and Allegorical, of the Earliest Ages* (1797), written as a learnèd mock of the excesses of Shakespearean commentators by the Rev. B. N. Turner, a friend of Dr. Samuel Johnson. This was a type of burlesque based on folk materials, begun in Dr. William Wagstaffe's *Comment upon the History of Tom Thumb* in 1711, and taken to its ultimate point in Hyacinthe Cordonnier's *Le Chef d'Oeuvre d'un Inconnu* (1714), on which see my *The Horn Book*, p. 339–41; and in a brief but telling spoof, "On Jollity," in *The New Boghouse Miscellany, or A Companion for the Close-Stool* (1761) p. 207, which I have quoted in full in *The Horn Book*, p. 435–36, and in my *The Limerick* (ed. 1970) p. XXXV.

As the Reverend Turner knew he was writing for a sophisticated adult audience, he did not feel he had to expurgate his nursery rhymes, which he also did not derive from any of the usual expurgated published collections but presumably from his own childhood memories, which is a very good way when there is no other. This was also the case, at least in part, with the staggeringly eccentric work by John Bellenden Ker (originally Gawler), *An Essay on the Archaeology of Popular English Phrases, and Nursery Rhymes*, of which a first volume was published in 1834 and three further volumes in 1837–40, riotously explaining hundreds of folk phrases and rhymes according to the author's peculiar mania.

Ker's gloriously unconscious humor has been much appreciated by almost all serious writers on nursery rhymes, since his ostensible purpose was to demonstrate laboriously that all or most folk-rhymes and sayings in English are really 'code' forms of mispronounced or misapprehended curses against the clergy, and similar secret matters, all in the 'ancient Dutch language' — known only to himself, needless to say. The heavily sexual tone of his mania has, however, generally been overlooked, obviously on purpose, though his original audience understood it perfectly and was greatly distressed. For example, the reviewer for the London *Times* at the period, who remarked:

> We entreat that the FILTH may be first expunged from the book. Mr. Bellenden Ker has attempted to explain some of the nastiest sayings of the lowest of the *canaille*. No one could have desired this information, even if Mr. Bellenden Ker could have given it — which he cannot; and, in making the attempt, he is unnecessarily dirty, without being in the least degree useful.

This is quoted in Ker's second edition (1835, vol. I: p. 223) under "Filth," followed by his standard *explanations* of the following new terms, obviously in free-association order: 'A Dirty Dog,' 'A Scoundrel,' 'A Rascal,' 'Pillory,' and 'Kiss My Arse.' Although Ker states concerning nursery rhymes (ed. 1835, vol. I: p. 247): 'I myself have heard, or seen more than three hundred,' he gives only a total of one hundred and thirty-three of these in his four volumes, many of which he evidently picked up from Turner's *Infant Institutes*.

After Ker's mad and confused attempt to set the record straight in the 1830's, there came almost total silence, lasting for over a century, as to the unexpurgated children's rhymes, sayings, jokes, games, and the like, except for the quiet antiquarian publication of John Aubrey's *Remaines* in 1881, from Lansdowne MS. 231 where it had lain unpublished for over two centuries. Meanwhile, the laundered nursery-rhyme literature grew into the absolute industry it still is, of which the star volume has remained the thoroughly expurgated *Nursery Rhymes of England* (1842) by James Orchard Halliwell, and the same editor's *Popular Rhymes and Nursery Tales* (1849), both recently brought back into print in London, 1970, by the Bodley Head. These expurgated collections have been the source of most nursery-rhyme books since.

The folktales Halliwell retails are, of course, just as expurgated as his selection of rhymes, and this sort of pre-expurgation by selection is also unfortunately the ruling case in almost the totality of even the best volumes of this kind, presumably collected directly from the children themselves in recent years. For example: Dr. Dorothy Howard's *Folk Jingles of American Children* (New York University thesis, 1939), and Dr. Brian Sutton-Smith's scholarly publications on the games of New Zealand children (much other material this researcher has collected in America remains unpublished), Carl Withers' *A Rocket in My Pocket: The Rhymes and Chants of Young America* (1946), Ray Wood's *Fun in American Folk Rhymes* (1952, very grossly expurgated); also my favorite volume of this kind, *Rimbles: A Book of Children's Classic Games, Rhymes, Songs, and Sayings,* published in 1961 by Mrs. Patricia Evans (now Carpenter), as well as Mrs. Edith Fowke's similar Canadian collection more recently, *Sally Go 'Round the Sun*; and especially Iona & Peter Opie's *The Lore and Language of Schoolchildren* (Oxford, 1959), which undertakes to cover the field with some completeness, but is in fact almost totally expurgated just like all the others. It will also be observed that practically all of the preceding works, and many more like them, concern themselves strictly with rhymes and songs. The children's *jokes,* riddles, and folktale scraps, which form practically the entire matter of the present volume, *A Joke for Every Occasion,* have almost never been handled at all, let alone authentically.

One very curious result of all this pre-censorship and expurgation has been the creation of a minor sub-literature — perhaps just a fad — in which, avoiding the mania of Ker's method, certain writers have tried to find their way back, *by intuition* as it were, to the bawdy and erotic originals they sense lie behind the laundered nursery rhymes and similar lore of the usual collections, somewhat in the fashion of salmon fighting their way back upstream to spawn. Thus we have Kendall Banning's *Censored Mother Goose Rhymes* (New York, 1926) and the same compiler's *Purified Proverbs* (1930), which might better have been called *non*-censored Mother Goose rhymes and *polluted* proverbs, since all that is done is to print the usual texts with certain key words xxxx'd out, the reader then being invited to create an off-color recitation out of the presumably innocent rhyme or proverb by reciting it aloud with a suggestively hummed 'Mmmmmmmmmm' to replace the xxxx's!

The same system was later applied to a brief anthology of standard poetic recitations, with much funnier effect, in Robert Carlton ("Bob") Brown's *Gems: A Censored Anthology,* an exceedingly rare little work printed for the author in Cagnes-sur-Mer, France, in 1931. (Copies: New York Public Library, and Brown University.) In this case, the 'censored' terms are blanked out by means of heavy black squares, rather than x's, the proposed method of mock-bawdy reconstitution by humming being, however, the same. Compare also a brief selection of nursery-rhyme parodies and similar, as "Mother Goose Vice Verse," by Alan Dundes & Joseph C. Hickerson, in the *Journal of American Folklore* (1962) vol. 75: p. 249–59, in an important issue of this *Journal* devoted entirely, and for the first time, to erotic folklore. These rare little volumes of the 1920's, and the parody rhymes in actual oral transmission, though admittedly funny to readers and tellers, have no authentic history beyond their jest. Yet they show with great clarity the strength of the underground realization that the usual collections and repertories of children's rhymes and other folklore are outrageously censored and faked, and that 'There is more here than meets the ear.'

II. THE SECRET LORE OF CHILDREN

THE FIRST crack in the dike, as to children's authentic folklore in England, came in November, 1913, with the proposed publication in *The English Review* of a portion of the Scottish antiquarian Norman Douglas' *London Street Games* (ultimately published in book form in 1916, revised in 1931). But, as first published in *The English Review,* an unknown amount of material – and in particular the last two speeches in the following quotation – had to be expurgated from Douglas' manuscript (ed. 1931, p. 20), of which the historical importance is that Douglas had the courage to submit this transcript of authentic children's dialogue for publication at all:

"Well ef I'm a liar yo're the biggest. So yer lumps it. I'm goin to be blowed ef I play wiv a lahsy blisterin blitherin blinkin blightin bloomin bleedin blasted barstard wot's got a movver [*mother*] wot's got a bloke wot's —"

" 'Ere, d'ye want a clip on the Kiber-pass [*arse*]?"

"Garn! Piss up yer leg, an play wiv the steam."

A bit later, at p. 29, Douglas notes briefly, as to the rhyme "Pounds, shilling and pence": 'There is an improper version of this, and of several others,' but the authentic texts are not ventured.

Douglas' enterprise was intended to supplement or supplant Lady Alice Gomme's lily-pure *The Traditional Games of England, Scotland, and Ireland* (2 vols. 1894–98, repr. New York, 1964) and the similar *Games and Songs of American Children* by William W. Newell (1883, revised 1903). Of the first of these the Opies justly remark, in *The Lore and Language of Schoolchildren* (1959) p. vi, that 'almost all her correspondents were country dwellers, and tended to be well-to-do. The great warren of city backstreets where the mass of the nation's children are bred and brought up remained *terra incognita*; and there is a slightly unreal feeling about most of the games Lady Gomme describes, as if the children had had to wash their hands and faces before playing them.'

As we shall see, the children also had to wash their hands and faces – and possibly their mouths out with soap – before supplying to their teachers [*n.b.*] the rhymes, games and other lore funneled on later to the Opies for their book, and the same unfortunate feeling of polite unreality therefore falsifies and distorts that work too. Norman Douglas' *London Street Games* were not only not faked, pre-censored and snob-selected in just that sense, but are also marvellously presented by the artist-with-words that Douglas was, of perfect ear and a lively sense of humor. This is especially grateful in his 'breathless catalogue' of the names of the games themselves (but without satisfactory descriptions), so strangely similar to Rabelais' list, four centuries earlier, of the games of Gargantua, in Book I, chap. 22, and of the folk-dances of France, as seen in the rediscovered manuscript fragments of *Gargantua & Pantagruel*, Book V, chap. 33. These last, having come to light only in the mid-nineteenth century, do not appear in the great Urquhart-Motteux translation of Rabelais, one of the glories of English literature, but will be found quite satisfactorily turned into English in the two more recent and more exact translations by W. F. Smith, and by Samuel Putnam.

Somehow in connection with his field research into children's games, Douglas was apparently brought up on a morals charge during World War I, as to an offense with boys. Whether he was guilty or not is unknown — he is not the only unwary collector of children's folklore who has been so accused. I once nearly ended up on a chain-gang in a Southern state on such a charge, though I admit I was not entirely innocent, being then only nineteen years old myself, and quite interested in the slightly underage Appalachian girl whose songs I was noting down. Whatever the case with Douglas, he was allowed to expatriate himself from Britain and no trial took place. It was obviously desired to avoid another resounding scandal like that of the Oscar Wilde trial hardly two decades before. Douglas spent the rest of his life in Italy, where his openly-avowed homosexuality did not cause him any trouble with the police, boldly publishing there his unexpurgated and classic collection, *Some Limericks* (Florence, 1928), in which the rhyme on the 'old man at the Terminus' (see *The Limerick,* No. 1124) is said to be his own bawdy mock of his earlier *contretemps* with English justice. He also made another unexpurgated folk-collection before 1920, of Florentine cursing and swearwords, as he discusses in *Alone* (London, 1921) p. 176, and in the introduction to *Some Limericks.* This was intended for publication as an appendix to *Alone,* but Douglas' publisher did not dare risk it then in England, and the manuscript is now lost.

Meanwhile, in Vienna, a bombshell had exploded of which the pieces are still falling around us. Sigmund Freud's publication at the turn of the twentieth century, *Three Contributions to the Theory of Sex* (English translation, New York, 1910), brought intensely into focus the hitherto inexpressible question of *the sexual life of the child,* in a way radically different from and going far beyond the usual savage condemnations of juvenile masturbation printed since the main wave of sexual repression in the eighteenth century. As Dr. Otto Fenichel has phrased it, in his encyclopedic *The Psychoanalytic Theory of Neurosis* (New York: Norton, 1945) p. 56:

It is generally known today that children exhibit numerous types of instinctual behavior which in content are identical with the drives which in perverse individuals replace normal sexuality. Indeed, it is difficult to observe children without seeing manifestations of this kind. Consequently, today it seems less appropriate to phrase the question: "Is there an infantile sexuality?" than to ask: "How was it possible that so obvious a phenomenon as [polymorphous perverse] infantile sexuality was not observed before Freud?" This striking oversight is one of the best examples of "repression."

Serious pediatricians since that time have slowly come out of their cupboard, and though they are now willing to agree that young children are interested in the sexual differentiation of their own bodies from those of their siblings and playmates — by sight and sometimes by touch — most pediatricians can still hardly bring themselves (in print) to admit that any actual sexual or proto-sexual activities ever do or should take place, not even masturbation, until the legal age of consent, and no kind of incest ever or at all! Also, the highly important realization that children's early sexual activities are very often what would be called in adults *perverse* (all types: you-name-it), which is the deepest and most significant level of Freud's discovery, is carefully never even mentioned.

In what is perhaps the best available hand-guide in English to child development, Arnold Gesell & Frances L. Ilg's *Infant and Child in the Culture of Today* (New York, 1943; with second volume entitled *The Child from Five to Ten,* 1946), various "Personal and Sex Interests" are bravely if briefly discussed concerning every age-level from five to ten, under the heading of "Self and Sex." But none of the children so carefully observed by Drs. Gesell and Ilg and their staff apparently ever masturbated — at any age up to ten — while the following is the entirety of what is given (vol. II: p. 324–25) concerning the secret sexual lore of children, and the playing of the erotic and aggressive sex games so easily observed among the five-and-ten year old little girls and boys of my own childhood (and parenthood), and perhaps of yours too: '6 YEARS: ... Mutual investigation by both sexes ... Mild sex play or exhibitionism in play or in school toilets. Game of "show." Some children are subjected to sex play by older children. May play hospital and take rectal temperatures ... 8 YEARS: ... Girls may be unusually responsive to touch and rough play with boys. Interest in peeping, smutty jokes, provocative giggling; whisper, write or spell "elimination" and "sex" words. Girls begin to question about menstruation ... 9 YEARS: ... Sex swearing; sex poems.' That is the total statement given.

Here, by contrast, is what a German psychiatrist, Albert Moll, found over thirty years before, as cited in his *The Sexual Life of the Child* (English translation, London, 1912) p. 262–63, as to the sexual folklore then circulating among slightly older German children, obviously almost identical with the similar folk-materials of the English-speaking children:

> Erotic and obscene books and pictures ... obtain a wide currency in schools, in part as printed pornographica, and in part passed from hand to hand in written form. Thus, from a number of girls' schools come reports of the circulation of thoroughly obscene writings among girls from twelve to fourteen years of age. Especial favourites are descriptions of the wedding-night, mostly in manuscript form; also an obscene version of the story of Faust and Gretchen; and quite a number of other improper poems pass from hand to hand in girls' schools. In boys' schools, the circulating matter consists rather of obscene printed books and pictures ... Obscene photographs are found even in girls' schools.

Boys in Britain and America have their doggerel obscoena too, such as "The Diary of a French Stenographer," and "The Bride's Letter" invariably attributed to Lord Byron! Of this last the editors of the unexpurgated song collection, *Snatches and Lays* (1962) remark: 'It is a work which, along with "The Confidential Clerk," occupies a very special place in Australia; who, as a schoolboy, has not paid his sixpence for a handwritten copy of one of these poems, or a penny to read them?'

Clearly, the circulated materials of this kind are intended and needed by the children as a form of graphic or practical sex education, far superior to the embarrassed flounderings by teachers and parents, who invariably — even today — attempt to keep everything at the theoretical level only, not only so far as the children are concerned but even playing down the described part of the father in the mother's impregnation. To the point where, as I have heard a young girl complain, 'You get a lot more practical stuff out of the story of the Virgin and the Pigeon,' in which the Virgin Mary is impregnated via the *ear*. Also, the items of the erotic folklore of children that come most often into the disapproving hands of elders and teachers in this way are just those items profiting least by oral transmission, and which have to be circulated in written or printed form owing in part to their length, or as being pictorial in essence. There is a whole German monograph on this subject by Dr. August Barth or Bartz, entitled *Kindliche Pornographen* (Vienna, 1915).

A rather mild collection of textual and pictorial materials of a similar kind was published in its monograph series by the American Folklore Society in 1975, Alan Dundes & Carl R. Pagter's *Urban Folklore from the Paperwork Empire*. Concentrating on the textual burlesques appealing principally to adult wage-slaves, this either omits or was unable to discover most of the really graphic such 'novelty' obscoena circulated in the form of drawings among adolescents and others in America, such as the erotic "Cat's Whisker" parody radio, and especially "The Delighter," a mock masturbation-machine for girls, on a Model-T Ford chassis (and revisions), along with numerous other items similar, which have been in circulation at least since the mid-1920's.

To the best of my knowledge, the first person who attempted specifically to collect the erotic folklore of children and adolescents in the English-speaking world has been myself, beginning in 1934 when I was sixteen years old and in the final year of high-school in Scranton, Pa. I had already been collecting and clipping non-sexual jokes for over four years, but had realized by then that only the sexual and scatological jokes were really popular or often repeated among my fellow-students, while the younger children preferred jokes of types turning on riddles and other word-play, these often sexual as well. I therefore concentrated from then on strictly on collecting the sexual and scatological folklore, particularly the very large though ever-changing float of erotic slang, insults, and other locutions (principally of boys), as well as their jokes, songs, rhymes and folk-poems — the latter usually in handwritten form, as noted above — as well as sexual superstitions and beliefs, and the description of the forbidden games, pranks, and initiations, including materials dredged up then from my own and the others' memories back to about 1925. This collecting was done at first in various towns of eastern Pennsylvania, New Jersey, and the South; later in New York City until 1953. Much of the recovered material will be found scattered through the two series of my *Rationale of the Dirty Joke* (1968–75), where it was not possible to group the materials according to age-levels, which would also have been somewhat misleading as many of the same jokes are told by adolescents and adults. Much more of the collected material still remains to be published, particularly as to the erotic and scatological songs and folk-poems.

An exactly similar but very brief collection, this time based entirely on recollection at the distance of half a century, was issued privately in Vienna, Virginia, in 1942, by the American ornithologist, Waldo Lee McAtee, as a *Supplement* to his *Rural Dialect of Grant County, Indiana, in the 'Nineties;* and some further but rather unrewarding original materials in this line by McAtee are preserved among his manuscripts in the Library of Congress. Another such collection, this time much more extensive and of great value, was compiled in 1952 by Kenneth Larson from memories of his youth in rural Idaho in the late 1910's, concentrating on erotic songs, jokes, and folktales. This has never been published, but a revision of the manuscript was later circulated privately in photocopy form: there are repository copies in the Folklore Archive and the Kinsey Institute Library, both at Indiana University. The great Vance Randolph "Unprintable" folklore collections of Ozark erotic songs, folktales, and other lore, compiled in 1949 and finally revised in 1954 for publication by myself, are repositoried in manuscript (and on the supporting recordings of the songs) in the Library of Congress, also at Indiana; with microfilm copies at Harvard, the University of Kansas, the University of California at Los Angeles, and elsewhere.

It will be observed that none of this material was or could be published at that time in America or England. When I was at last able, in the early 1950's, to find a New York publisher willing to undertake a serious erotic folklore series, the late Henry Schuman, his untimely death brought the project to an end, and it could then only be continued in Paris, and as to limericks, a type of folk-poetry popular mostly among adults. Meanwhile, the important psychoanalytic study by Dr. Martha Wolfenstein, *Children's Humor: A Psychological Analysis,* was issued by the Free Press, at Glencoe, Illinois, in 1954. This includes both jokes and punning lore current among children, courageously presenting the sexual materials and analyzing these in depth. This is still by far the best analytic work on children's folklore transmitted by the children themselves, and shows the ideal direction for future study when more of the raw material will be on record.

Not everyone agrees, perhaps, with the suggestion just made, as witness the rather simplistic review by Stefan Kanfer in *Time* magazine (May 3rd, 1976), of a profound and valuable work on fairy-tales and the child, by the great child-analyst Dr. Bruno Bettelheim, which the reviewer attempts to crush with anti-analytic and Philistine ridicule about seventy years out-of-date. The killing stroke is presumably a quotation from Prof. Vladimir Nabokov, hardly a disinterested observer since he is also the author of a 'humorous' novel on adult male paedophily, entitled *Lolita,* and here hooting at what he calls 'the fundamentally medieval world of Freud, with its crankish quest for sexual symbols (something like searching for Baconian acrostics in Shakespeare's works [*or in Nabokov's?*]) and its bitter little embryos spying, from their natural nooks, upon the love life of their parents.' Behind the know-it-all pose here, one discerns the modern proudly neurotic and obscuranticist mind to which such a review is intended to appeal, and which nervously prefers all its folktales to remain unanalyzed and 'ununderstandable,' and its nonsense to remain safely — nonsensical.

The new generation of collectors of unexpurgated folklore among both children and adults has come into existence since the 1950's, in part owing to the newly-available technique of collecting sung or spoken folklore by means of tape-recording. While the tape runs, reel to reel, sometimes for a period of an hour or more, everything that the joke-tellers or singers may offer is automatically recorded without distinction, and often without self-consciousness on the part of the tellers, who become less and less motivated, as time passes, to the usual mental pre-expurgation of their repertory. By these means, the American folklorist Roger D. Abrahams was able to present to the University of Pennsylvania in 1962 a remarkable thesis entitled *Negro Folklore from South Philadelphia,* and composed of transcripts of the jokes and 'toasts' (rhymed recitations) spoken into his tape-recorder by a group of Negro youths in the Philadelphia ghetto.

A selection from this thesis was courageously published in book form as *Deep Down in the Jungle* (Hatboro, Pa. 1964) by the short-lived but seminal publishing firm, Folklore Associates, headed by Dr. Kenneth Goldstein. This book has since been revised (Chicago, 1970) though not improved, but much of the material collected in the original thesis still remains unpublished. An even more startling collection of unexpurgated Negro 'toasts,' not including any joke texts, has more recently been issued by Prof. Bruce Jackson, as *"Get Your Ass In the Water and Swim Like Me": Narrative Poetry from Black Oral Tradition* (Harvard University Press, 1974). Here the informants were largely older youths and young men, some of them prisoners.

Jackson's introduction is a masterpiece of low-pitched but elegant analysis of his materials, in the folklore sense, and one can fault it only for the short shrift given to any historical treatment of its subject. The resolutely rootless or non-historical approach is, in general, the main defect of almost all recorder-based and 'performance-oriented' folklore collections over the last two decades. Many of these (though not Prof. Jackson's collection) are frankly staggering in their lack of historical depth or perspective, and ludicrous in their insistent and pretentious jargoning, usually on the basis — when all is said and done — of a few hours of recent tapes, grafted onto a whole-souled unconsciousness of the possible existence of any documentary sources or texts older than a narrow academic spectrum of similar publications over the ten or fifteen years preceding. *Roll them tapes!* One magazine editor, a few years back, to whom I complained about his blue-pencilling out all references to books or even incidents earlier than a cut-off date of

1930, bowled me over completely with his matter-of-fact explanation: 'Well, you know,' he said painfully, 'our people don't like reading about *deaders.*'

As to the modern Negro 'toasts,' I have tried to trace these to their congeners in Scottish bragging folklore of the sixteenth century and elsewhere, in *Rationale of the Dirty Joke: Second Series* (*"No Laughing Matter"*) p. 782–97; and in particular in a set of long historical and textual studies on "Bawdy Monologues and Rhymed Recitations" in the *Southern Folklore Quarterly,* Autumn 1976 issue, published by the University of Florida at Gainesville. Until the publications by Abrahams and by Jackson, only sporadic mention was ever made of the Negro 'toasts' in folklore literature, and I believe I must have been the first white person purposely collecting these. From about 1944 on, I hand-transcribed many such 'toasts' at a cost of twenty-five cents per declaimed text (the accompanying shoeshine itself costing ten cents more) from the very young Negro bootblacks at that time lining Forty-second Street behind the New York Public Library, with their little homemade shoeshine boxes, and trying to attract customers and while away the sunless days by means of solo soft-shoe dances and verbal games like these.

In countries other than America, the situation in the publishing of children's folklore has become much more liberated in recent years, beginning with Ian Turner's *Cinderella Dressed in Yella,* a collection of children's rhymes published without expurgation in Australia in 1969, and now being revised for forthcoming London publication. The most extensive and in many ways the most remarkable such collection is that now in progress, under the general title of *Studien zur Befreiung des Kindes* ("Studies toward the Liberation of the Child") by Ernest Borneman of the University of Salzburg, Austria. Two volumes have so far appeared, both mostly on songs and rhymes, entitled *Unsere Kinder, im Spiegel ihrer Lieder, Reime, Verse und Rätsel,* and *Die Umwelt des Kindes, im Spiegel seiner "verbotenen" Lieder, Reime, Verse und Rätsel* (Olten, Switzerland: Walter-Verlag, 1973–74). These large volumes, sensitively collected and edited, are of the most extraordinary value, and it is hoped that the series can be continued from the enormous collectings already made among German-speaking children by Borneman.

In France, the field is dominated by the recent and very frank and full study, *Le Folklore obscène des enfants* (Paris: G.-P. Maisonneuve & Larose, 1974) by M. Claude Gaignebet, author with Marie-Claude Florentin of another remarkable monograph, *Le Carnaval* (Paris: Payot, 1974). Gaignebet's *Folklore obscène des enfants* is a key work, textually, historically and interpretively, and further study of the subject must begin there. Of unusual value is its careful historical orientation, drawing comparative materials from as far back as Rabelais' *Gargantua & Pantagruel,* Book I, chap. 22, in the 1530's, and from the oldest known book of children's lore, *La Friquassée crotestyllonnée* (Rouen, 1604; and modern reprint edited by P. Blanchemain, 1878). Mostly scatological, this gives the '*antiques modernes chansons, jeux et menu fretel des petits enfants de Rouen*' in the sixteenth century. Gaignebet also draws on the valuable collection of Franco-Swiss children's folk-rhymes, Emil Bodmer's Zürich thesis, *Empros, oder Anzählreime der französischen Schweiz* (Halle, 1923), and on the more recent and definitive similar French collection, Jean Baucomont's *Comptines de langue française* (Paris: Seghers, 1961), begun in the 1930's. As to children's games and similar folklore in Rabelais, the basic contribution is still "Les Jeux de Gargantua," studied by M. Jean Psichari and others in the *Revue d'Etudes Rabelaisiennes* (1908–09) vols. VI–VII.

Four centuries later now, French children are still far from intimidated as to their erotic folklore, especially their bawdy *comptines* (rhymes) and songs, many of which have tunes of great age and exceeding beauty, such as "*Fillarette*" and "*Les Filles de Camaret,*" known to most students and young soldiers. The most popular song among children in France today is a music-hall item, "*Le Zizi*" ("The Weewee"), which even includes a stanza satirizing the penis of the Pope. Though this is currently sung by girls and boys six and eight years old in schoolyards throughout France, during their recreation period when they escape momentarily the surveillance of their teachers, it created a newspaper scandal a few years back when issued as sheet-music for adults, and when a recording of it was played over the powerful Luxembourg radio station in 1974.

The Opies in their *Lore and Language of Schoolchildren* (1959) p. 95, under "The Improper," tell of an exactly similar case in Wales, when a 'whole audience of 450 – dear little girls aged five years to eleven years –' spontaneously broke into the following chorus when the tune of "Men of Harlech" was played by the orchestra at the Coronation Tea:

> I'm a man that came from Scotland,
> Shooting peas up a Nannie goat's bottom ...

The Opies' informant insists (and so do they) that the children were 'blissfully unconscious of what they were singing,' but this pious whitewash rather slides to the ground when, three pages later, we are told of another 'group of girls playing with a skipping rope in a Wiltshire village' in 1952, while singing a little song against Kaiser Bill, if not against Bonaparte, ending:

> He say if the Bone Man come,
> Stick your bayonet up his bum.

As between the peas shot up a Nannie goat's bottom, and the bayonet stuck up the Bone Man's bum, the unprejudiced reader finds it difficult to sense the 'unconsciousness' of one, and the purposefulness of the other, which the Opies would distinguish.

It is illuminating to quote here their conclusion as to 'impropriety' in children's folklore, p. 95, a passage which leaves the Opies' book somewhat beyond even that of Lady Gomme – whom they criticize on just this point, as quoted above – in would-be patrician elevation and squeamishness:

> Genuine erotic verse ... is unusual. That there are villains among children, as among adults, the *News of the World* offers frequent testimony; and from somewhere the ogre child [!] acquires his strange salacious prescriptions, taking criminal pleasure in pressing them on juniors, and inscribing them on the walls of the school lavatory. But we are not here discussing delinquents ...

After such a caveat, lumping all the genuine erotic lore of children with 'criminal' and 'delinquent' toilet-graffiti, acquired 'from somewhere [by] the ogre child,' all the Opies can permit themselves to print under "The Improper" comes to a handful of weak-sister items, mostly at the nursery scatological level, concerning 'bums' (buttocks), lost and dirty drawers, and sliding on one's ask-me-no-questions; with a few slightly stronger rhymes carefully alluded to in prose transcriptions only (p. 96). That takes care of "The Improper."

I do not wish to seem to be selling short the Opies' useful compilation, *The Lore and Language of Schoolchildren,* and its continuation as *Children's Games* (1969). Their failure here is all the more disappointing in that their earlier *Oxford Dictionary of Nursery Rhymes* is a modern gem of unassuming yet very thorough literary research. Even at this level of library documentation, the *Lore and Language* volume falls particularly short, as when the authors do not recognize (p. vi) in the well-known ball-bouncing rhyme of girls, "One, two, three, a-lairy," where the leg is slung over the ball at the word 'a-lairy,' the old English term *aliry,* meaning crosswise, as of the legs — itself a remarkable example of ancient vestiges surviving today solely in children's lore, and without ever making use of transmission by the printed word. One thinks often, in studying such survivals in the lore of children, and there are many of them, of the explorer Alexander von Humboldt's account of the old parrot, as told in T. H. White's *Bestiary: A Book of Beasts* (1954) p. 114: 'In South America he met with a venerable bird who had the sole knowledge of a dead language, the whole tribe of Indians (*Atures*) who alone spoke it having become extinct.'

The Opies' real failure stems from their own and their schoolteacher-informants' clear intention *not* to collect and not to give the full and true record of modern British children's oral lore, rhymes, games, and all the rest of it, except insofar as the children could be restricted to no more than a mild verbal unseemliness (as that concerning dirty drawers: a favorite theme) not too shocking to the class snobbery of the adults involved, all of whom were also in authority positions over the children quizzed. In the deepest sense, such a project could never have succeeded in being anything but soulless and superficial, owing to its over-ambitious scope on the one hand, and especially to its method of collection, which carefully insulated the actual editors and the children away from each other by hundreds of miles. This fact is somewhat disguised by the Opies' prefatory statement, p. vii, that their work is 'based on the contributions of some 5,000 children attending seventy schools,' which is certainly something of a *suggestio falsi,* considering the impersonal method of collection actually used.

Though it nowhere mentions this fact, *The Lore and Language of Schoolchildren* is based in largest part on written materials channelled to the editors by some seventy school principals and other collectors, to whom they sent a mimeographed questionnaire several pages long, entitled *The Oral Lore of School Children* (a copy of it lies before me as I write), listing twenty-five questions, mostly as to games, rhymes, and sayings, on which the children were to be quizzed by their teachers, either orally or in writing. These replies could be expected to be well-expurgated beforehand, of course, both by the intimidated children and by their solicitous schoolteachers, themselves intimidated in turn by being all listed and named geographically on pages xi–xv, though the crucial questionnaire is neither mentioned nor printed at all. Perhaps the editors felt this was the only way in which they could handle so ambitious a project – 5,000 children! – and so complex a subject-matter, while staying safely away from any contaminating social or verbal contact with any real children but their own.

The present work, *A Joke for Every Occasion,* by Sandra McCosh, avoids the Opies' mistake, and makes use of the almost exactly opposite method of collecting and editing, though a questionnaire was used in part. Unassuming and unexpurgated, collected in only half a dozen controlled locations rather than seventy or more, and without historical tracings, Miss McCosh's work does not strain for superficial broadness and social acceptability, but strikes purposely for depth and total authenticity, and achieves this visibly and at once. There are none of the Opies' pretentious distribution-maps *à la* Kinsey, no graphs and no charts, and – as distinguished from certain recent folkloristic studies – nothing (and nobody) was run through a computer. Miss McCosh does not state that this is the totality of English or American children's jokes and puns; she presents it strictly as a sampling, but goes very deep.

Instead of filtering the children's secret lore through the medium of watchful teachers in postures of authority, with everybody on their best behavior for the honour of the school (and possibly televised *fakelore* performance?), the children were here met in a personal and permissive situation by the researcher, who is a bright and friendly young woman of just the kind that children like and trust, who tried to put them at their ease and gain their confidence. Without this sort of preliminary, and the creation of this sort of ambiance, nothing authentic can ever even be overheard from children, who are usually extremely secretive about the lore they know adults may disapprove of, and sometimes even about the magic of their names! *'What's your name?' 'Pudding-and-tame! Ask me again and I'll tell you the same.'* (An occult evasion that the Opies very correctly trace back two centuries or more, at p. 157; 'Pudding-of-Tame' being in fact an old name for the Devil.)

A Joke for Every Occasion was undertaken by Miss McCosh, then an American graduate student, while preparing her thesis at Leeds University in England, in 1973–75. She began by using a questionnaire, which is printed before the texts of the jokes below, with the idea of getting the children 'started' in this way. With children aged 9–10, the questionnaire took about one-half to three-quarters of an hour to fill out. The children were allowed to talk to each other and consult about the jokes while filling out the questionnaire, and no effort was made to keep the children in rigid classroom order.

Early in her research among schoolchildren in Leeds and London, Miss McCosh realized that the teacher-controlled questionnaire system employed by the Opies cannot give a reliable picture of the children's true repertory at any subject-level. In fact, even the mere presence of the teacher generally dries up and represses the verbal offering – let alone the writing down – by the children of that part of their lore which might be considered 'rude' (obscene). In one significant instance that she notes, when the children artlessly asked whether they might give 'rude' materials too, the teacher snapped that they weren't supposed to know anything 'rude' in that school! The researcher therefore turned to the auxiliary help of the tape-recorder method, which had already been shown by Roger Abrahams' work to be so fertile of results with Negro youngsters in Philadelphia. She also diplomatically arranged, where possible, that the recording was done when the regular teacher was absent, by preference during the recreation period.

The extensive riddle texts in this collection, and similar joking materials not quite rising to the level of jokes, are very significant of the age-levels involved. Peter Farb, in his fascinating popular book, *Word Play: What Happens When People Talk* (New York, 1973) p. 100, in the section on "Verbal Duelling," seems to suggest that young children do not know the difference between a joke and a riddle. He says:

> At first thought, the riddle might appear to be an even simpler form of verbal duelling than opening a conversation or beginning a phone call. Indeed, most English-speaking communities attach little significance to riddles and usually regard them as a simple pastime for children. In fact, the majority of American children *are* strikingly punctual in acquiring a repertory of riddles at about age six or seven, and at that age they tell about three times as many joking riddles as jokes in any other form. During the next several years, riddles continue to make up about half of a child's store of jokes, and it is not until about age eleven that they are discarded in favor of anecdotes. A few children between the ages of six and eleven can tell the difference between a joke and a riddle, although most of them will ask a riddle when they are requested to tell a joke.

In a deeper sense, the riddles represent and replace aggressive jests for younger children, to achieve the same pleasurable effect for the teller that is sought in 'punchline' jokes of the standard anecdote type told by older children and adults. The point about riddles is that the listener-victim is *never* expected to be able to give the 'right' answer (so also in "Knock Knock" jokes), and the answer is then delivered by the teller himself, thus achieving the same triumph as is experienced in giving the 'punchline' by the teller of the usual jokes.

As now revised from the original thesis and here presented to the reader, Sandra McCosh's *A Joke for Every Occasion* must create a new era in the collecting and publishing of children's folklore in the English-speaking world, especially in its proposed backing-up now by the revised edition of Ian Turner's equally frank collection of rhymes, *Cinderella Dressed in Yella*. Since the present work represents almost the totality of what was recorded by questionnaires and tapes in both England and America, there can be no question of either expurgation of the sexual and scatological materials, or of any overemphasis on these beyond the true proportions they obtain in the children's private lore.

If anything, I would judge that there is far less erotic material in Miss McCosh's book than can be elicited when children are frankly encouraged, after their confidence has been gained, to recite all the jokes, songs, and sayings they *never* recite 'when grown-ups are around.' Some kinds of secret lore, such as games, initiations and competitions of a sexual kind (also the scatological) are also never engaged in when adults are anywhere in the neighborhood, and these are among the most difficult to collect, except by personal memory in later years. I have often frankly asked both children and adults for their sexual repertories, when I felt I knew them well enough to do so, and have never once been told by children that they do not have any such lore. Though I have sometimes been required not to look at them, or to turn my back while writing down at their dictation what they spoke or sang.

III. THE ATTACK ON THE CHILD

THERE IS something more to say here, more important in many ways than the textual and bibliographical precisions that have gone before. As opposed to the notion that most people love or even adore children, and would do anything to make their young lives happy, filled with childish prattle, folklore, games, and the like; the cruel fact is that children have been a main object, over many thousands of years, of violent cultural assaults in almost all parts of the world, to force them to accept, and to warp them firmly and finally into their intended rôles as adults, in cultures that can only be called sociopathic. Our own culture is certainly one of these. As one obvious proof, I was brought up, and I imagine many of my readers will have been brought up, in a milieu where violent physical beating by adults, with sticks and straps, or (at best!) intense psychological humiliation and crushing of the child's spirit, by means of insults, physical immobilization, deprivation of love, and some torments quite unspeakable, were accepted as perfectly normal and usual parts of the child's education for social life.

This is not the place to write the long and dolorous history of cruelty to children, nor even of the Societies intended to prevent this; nor of the crude commercial exploitation of children – I mean their bodies, not their pocket-money, but that too – for many centuries now. I hope no one will ever write such a history: I can imagine only too clearly the hypocritical motives of most of the audience for such an (inevitably) illustrated sadistic romp, which would make John Foxe's sixteenth-century *Book of Martyrs* seem merely crude. As to the children's literature which is presumably the mildest expression of this sort of intimidation of the child by the adult world, let me cite only one perfect statement from that pre-excellent handbook, George Sampson's *Concise Cambridge History of English Literature* (1941) p. 617, his section on "Children's Books":

> A terrible fact in the history of controversy, whether political or religious, is that the minds of children are the favorite battleground of ruthless adults. The religious fanatics of the sixteenth and succeeding centuries tormented the minds of children with fears of speedy death and the almost unescapable certainty of hell-fire. Thomas White, Minister of the Gospel, in *A Little Book for Little Children* (1702) – there were two books of this name – urges the young not to read Ballads and foolish Books, and offers them instead horrible stories of martyrdoms drawn from Foxe. The anonymous *Young Man's Calling, &c.* (1685) outdoes White in examples of martyrdom. The most widely read of these oppressive compilations was James Janeway's *Token for Children: being an Exact Account of the Conversion, Holy and Exemplary Lives, and Joyful Deaths of Several Young Children* (1720?) a supreme example of morbid and gloating piety.

Janeway's example was widely followed in nearly two centuries of pious ejaculations and edifying meditations by reverend jackasses on the deaths of small children. A whole library of these unwholesome exudations of Christian sadism could be collected, one of the last and probably the least excruciating being the poem, *A Little Child's Monument,* late in the nineteenth century, by Roden B. W. Noel, groom of the privy chamber to Queen Victoria, in memory of his son who had died at the age of five.

The meaning of all this 'morbid and gloating piety' can only be understood in relation to the witchcraft hysteria which had preceded it in the seventeenth century, and from which the little children were secretly to be saved by happy death. This is alluded to in the Rev. White's admonition, cited above, for children 'not to read Ballads and foolish Books.' Bawdy ballads, as is well known, were inspired by the Devil, who also presided in person at the Witches' Sabbats ('buff-balls' of naked dancing by young and old of both sexes) at which these impious songs and parodies were sung, especially in Scotland, to irresistibly aphrodisiacal fiddle-tunes taught to the fiddlers by Old Nick himself, and later transplanted to the American Ozarks, still retaining their curiously obscene titles as collected in 1954 by Vance Randolph.

This is a much larger subject than can be handled here. The key is given in the blazing rhetoric of *The Sorceress,* by the great French historian and stylist Jules Michelet, of which an excellent English translation was published about 1900; and in the continuation of this by Margaret Murray in *The Witch-Cult in Western Europe* (1921) and *The God of the Witches* (1933). Modern daimonism and its fiercely evident 'urge toward evil,' combined with the mushy-minded vogue for every kind of occultism and mock-psychology all around us, make very clear how these secret cults hung on – and hang on still – as a folk resistance to repressive Christian anti-sexuality, under the name of 'witchcraft.'

Another significant point is made in Philippe Ariès' thought-provoking *Centuries of Childhood* (New York, 1962), in which, says Jon Bartlett in the Canadian folksong magazine, *Come All Ye* (Vancouver, Nov. 1974), it is observed that: 'The secret world of children – of ritual, game, and language – has not always been such. Indeed, the very concept of childhood is a fairly modern one. In the thesis of Philippe Ariès that, until about the seventeenth century, the only significant social division was between what we would now call "babies" (who have always needed special attention) and everyone else. Games such as hide-and-seek and leap-frog were not restricted to children (see, for example the paintings of Breughel ["Children's Games" and "Proverbs," and the engravings of Abraham Bosse]), and the great festivals and celebrations of the year were not limited solely to adults.'

It was precisely these festivals and celebrations that worried the witch-hunters and anti-child moralists most, owing to their frequent connection with the pre-Christian ('witch-cult') ceremonials of Solstice and Equinox, as well as the open sexuality and even mockeries of Christian ritual earlier allowed at Carnaval, and to the Goliard poets at the Feast of Fools. At the public level, ostensibly, the Protestant Reformation and the Puritans afterward had brought an end to all that, except for the Jewish holiday of Purim (also obviously part of a pre-Christian worship) and the secret survivals of magic and superstition in children's games and charms, to which the best key is still John Aubrey's contemporary *Remaines of Gentilisme and Judaisme* (MS. 1686/7, first published completely in 1881). See also the texts of the authentic medieval *Carmina Burana* – not the neo-pagan Nazi ceremonial to movie music by Carl Orff, in the 1930's – and Johan Huizinga's *Homo Ludens* (English translation, London, 1949). The most perfect indictment is perhaps the little rhyme printed in the work that follows (No. 74), as collected in 1973 from a nine-year-old girl in Leeds – '*Our children will be our judges!*'

> All the teachers at our school go to Church on Sunday
> To pray to God to give them strength to whack the kids
>   on Monday.

There have been defenses of the child, of course, but not very many. Mostly, everyone was agreed for centuries and still agrees that children are crude little beasts who must be beaten into learning a few rudiments of knowledge ('reading, writing, and 'rithmetic') by means of which they can later be set to doing useful work profitable to their parents and employers. Many countries, such as France, still have no higher concept of either children, education, or human life than this. Perhaps the most significant defense of the child was therefore that of the Czech educator, Jan Comenius, in the crucial seventeenth century, who tried to create school-systems where children would be taught without cruelty or force, and *according to their natural aptitudes.* To show how this should be done, he published in 1654 his very influential *Orbis Sensualium Pictus,* the first children's textbook with illustrations adapted for teaching.

At the literary level the defenses really began with that by Jean-Jacques Rousseau, who phrased this paradoxically as a defense, instead, of the presumably noble and unspoiled 'Savages' of America and Oceania, since he disliked and resented real children, especially his own. The most sincere cry was surely that of William Blake, in his *Songs of Innocence and of Experience,* issued during the French Revolution in 1789–94, but, like all the rest of Blake's books but his first *Poetical Sketches* (1783), in such excessively snob-directed limited editions as to have had absolutely no effect on any century but our own. The windy celebrations of childhood by bearded American poets like Longfellow and Whittier, of the "Barefoot Boy" school, ending with Eugene Field in the 1890's, need not concern us here: it is all beard-wax and buncombe, and sometimes (as with Whitman) disguised perversion.

Actually, everyone but Blake, and Mark Twain a century later in *Huckleberry Finn* (1885), betrays the notion that childhood is charming to vapor about but that the child *must* ultimately be tamed and 'educated,' and by hard knocks — of Fate, to be sure — when necessary. An exception should be made for Elizabeth Barrett Browning's poignant *The Cry of the Children,* written in 1844 before her marriage, a 'searing and unanswerable accusation ... the first and fiercest exposure of the price paid for Victorian commercialism.' This has been unjustly overshadowed by the perhaps equally sincere but rather fustian tear-jerker, *The Song of the Shirt* by Thomas Hood (published in *Punch,* 1843), which concerned itself with the fate of the exploited mother rather than the factory-driven child under early mad-dog capitalism.

Defenses of the child were and have remained the exception, and only the ones by women seem really trustworthy, such as the recent *Les Enfants d'abord* by Christiane Rochefort; whereas the defenses by men sometimes curiously vacillate, alternate with open attacks on the child, or at least break out unexpectedly in nasty teasing or gloating. Consider for example the beautifully-written children's book, *Mistress Masham's Repose* (1946) by T. H. White, the most perfect parody or continuation ever made of Swift's *Gulliver's Travels,* where, in a work otherwise simply dripping with charm and fantasy, the ten-year-old girl protagonist is suddenly dragged off by her evil guardians to an operating torture-chamber – from which she is saved finally by the Lilliputians, to be sure. Occasionally, an intended 'children's book' is wholly overwhelmed by the author's evident hatred of children, alternating with a sick and neurotic attraction expected in the audience to childhood themes, as for example in the cruel pages of Richard Hughes' *A High Wind in Jamaica* (1929, also entitled *The Innocent Voyage*) and the perfectly ghastly *Lord of the Flies,* by William Golding, neither of which books can be given to children to read.

Less cruelly, certainly, but likewise filled with the same odd alternations, the lovely and doubtless unconscious uterine birth-fantasies of the Rev. Charles Kingsley's *Water Babies* (1863) demand, as a sort of entrance-fee to the watery womb, that the beaten and grimy little chimney-sweep be hunted over the bare mountain like an animal, and then die of exhaustion and drowning, while the saccharine counterpoint of good little children sing happy songs at their country school. A century later, the similar birth-fantasy of Maurice Sendak's *In the Night Kitchen* (1970) is obviously not unconscious at all, and reads like a jolly adaptation of Freud for the kiddies. Its charm is belied, however, in the very same artist--author's grisly book of monsters for children, *Where the Wild Things Are,* which draws its inspiration more from Hilaire Belloc's *Bad Child's Book of Beasts* (1896) if not from the Marquis de Sade. (The necessary subterfuge is that the little boy finally becomes the king of the monsters.)

Less dangerously to the child, certainly, and were it not for the inversion of the dates, one might call Frances Hodgson Burnett's heavily symbolic story for children, *The Secret Garden* (1911) a child's version of D. H. Lawrence's *Lady Chatterley's Lover* (1928). Actually, one would not be surprised if Mrs. Burnett's lovely book were Lawrence's unavowed inspiration: in the earth-male or Great God Pan crooning to his animals in the jawbreaking dialect

(Dickon/Mellors), *vs.* the rich but impotent upper-class cripple writhing in his wheel-chair (Colin/Chatterley), the young girl perturbed by the untended roses of her 'Secret Garden,' and all.

Meanwhile, the nineteenth century raised to an art and finally to an industry the flood of hortatory and threatening 'children's literature' intended to tame the unruly child and deform his soul to suit civilization, as his feet were deformed to fit pointed shoes: Victor Hugo's ineffably cruel parable of the endless grin cut into the living flesh of the child's face by the baby-stealers in *The Man Who Laughs* (1869), which said it forever. The classic in this line, in conscious ferocity against the child, is of course Dr. Heinrich Hoffmann's *Struwwelpeter* (1845, and translated from the German into English doggerel verse by the same Mark Twain who wrote *Huckleberry Finn*). This is entirely concerned with open killings and symbolic castrations of naughty children, especially the bad little boy, Struwwelpeter, who *will not comb his hair*! As a truly remarkable proto-analytic article by Dr. Rudolph Friedmann has been devoted to this acutely influential horror-work, in my lay-analytic magazine, *Neurotica* (No. 9, 1951; and enlarged in Dwight Macdonald's *Parodies,* 1960, p. 494–501), little more need be said about it here. In his nympholept parody of psychoanalytic prose, Dr. Friedmann says everything and more, particularly in his sinister closing line: 'The death of the child is the birth of the parents.'

Far from being merely an aberration of Teutonic cruelty, *Struwwelpeter* dominated its century and is with us yet, not only imprinted in the psychic structure of the generations of German children brought up on its rules, but in a horde of imitations. Of these, Wilhelm Busch's *Max und Moritz* was only the first in continuing the same themes at a more vulgar level, as does the famous American 1910's comic-strip plagiarism of Busch's endlessly naughty-and-punished little boys as "The Katzenjammer Kids." Compare also the mere textual elaboration of the same themes in George Wilbur Peck's *Peck's Bad Boy and his Pa* (1883), wildly milking the same sadistic vein of humor from the alternating pranks against the father, and the flagellatory punishments of the 'bad boy.'

With excuses like these, no extreme of cruelty against the child is forbidden. See the incredible 'humorous' illustration of the angry tailor cutting off the head of the bad little boy with an enormous shears, for mocking him; then killing himself in prison with the same shears. This is reproduced in *Neurotica* No. 9: p. 23, from Busch's further collection of 'Droll Tales and Merry Designs,' *Naturgeschichtliches Alphabet* (1880). There is also still in lively existence a presumably humorous sub-literature of frank attacks on the child, in both words and jolly pictures, by young fathers jealous of their newborn children, whom they visualize themselves and us as joyously beating up with boxing gloves, bats, clubs, hammers, and sometimes special flagellation ('spanking') machines intent on destroying the child.

Nothing is symbolized any longer in the presumed children's literature of modern times. All is unabashed violence, cruelty, explosions, murder, and death; and the children are of course encouraged to enjoy themselves fantasying on these same adult-supplied themes. The authors and illustrators of such literature (and the matching movies, comic-books, and television) recoil today at nothing ... nothing. Even a torso-murder, with the corpse's arms and legs gruesomely hacked off, is shown in the snob-illustrated nursery-rhyme book, *Three Young Rats,* by Alexander Calder & James Johnson Sweeney (New York: Museum of Modern Art, 1944–46) pages 107, 113, and with *worms,* page 127, the hands-down winner in the "Most Disgusting Children's Book" sweepstakes until some more recent items by Tomi Ungerer. And the *omnia opera* of Edward Gorey (*Amphigorey,* 1974): really just anti-children gloats, especially the fashionably 'sick' and campy sadisms-in-verse of his *The Listing Attic* (grisly limericks: 1954), and *The Gashlycrumb Tinies* (1963), the most repulsive of current anti-child and anti-family romps. And all, of course, under the gallows-laughter excuse of 'sick' or 'camp' humor, in which evil things are curiously admitted to be psychologically sick and are *therefore* purported to be specially funny. The modern equivalent of the older centuries' permitted lunatics in the streets: 'God's fools.'

An illustrated English book, apparently entitled *The Grump,* and dating from the early twentieth century, has the children shown being frankly stuffed into a sausage-making machine, and fed to Mr. Grump for supper. This is left only as an ugly implication in the folktale of "Hänsel & Gretel" and their cannibalistic witch, of which several hideously illustrated modern editions exist by Maurice Sendak and others, aside from the opera by Engelbert Humperdinck (1893) which is for some reason always shown to children on Christmas Day. It is worth underlining that, in general, both the authors and artists nowadays specializing in children's books, comic-books, animated cartoons – a real battlefield of cute little animals mutilating and destroying each other – and most other juvenile literature and television 'media' pap, are among the sickest degenerates and most aggressive neurotics running around loose. They should be stuffed into their own sausage-making machines (one of their milder fantasies), or at the very least be prevented by force from having anything whatever to do with children or their literature. But no one – except one psychiatrist, Dr. Fredric Wertham, has ever had the courage to say so.

One should also not overlook the writers and others whose attack on children takes the crudest and queasiest form, of sexually exploiting their bodies in fantasy or in fact. The classic example is the well-loved Lewis Carroll, who was finally prohibited from coming to the home of the little girl to whom he dedicated *Alice in Wonderland* (1865), owing to the naked photographs he had been making of a dozen other little girls, if not of her. So also America's favorite humorist, Mark Twain, who became almost an archetype of the 'Dirty Old Man' when a widower in his seventies, sporting white cashmere suits to show his total purity, and surrounding himself with a carefully non-sexual harem of little girls from eleven to seventeen. These he called publicly his 'Angel-Fish Aquarium,' but considered them privately – as shown in the last manuscript he ever wrote, the "Ashcroft-Lyon" document – as the juicy young virgins from whom he doubtless hoped for some sort of rejuvenation and a cure for his sexual impotence. See further my long introduction to Twain's hitherto unpublished *The Mammoth Cod* (Milwaukee: Maledicta, 1976).

Owing to the libel laws, it is not possible to discuss right here any living writers of children's books, though it would not be hard to do, covering both heterosexual and homosexual cases. One that I cannot forbear to mention is that of perhaps the most famous modern illustrator of children's books, who has behind him a long *sub rosa* publishing history of privately issued pornographica, concentrating on detailed orgy scenes of children, often with their parents or other adults. This man's early work sells today at fabulous prices among European erotica collectors, much of it in the form of unpublished watercolor sketches of paedophilic and incestuous scenes, which even the underground publishers had refused to touch. Things have changed: aside from the children's-book illustrators who graduate into this work from an apprenticeship at drawing the sick fantasies of sado-masochism for *Nutrix* comics, and other horror-publications similar, one well-known illustrator of children's books today has openly published under his own name a portfolio of sexually perverted imaginings, not really so different from the material in his ostensible children's books.

The bogus public literature intended for children by these and other worthies has in our century increased to monumental proportions that would have made those early industrialists of the children's-book industry, Samuel Goodrich ('Peter Parley') and William Holmes McGuffey, pea-green with envy. Most of this literature, and the matching 'media' proliferations, are based squarely on the simple Newtonian principle of 'equal and opposite reaction' laid down first in the eighteenth century by the early nursery-rhyme editors and publishers, as discussed at the opening of this essay: *Childhood sexuality and the harmless bawdy lore of children are to be replaced at every level by violence, horror, and death.* The children do not ask for this; adults force it upon them with all the crushing power of printing-presses, motion pictures, television, and the socially organized and institutionalized spectacle-sadism of 'death shows' and the mass-genocide that will doubtless come next, on the style created by Hitler. 'The effect of this imbalance,' says Christine Hoffmann, 'is devastating. Children are ambushed from infancy by violence in every form of medium. From television, comic-books, and a score of other sources they learn to suppress instinctive emotions of love and sex, and to hate everything from authority figures to the opposite sex.'

Every nursery-rhyme collection, every children's library, every child's private library of comic-books, is today a living museum showing this principle of *permitted sadism substituted for prohibited sexuality* in lavish operation, while motion pictures, animated cartoons and television are the full-color Chamber of Horrors or advanced course for the young graduate sadists, pyromaniacs, and other degenerates. I have made this substitution of an allowed sadism for a censored sexuality the subject of my monograph, *Love & Death: A Study in Censorship* (New York: Breaking Point, 1949), covering in particular murder-mysteries, comic-books, and the literary and real attacks of adult men and women on each other. Instead of going out of date, this monograph seems to become more timely every year, except that the most recent offerings are far more horrible and bloodthirsty — especially in motion pictures and television — than anything being promulgated during the 1940's, with the possible exception of the Atom Bomb.

Rather than give any further analysis myself, I would prefer to draw back again to the smallest scale, and cite here in full a famous document, bravely issued in Manchester, 1952, by Geoffrey Handley-Taylor, and inspired perhaps by the demands of Prof. Allen Abbott in 1937 and Geoffrey Hall in 1949 for reform of at least the nursery rhymes, shovelled out for centuries now by doting parents in Britain and America upon their youngest children especially, as being perfect memorizing matter with which to stuff these youthful brains.

> The average collection of 200 traditional nursery rhymes contains approximately 100 rhymes which personify all that is glorious and ideal for the child. Unfortunately, the remaining 100 rhymes harbour unsavoury elements. The incidents listed below occur in the average collection, and may be accepted as a reasonably conservative estimate based on a general survey of this type of literature.

 8 allusions to murder (unclassified),
 2 cases of choking to death,
 1 case of death by devouring,
 1 case of cutting a human being in half,
 1 case of decapitation,
 1 case of death by squeezing,
 1 case of death by shrivelling
 1 case of death by starvation,
 1 case of boiling to death,
 1 case of death by hanging,
 3 cases of death by drowning,
 4 cases of killing domestic animals,
 1 case of body snatching,
21 cases of death (unclassified),
 7 cases relating to the severing of limbs,
 1 case of the desire to have a limb severed,
 2 cases of self-inflicted injury,
 4 cases relating to the breaking of limbs,
 1 allusion to a bleeding heart,
 1 case of devouring human flesh,
 5 threats of death,
 1 case of kidnapping,
12 cases of torment and cruelty to human beings
   and animals,
 8 cases of whipping and lashing,
 3 allusions to blood,
14 cases of stealing and general dishonesty,
15 allusions to maimed human beings and animals,
 1 allusion to undertakers,
 2 allusions to graves,
23 cases of physical violence (unclassified),
 1 case of lunacy,
16 allusions to misery and sorrow,
 1 case of drunkenness,
 4 cases of cursing,
 1 allusion to marriage as a form of death,
 1 case of scorning the blind,

1 case of scorning prayer,
9 cases of children being lost or abandoned,
2 cases of house burning,
9 allusions to poverty and want,
5 allusions to quarrelling,
2 cases of unlawful imprisonment,
2 cases of racial discrimination.

Expressions of fear, weeping, moans of anguish, biting, pain, and evidence of supreme selfishness may be found in almost every other page.

Here, as just one sample, is a charming morsel quoted with high approbation in Clifton Fadiman's "Babel and Babylon," in *Any Number Can Play* (1957), marvelling 'What terror . . . gasps out of these stanzas, with their dreadful iteration, sung to children when all England waited in fear of Boney:'

> Baby, baby, if he hears you,
> As he gallops past the house,
> Limb from limb at once he'll tear you,
> Just as pussy tears a mouse.
>
> And he'll beat you, beat you, beat you,
> And he'll beat you all to pap,
> And he'll eat you, eat you, eat you,
> Every morsel, snap, snap, snap.

This list would, of course, be considered very mild stuff indeed today, at any level above that of the nursery. Ask any ten-year-old child you know, or simply sit down with him (or her) and read the comic-books children read, or watch thoughtfully the movies and television they watch – in fact, that you yourself may purposely be putting before their eyes, or accompanying them to see. Again, people who deplore this state of affairs are always apt to overlook that children do not and cannot themselves proliferate this ghastly horror-literature, and the Grand Guignol of television which is now replacing it, any more than they are the authors of that lesser Guignol, of Punch and Judy belaboring each other and everyone else, that preceded it.

We know that children learn to *enjoy* it, just as they enjoy narcotic and hallucinatory drugs when these are peddled to them. The question is, why are money-grubbing and perverted adults allowed to pervert children? These big 'media' industries, capitalized in the billions, have found their profit in this purposeful perversion of children, while idiot parents sit by, smiling permissively and — truth to tell — defiling themselves happily in the same sadistic spectacles. Of attacks on the child, this is certainly the most dangerous that has ever existed, and at a really frightening level that makes unimportant the merely quaint older system of beating the children physically in home, school, and factory, while berating them as idle sinners in print and threatening them with damnation.

One thing is sure: there is more and worse to come. The Attack on the Child has now broadened out into an *ideal* in our civilization, the Pharaonic ideal of King Herod in *Matthew*, ii. 16, who wanted simply to kill all the children. Does this seem overstated? Yet what else is the conscious and noisy intention of that broad segment of the civilized world today, who would not accept birth control owing to their religious prejudices and superstitions in the 1930's when there was still time, and who therefore today are demanding that there should be *no more children*, or the fewest possible needed to keep all the billion wheels of materialistic Western civilization meaninglessly turning. 'Zero Population Growth!' — the new rallying cry of overpopulation alarm-criers and newly-worried environment polluters. A chorus now curiously swollen by the voice of the Lesbian fringe of the Women's Liberation movement, who, fearing and having failed at motherhood themselves, wish to make us believe that woman can never be really free until she is nothing more than a neuterized wage-slave like man; with pants, sterilization, and all the glorious rest of it.

Meanwhile, simultaneously, miracles of medical science and surgery are lavished, and are to be lavished in an increasing scale, on keeping the old people alive — as long as possible or longer — under the propaganda denomination of lengthening the span of life. '*We Will All Live To Be 200 In the 21st Century!*' screams a pathetic headline in a cheap magazine before me. All of us, that is, except the well-birth-controlled and aborted children. They are not to be born at all. *Place aux vieux*!

And what is our glorious future-without-children to consist of? Well, servo-mechanisms and computers will of course do all the necessary work (and thinking), we are assured, while 'Golden-Age Youngsters' in their sixties and seventies slide gracefully into their 'Third Age' – or is it the Fourth? – while masticating unaccustomed delicacies in exotic restaurants with their new, state-supplied false teeth. And soar in the jumbojets of the future, on their 'Be-Good-To-Yourself' retirement-plan flights, to glamorously unknown foreign locations (whose native populations have all long since been starved to death, except for a few necessary guides and prostitutes of both sexes: *Population Zero*!) while watching cowboy-&-gangster murders and spy-tortures on the in-flight movie screen, and the germ-free nipples in their aging ears play a soothing soundtrack of gunfire and explosions to calm their souls. They are right, of course. With adults like these, who needs children? If the food runs short, *eat* the children, as Dean Swift suggested.

The essential trick, the nimble-go-thimble that makes the whole social swindle work, is the substitution of violence – which one can slaver over at any age – for the sexuality that remains mostly the prerogative of the relatively young. That is why the young must be conditioned to want and *need* violence, at least in media-supplied fantasies, until the time when violence a little more real will be made available. I have tried to outline this not-very-well hidden plan for the future in *Love & Death,* and it has also been done, much better, in two books by the one – just one – courageous psychiatrist who was willing to stand up on a platform with me and attack the peddling of violence-fantasies to children, Dr. Fredric Wertham in his *Seduction of the Innocent* (1954) and his much deeper and more frightening *A Sign for Cain* (1966). Here Wertham broadens out the whole question, in the realization that all this glorification of violence and savagery for children and adults, this diseased paddling and peddling in blood and horror, is simply the purposeful psychological softening-up of the entire and final generation of children destined to operate the genocides to come.

It has been customary now for three centuries to express a good deal of smug self-congratulation about the sex-substituted violence of children's literature, or, rather, to brag of its presumable lack of any sexuality at all. "The Pornography of Children's Books," as suggested by Joan Gould, is a study that remains to be written. Meanwhile, the recent collapse of the same old three centuries' anti-sexual censorship throughout much of Western Europe and America has brought a generally offensive type of pictorial pornography into mass circulation in magazines, motion-pictures, and the street-life of most large cities in the West. This makes it difficult to keep the pure sadism intended for the juvenile audience hermetically separate any longer from the impure pornography presumably intended for adults. The usual solution has been to prevent children from seeing sex films, by means of a police-enforced "X" rating, while encouraging them to see all the violence films and television grue they please, if accompanied by an adult ("PG" classification: 'Parental Guidance') – the very same adult who will accompany them into the psychiatrist's office a few years later, but can never understand why.

Anti-pornography crusades are mounted by religious groups, and indignant exposés are published in powerful propaganda organs, such as *Time* magazine (April 5th, 1976), excoriating pornography as the new plague. But the emphasis is invariably on the undesirable pornography of sex; never on the far more undesirable and anti-human pornography of violence, which is in essence a socially institutionalized amok. It is frittering and fraudulent to strike poses about "The Porno Plague," while pointedly omitting to mention that the plague actually engulphing us is not the pornography of sex but the perverted pornography of violence, catastrophes, sadism and death.

Two motion pictures have typified the two antagonistic genres – fortunately still separate – of sex and violence: the first and most popular of the 'hard core' sex-movies publicly shown, called *Deep Throat*, of which the title is also its scenario; and the outstanding best-seller among the sadism movies, *Jaws*, in which we see a killer-shark devouring alive its human victims, who vomit their last gutload into the paying audience's face. *Deep Throat* grossed thirty million dollars at the box-office. *Jaws* grossed one hundred and fifty millions. Extrapolated onto the national scene, that means five times as many Americans (including permitted children) preferred to enjoy straight sadism rather than exotic sex, at least as a spectacle. Five to one: think it over.

Add to these figures the total box-office gross on all the sex-shows, books, magazines, films, etc., combined; versus that of mere-ly the new violence films, like *Earthquake, The Towering Inferno* (double-featured as "Shake and Bake!" but two sex-shows as "Cream and Scream!" would be in bad taste), plus *Rollerball, The Exorcist, The Godfather, Mandingo* — an anti-Negro torture-show, pretending to be an historical exposé of slavery — *Soldier Blue, Bonnie and Clyde,* and a thousand other crime and horror gloats, raking in the money for over seventy years now, and in all countries. The total sex porno scene is a picayune million-dollar racket, run by authentic perverts, god knows. The Pornography of Violence is a billion-dollar industry, also run by perverts, but with unlimited banking credit and media time. After the fantasy orgasms of sex porno have come the 'live shows.' After the bloodbath fantasies of violence pornography, with its juicy catastrophes and closeup cow-boy killings, must come the 'death shows.' Take your pick.

In fact, the death shows are here already. Aside from the endless war-horror propaganda photos (and faked drawings) in national magazines, movies, and the like, plus the endlessly-repeated 'news' shots over television of assassinated political leaders and helpless hostages grovelling in their blood, there is now even a 97-minute television documentary called *Dying,* being shown nationally all over the United States, excruciatingly savouring for an hour and a half the pre-death agony of three separate people dying of cancer. This supreme example of death-gloating, peddled to the entire viewing audience of a nation under the vile hypocritical pretense of 'sympathy,' took two years to produce — while photographing the slowly-dying victims and their daily lives — and $330,000 were spent on making it, most of this money coming from the National Endowment for the Humanities (*sic*). Less pretentiously disguised about their crude sadism, there are already available almost endless movies and plays, keyed completely to the spectacle of human and even animal deaths, including one presumably *avant garde* item showing the progressive stages of putrefaction of the dead body of a dog. One assumes this was paid for by the National Endowment for the *In*humanities.

It is difficult to understand all the publicity fuss made about just one of these death shows, called *Snuff*, which ends with one miserable girl killed before the audience's eyes, just like *Bonnie and Clyde* years back. Perhaps *Snuff* was too unsubtle about the sexual overtones involved in killing and presumably dismembering a naked woman. Yet that is where *Jaws* BEGINS its hundred and fifty million dollar success. And goes on from there. Gullet for gullet, would you rather risk your body politic to *Deep Throat* or to *Jaws*? Is it the exotic eroticism of the one, or the spectacle sadism of the other, that will really bring America and the West to the total pornotopia of violence prophesied in *Brave New World, Rollerball, Death Race 2000*, and *A Clockwork Orange*?

One important final point. *Time* ends its exposé by observing dourly that there is no pornography problem in Russia. Nor in China. That is because neither culture allots paper pulp or media time to socially undesirable activities like the pornographies of sex and of violence, to which we in the West allot respectively millions and billions. The Russians and the Chinese have lots of sexual problems, just like us, but they siphon off these repressions into solving their social problems, exactly as Freud suggested.

We in the West are being touted instead into forgetting our overwhelming social problems by throwing ourselves into the mudbath of sex porno and the bloodbath of violence, catastrophes, sadism and death. Violence-pornography is the new *Opium of the people*, long after Marx. We have opened the doors of those two tremendous mysteries — sex and aggression — and are using the secrets we have found there to destroy ourselves. That is why Russia and China are quite confident that they will bury us. When we have sacrificed our children on the altar of gold, to the Molochs of the violence industry, and our dirty dance on the volcano of violence is finished.

G. LEGMAN

La Clé des Champs
Valbonne (Alpes-Maritimes)
FRANCE

PREFACE

The world of children, as shown in their jokes, is a fascinating and often strange place, where animals can speak, shapes and actions are distorted, and most anything can happen within basic limits set by the adult world. Children's jokes depict a strong contrast between a surface or funny level and a deeper and more serious meaning and significance. This duality also represents the contrast between the child and the adult, the child's world and the adult world. The child must learn to adjust to and live within the adult world with all its encompassing rules, laws, and restraints, and his jokes give him one medium to try and merge childish fantasy with reality. The more serious and significant meanings of jokes are often ignored in favor of the light and funny aspects of them, for jokes are "just funny," and therefore can be used to disguise and hide thoughts, emotions, actions and criticisms that can't be voiced openly for fear of punishment or causing too much anxiety and tension. The success of a joke often depends on hiding this contrast between what is literally and vividly said and what is actually subtly implied on a deeper level, and on the whole children are unaware of any other meaning besides that the joke is funny and that they laugh. A joke is no longer funny if it comes too close to stating what the child is afraid to say, think or feel openly.

This duality of children's jokes which contrasts the child with adult and shows the process the child must go through to become an adult, continues into many different aspects of the jokes. Innocence versus knowledge, youth versus old age, the fool versus the wiseman, are all elements found in the jokes. On the surface the child is innocent, young and the fool, but underneath the image changes, and the tables are reversed; it is the adult who is stupid and the fool, and the child triumphs. Taught to grow up quickly and become an adult, but treated like a child, he learns through his jokes, especially about sex, and he shows he knows much more than his parents realize, or want him to know.

A major contrast found in the jokes is the difference between the mild gentle form of the joke, and the actual aggression expressed and the pain caused by the jokes. Children's jokes are usually fairly mild, and the aggression level is fairly low. There is certainly the aggressive element present of making the listener feel like a fool because he doesn't know the trick answer to the riddle or joke, and within the subject matter of the jokes there is aggression expressed towards various groups of people, usually adult authority figures. On the whole the jokes aren't strongly aggressive, and don't try to force the listener to suffer the same anxieties and tensions that the teller suffers. The enjoyment and amusement the child gains from the jokes comes perhaps from the vivid image created by the words rather than from the actual aggression or hostility expressed.

Here again is another contrast that ties in with the surface-deep, funny-serious meaning, the pictorial image versus the subtle verbal thought. Children's jokes on the whole lack subtlety of action or words, but instead create and rely on a strong pictorial image for the amusement. Jokes such as No. 852, where the pregnant woman swallows various objects, including a couch, create for the listener and teller a vivid picture, and the absurdness of the image is funny, no matter what the underlying serious significance the joke may be. Even simple puns tie a physical action or object to a mental concept or thought, such as the man taking a ruler to bed to see how long he slept. (No. 450) The images and pictures formed in the jokes, even if the child lets his imagination and fantasy run wild, are still concerned with concrete objects and actions, and not abstract ideas and thoughts.

The jokes that a child tells usually correspond to his physical mental, and emotional development. Although his understanding of the joke and why he thinks it is funny may be different from that of the adult, rarely does a child tell a joke that he doesn't understand in some manner, for in that case he is apt to fail in telling the joke and look foolish in front of his peers and to adults (usually his parents). As his understanding and vocabulary build and grow, so will his jokes change from short quick riddles and puns popular with the younger children, to complex jokes and anecdotes. Correspondingly, as he grows older, the child's jokes will reflect a greater aggressive level, become more subtle and abstract in thought and action, and adult-like in form.

Children learn early (some at the age of 3 or 4) that jokes are one form of communication, a form that can gain them acceptance and popularity. Although not every child tells jokes, most learn to appreciate them and to laugh. Those who adopt this form of communication try to perfect their art, learning how to tell the story properly, how to keep their audience interested, when to spring the punchline at the right psychological moment, and gathering a larger repertoire of stories and jokes so that they can keep talking and remain the center of attention. Many of the jokes children tell have been around a long time, having been passed from child to child, generation to generation, like joke No. 491, "Who wrote the Cliff Tragedy? Eileen Dover," or No. 360, "What goes 99 bump? A centipede with a wooden leg." For the children, only one criterion is used to tell if a joke is popular and in oral circulation – it is funny and it allows or causes the children to laugh.

Children's jokes therefore, represent a merging of reality with fantasy, the physical world with a mental world, the concrete with the abstract, and pictorial images and actions with verbal thoughts. The humor of the situation is found in the clash or incongruity between these spheres, as the child struggles to think and act like an adult, learning to accept life as it is and not as he would like it to be.

The purpose of this research was to discover how children view the adult world through the medium of their jokes and humor. In order to answer this question I needed both children and their jokes.

In England, two locations were used, Leeds and London. The main bulk of this material was collected with the use of a tape recorder, but questionnaires were also used. Most of the collecting was done in the school year 1973-1974. Four schools were chosen in Leeds, and two schools were selected in London where only questionnaires were used (see Appendix No. 1). On a return trip to London in 1975, the taping method was used at a third school.

In the United States, jokes were collected from children at schools in San Francisco and San Diego, and at a Navy swimming pool in San Diego, all with the use of the tape recorder. Jokes remembered by older people from their childhoods were also collected, and these jokes came from Colorado, Oregon, New Jersey, New York, and California.

The original age group chosen to study was from 8 to 11, but in Leeds these limits expanded to include age 6 through 13. In London, the children ranged from 7 through 11, and in the United States from 6 to 16. The majority of the children were aged 8 to 11.

The approach to the jokes was basically psychological – why do the children find these particular jokes funny, how do they view the adult world they live in through the jokes, and what themes are present in the jokes? When I asked the children why they liked their jokes, the only answer consistently given was that they were funny. Any deeper psychological reason why they might like the jokes is unknown or ignored by the majority of the children, although a few of the children realize that they like a particular joke because it makes a certain adult, either a teacher, policeman, or parent, look foolish.

The jokes were divided into twenty-five categories, the first ten by the type of joke, such as parodies, riddles, and knock knock jokes; and the last fifteen by the subject matter – ethnic jokes, elephant jokes, sexual jokes, etc. A further nine themes were cross categorized throughout all twenty-five groups; themes that in some cases were more general than the original subjects, and in other cases more specific. These included topics such as sex, odd characters, and animals. With the jokes sub-divided into sections and themes, I was ready to determine what these jokes meant to the children, and what general trends, if any, existed in this large body of material.

Even though I had some difficulties in collecting the children's jokes, which I will discuss below, I was able to adapt to the child's world and viewpoints, and laugh with them at their jokes. I usually had no difficulty in getting the children to begin telling jokes, and once started, and after they realized I was an appreciative listener, there was no stopping the flow of jokes.

In England, I found I was popular among the children for a variety of reasons; one, I was from California where their favourite pop stars were from; two, I had an American accent which they admired; and three, they got out of their regular work and classes to tell jokes, At one Leeds school the boys wanted me to return in the afternoon so they could get out of maths to tell jokes. The teachers also cooperated, for they got a break from teaching and from the children. In the United States, similar reasons made me popular with the children and teachers, except a reverse of the accent held true; the children thought I was English and liked my accent.

Although the American and English cultures are very similar, and the language is basically the same, I discovered some English jokes that I just didn't understand. Humor is particularly difficult to explain – the joke isn't funny when you have to repeat and explain it – and it relies on basic knowledge, such as cultural values, ideas, and tension spots that are understood and taken for granted by a group's member, and are again very difficult to explain to an outsider. Most of the jokes that I didn't understand were ones based on brand products, TV shows, stars and heroes, and esoteric stereotypes of other ethnic and cultural groups present in England and different from my background. After living in England for a year I picked up a lot of necessary information for understanding English humor.

Some of the jokes that are based on insider's information in England are joke No. 816 – a golden wonder crisp; No. 817 – Tunes help you to breath more easily; No. 1002 – stork margarine and penguin biscuits; No. 521 – Tommy Cooper and 'just like that'; No. 520 – Larry Grayson and 'shut that door'; and No. 384 – Wheetabix the Builder.

Similar jokes that are typically American are No. 418 and No. 538 – Betty Crocker; No. 295 – a ball-point banana; and No. 489 – Marshall Dill (Marshall Dillon of Dodge City).

Many other jokes could be given as examples for both cultures, especially differences between England and the United States, of different words for the same object, such as crisp = potato chip; knickers = panties (underpants); biro = ballpoint pen, etc. I found at first I needed an interpreter to explain the English products and people, and fortunately I had a roommate who gladly explained any points and listened to my tapes to decode certain words that were unintelligible to me, either in their usage, or with the accent. At times the accents were just too much – especially the Yorkshire accents in Leeds. I also had problems with the speed of the children's talking, even in the United States. I started each taping session asking the children to speak slowly so I could understand what they were saying.

A serious shortcoming of the taping method is having no record at all of the children's facial and body movements and expressions. It is hard to record on paper what the person emphasized and how different words were accented, and the jokes lose a lot of their vitality and humor when they are only read. Each joke teller imparts a bit of his own personality into each joke, making it his version of the joke. The first four boys interviewed, aged 12 and 13 from Leeds, each had their own manner and style of telling jokes, and each one was an expert joke teller. My favourite joke was one told by one of these four boys about a budgie, complete with a strong voice emphasis and expression, and an unusual head movement signifying the death of each bird, but much is lost in the written paper version. (No. 1130)

A major difficulty with using questionnaires was the difficulty of reading the children's handwriting, and deciphering their spelling. In most cases, the child's spelling was corrected, such as 'ded' to 'dead', but in some cases this was impossible, and their spelling was retained, along with their grammar and punctuation.

A problem specifically related to collecting children's jokes is the necessity of laughing at each and every joke, even if I'd heard it five times before. The children were giving me something they valued, and they expected me to show proper appreciation of their jokes. I got extremely tired of the wellerisms about the chimneys and telephones (No. 607 and 609), but when I received three versions of the same joke, one right after the other, I had a hard time laughing. (No. 868). Also, what is funny to a child is often not funny to an adult, such as the many jokes I heard about toilets and the need to use them.

Overall, the project was extremely successful. Even with the difficulties of reading the handwriting on the questionnaires, or of decoding the tapes, over 1000 jokes were collected, many more if duplications and variations were counted. The children confided in me, perhaps because they realized they would probably never see me again, and that I couldn't affect them or punish them in any way. And for a short time, I became a child again, viewing in a strong and vivid pictorial way the world of a child.

ORIGIN AND TRANSMISSION OF JOKES

The origin and transmission of jokes are an interesting problem. When asked, children usually say they got the joke 'off a friend' or another person. In England, other sources are current T.V. programs such as Dave Allen (Irish jokes), The Comedians (variety), and Jokers Wild (variety), comic books (Shiver and Shake, The Topper, Wizzer and Chips, Sparky), and rag mags (pamphlets published and sold by all the universities during rag week containing jokes and pictures, the money going to charity). In the United States joke books are very popular. When the elephant joke cycle was popular, elephant joke books were published, and many other joke cycles have jokebooks dedicated solely to that type of joke, like the Polack or Jewish jokes. Jokes seem to suffer very little from the effects of publication, although to continue in popularity a joke must also be found in oral circulation.

Children tell jokes most anywhere, although the school, either during class, playtime or before or after school, seems to be the most popular time and place, with home running a close second. In keeping with where they tell jokes, most children tell their jokes to their friends, with their parents the second most popular recipient. Almost all of the jokes a child learns will be told to his parents, except for the sexual ones, which he isn't 'supposed to know' and that he could be punished for. Although parents hear most of their child's jokes, the child learns few jokes from his parents.

The transmission of jokes is an amazing phenomenon, in that the children's joke repertoires are similar from Leeds to London, but also, there are similarities in the jokes told in England and the United States. The greatest similarity can be seen in the joke-riddles, which are easy to learn and repeat, but long jokes too were found in both cultures. One very popular joke cycle, the elephant jokes, had international fame and was told in the United States, England, the English-speaking parts of India, as well as Germany and perhaps other countries as well. As travel becomes more frequent, especially international travel, jokes go too, crossing cultural and language barriers. Service men stationed abroad also carry their jokes with them. An interesting transmission line was suggested – as stock brokers call each other from London to New York and vice versa, and are waiting for information, they exchange jokes. Jokes are also said to be transmitted around the United States on the telegraph wires at night when the lines are being checked, and the taxi cab drivers are great transmitters of jokes. However they travel, jokes make themselves at home in their new location, and have in many cases taken the place of the folktale, which people no longer have time to listen to. The short joke form, adapted to today's fast pace, has become a member of the international jet set.

A few of the children said that they made up jokes themselves. The younger children were probably referring to joke-riddles, which follow a formula. Once the formula is known, countless jokes can be made up. One 8-year-old girl from Leeds said she made up the joke "What is yellow and goes round and round? A banana in a washing machine." (No. 294) This type of joke can be about almost any object and action, and one popular with the London children is "What is white on the outside and green on the inside? A frog sandwich." (No. 285) While still staying within the bounds of a set formula, the children can use their imagination and experience to make up jokes that baffle the listener, but actually have simple logical answers. These jokes also have the advantage of being short, simple, and easy to remember.

A second joke that was possibly made up by a child is No. 497, "When is a bus not a bus? When it's a street." Although this joke doesn't make sense, it does follow the formula of a similar joke "When is a door not a door? When it's ajar." (No. 500) The formula has been learned but the meaning isn't clear.

As for the joke proper, I know of only one joke that a 12-year-old English boy made up. This is No. 836 about Black men trying to sneak into England by the use of coffins. This joke was told by one of the most experienced joke tellers I talked to, one of four boys aged 12 and 13 from School 1 in Leeds. The boy who made up the joke did not tell it, but his friend did, showing that the joke was beginning to pass into oral circulation and acceptance. The joke is well organized and portrays current ideas and stereotypes of immigrants and Black people in England. Although there is no proof that the boy actually made up this joke, I see no reason why these boys couldn't make up jokes, for all four of these boys are very fluent joke tellers. They know enough jokes and joke motifs to be able to compose new jokes, they often told jokes, especially among themselves, and they are from an area and of an age to be aware of current events and current problems. Even the jokes they have learned from other sources, because they tell them, show that they have some understanding of the situation. Jokes about the dumb Irishman, or greedy Jew, are very popular, and as they said, 'we have nothing against the Irish, but they're supposed to be stupid and Jews to be mean.' They have incorporated the current stereotypes of these groups into their jokes and thinking, and are aware of them, even if they realize they aren't real or true. Most jokes, but especially sexual jokes, aren't told by the child until he has some understanding and comprehension of the joke, or he might make a fool of himself by telling the joke incorrectly. By incorporating a joke into his repertoire, the child shows that the joke has some meaning and function for him, and it can demonstrate how far he has mentally and emotionally developed.

Other possible jokes the child might have made up are ones where the punchline concerns the character's need, desire or use of the toilet. These jokes are particularly popular with the 8 and 9-year-olds, such as the 8-year-old boy's joke about the 6 foot raspberry pudding pie from outer space (No. 917). What is funny to the child is this great desire to use the toilet, and the long drawn-out accounts, probably the beginnings of the shaggy dog structure, end with this element. Again too, the picture created is very vivid and alive. Their imagination is used to create fantastic situations and characters, but in the end, they are brought down by the common human need to use a toilet.

HISTORICAL TRENDS

Jokes can travel in large cycles or groups, usually comprising a general charcter, or stereotype; and the humor arises from showing or high-lighting various aspects of this stereotype or character. These cycles can be divided into four different types: 1) cross-cultural, found in both England and the United States; 2) delay of transmission from one culture to the other; 3) same form and attitude but the actual character has been changed; and 4) cycles existing in one culture but not the other.

Studies have been done to show how and why a particular cycle has fit into the history of the culture at that moment in time (Dundes and Abrahams, 1969), and how a certain cycle has paralleled the psychological development and growth of the child (Wolfenstein, 1954). It is not my aim to determine why various cycles now exist among the children in England or the United States, but to point out the various types and how they have changed over time.

1. Cross-cultural: The elephant joke became popular in the United States and England (as well as the English/American groups in India and in other European countries) in the early 1960's. Jokes similar to the elephant joke, using the same format, were also popular, such as:

What's black and dangerous and sits in a tree?
A crow with a machine gun. (No. 251)

What's green and swims in the ocean?
Moby Pickle. (No. 277)

The elephant joke became so popular that books of elephant jokes were published, and they were popular with adults as well as children. Some of the jokes popular with adults had a sexual connotation:

Why does an elephant have 4 feet?
It's better than 6 inches. (Dundes and Abrahams, 1969, p. 230)

Although there existed many more the straightforward, non-sexual type, such as:

Why did the elephant paint its toenails red?
To hide in the cherry tree. (No. 695)

Presently in England and in the United States, the elephant joke has gone out of fashion and is no longer in circulation. I collected this type of joke from some informants over 18 who remembered them from their childhood, and from a few children who had seen them in an English comic book, but on the whole elephant jokes aren't popular now. Jokes of the 'what's — (color) and — (action verb)' type, similar to the elephant joke, are also dying out, although more of these were told by the children than of the elephant jokes. A joke popular in London in some ways shows the death of the elephant joke cycle:

Two elephants fell off the cliff. Boom Boom. (No. 717)

Dundes and Abrahams have investigated the latent content of the elephant joke, relating it to certain psychological and social factors in the lives of those who tell these jokes. The elephant, big, apparently clumsy, yet tremendously powerful and surprisingly adept, is the epitome of sexual power, and his immensity (especially of his phallus) and his alleged ability to procreate even under the most trying conditions, continually reoccur in the jokes. Dundes and Abrahams have related this superphallic elephant to the Western Oedipal strivings of the children in their families, as well as to the rise of the Negro in the Civil Rights Movement in the United States in the early 60's. The association of the elephant and the Negro, both coming from the jungle, and both being presumably sexually superpotent with large genitals, as well as concern with color, have led to this conclusion. Through fantasy, the elephant as the adult sexual rival and/or Negro is harmlessly killed and conquered in the jokes (Dundes and Abrahams, 1969, p. 225–239)

I assume that some of the same reasons exist for English people to tell elephant jokes as for Americans, but the motives for them to circulate have passed into other joke forms. The elephant joke now lives only in memories, comic books, and elephant joke books. (For additional elephant jokes, see Bibliography.)

2. Delay of Transmission: The Cruel Joke series or "sick joke" circulated in the United States in the late 1950's and early 1960's. I used to tell them when I was about 8 (1958) and they were of the form:

Mommy mommy, it's dark down here.
Shut up or I'll flush it again. (No. 1110)

Mommy mommy, can Johnny come out and play?
But you know Johnny has no arms or legs.
That's okay, we want to use him as second base. (No. 1111)

The first line of the joke is a simple request or statement, but the concluding statement throws the joke into a different realm of meaning. Either the "mommy" or the child is seen as the sick person, who both commit nasty, cruel and aggressive acts; the mother toward her child, or the mother and/or child against a third person.

Although these jokes came to England in the early 60's, which is only a short delay in transmission, they are presently circulating in England, but mainly with the older children, aged 11-18, and adults. They also appear to be much more popular now than in the 60's. The jokes are of the same form and content:

Mummy mummy, can I lick the bowl?
No, flush the chain like everybody else does. (No. 1112)

Mummy mummy, it's hot in here.
Shut up and get back in the oven. (No. 1113)

When someone tells one of these "cruel jokes," you hear comments like "How sick!" but one of this sort leads to others being told as well. Several years ago when the Biafran people were starving, similar cruel jokes existed about them as well. Presently in California there is a cycle of jokes called the "dead baby" jokes told by adults, and based on the same format.

How do you make a baby float?
3 scoops of dead baby in a glass of root beer. (SD:b.24.75)

(For additional cruel jokes see Bibliography.)

   3. *Same form and attitude, but different character:* Jokes that fit this category are ethnic jokes. These are based on a culture's stereotype of a certain ethnic group, and Dundes (1970) has researched clusters of characteristics that make up the stereotype and define the ethnic group for a specific culture.

   Two main ethnic stereotypes in the English material are – the Jewish and Irish joke cycles. The children define the Jew as mean, stingy with his money – a skinflint, with a desire to make a lot of money, and crafty. The Irish are stupid — "thick," dirty and poor; and, in relation to the Scottish and English, the Irishman is almost always the butt of the joke. The Englishman is always correct and posh, and the Scotsman is in the middle, or sometimes 'tight with his money,' crafty, and stingy.

In the United States, the Polish jokes (or Italian or Puerto Rican) take the place of the Irish jokes. (In Montana the North Dakotans are the butt of the joke, and in Texas, the "Aggies" — students from the State Agricultural College). The "Polack" is stupid, dirty, poor, inept, and vulgar, boorish and tasteless. The Italian can also have these same attributes, and also lacks courage. A similar stereotype is found for Jews: concern with making money, and always looking for a bargain or trade; desire for status — males in becoming professional men and females by marrying professional men, usually doctors and lawyers; a large Jewish nose; and pro- and anti-Semitism. (Dundes, 1970, p. 186-203)

The similarity of form but different character can be seen by comparing the Irish jokes with the Polish/Italian jokes.

1. a. What does it say on the bottom of a Guinness bottle?
   Open other end. (No. 729)

   b. What does it say on the bottom of a coca cola bottle in Poland?
   Open other end. (Dundes, 1970, p. 201)

2. a. How to keep an Irishman busy: Give him a card which has printed on both sides: — Please turn over. (No. 783)

   b. How do you keep a Polack busy?
   Give him this, (a square piece of paper on both sides of which is written, "Please turn over.") (Dundes, 1970, p. 201)

3. a. How many Irishmen do you need to paint?
   One to hold the ladder, one to hold the paint, and 100 to move the wall up and down. (No. 735)

   b. How many Italians does it take to change a lightbulb? 3 — one to hold the bulb and 2 to turn the ladder. (Simmons, 1966, p. 478)

   c. How many Italians does it take to make popcorn?
   4 — one to hold the pan and 3 to shake the stove. (Welsch, 1967, p. 185)

Many more examples could be given to show how the joke cycle is similar in both cultures, even though the butt of the joke has changed from the Irish to the Polack or the Italian. This shift in the United States can partly be seen as the rise of the Irish in the social and economic levels while the Italian and Polack have taken his place as the group that is trying to get jobs and rise in status. A difference can be seen in the intensity of the anti-stereotype; the Irishman is poor, and "thick," and dirty, but the Polack and Italian are even dirtier, poorer, and incredibly stupid, as well as being incapable, gross, uncouth and tasteless. Jokes such as:

Why does a Polack carry shit in his billfold?
For identification. (No. 750)

Why does a Polack wear a hat while taking a crap?
So he'll know which end to wipe. (Dundes, 1970, p. 200)

What is an Italian luau?
A bunch of guineas (Italians) sitting around a cesspool with straws. (Simmons, 1966, p. 478)

What is a Polish barbeque?
A fire in a garbage can. (Dundes, 1970, p. 200)

These are typical of the ethnic cycle in the United States, but I did not find in England any of these as typical of the Irish joke cycle, or at least I didn't collect any that were this anti-Irish. (For additional Irish, Jewish, Polish and Italian jokes see Bibliography.)

A second joke cycle that fits this category is the "moron" cycle which was extremely popular in the United States in the early 1950's, especially with children aged 7-11. Jokes of this sort were of the type:

Why did the moron throw the clock out the window?
To see time fly. (No. 472)

Why did the moron take the ladder to school?
He wanted to go to high school (No. 447) (Other versions: England – boy; US – Silly Billy)

The moron was thought to be old, about 40-50, usually a man, and extremely stupid and foolish. The humor arose from the ridiculous things he did with a logical reason based on his misunderstanding of the actual situation. As far as I was able to determine, the moron as a character was never found in English jokes, but the same or similar jokes with different characters are presently in England. One joke:

Why did the moron drive his car over the cliff?
To test his air brakes.

This has been attributed to an Irishman, and in the United States to a Polack:

Why did the Irishman drive a 2-ton truck over the cliff?
To test his air brakes. (No. 730, 772)

Others are attributed to a non-descriptive person:

Why did the man take the pen and pencil to bed?
To draw the curtains (No. 448)

Why did the man bring a ruler to bed?
To see how long he slept. (No. 450)

Why did the nurse tiptoe to the medicine cabinet?
She didn't want to wake the sleeping pills. (No. 473) (also Silly Billy)

Why did the vicar go into the church with a machinegun?
To make all the people holy. (No. 476)

All of these jokes have been attributed to the moron as well, but the figure in these more modern-circulating jokes is closer to reality. The child can recognize a boy, a man, a nurse, or a vicar as a real person, and capable of committing these foolish acts: but a moron, whatever or whoever that is, is hard to picture. The concept therefore, of a moron or "fool," the dumb innocent person, has been transmitted from the one culture to the other, even though the moron has changed names. In the United States as well, the moron as a character has dropped out of circulation, and he now appears as Silly Billy, another hard-to-define character, but easier to imagine as a human being. The function remains the same, the mocking of a foolish person, with perhaps the underlying suspicion that you could make the same mistakes.

See the happy moron
He doesn't give a damn
I wish I were a moron –
My God! perhaps I am. (Wolfenstein, 1954, p. 132-133)

The moron can also be envied; he always survives to commit another blunder, and yet he seems oblivious to harm and punishment, never learning from his mistakes. Dr. Wolfenstein says well: " . . . the child sees the moron as falling into traps which he is much too smart to succumb to. However, the moron is also enviable in his freedom from anxiety, not seeing the hazards he risks." (Wolfenstein, 1954, p. 132-133)

4. *Present in one culture only:* The Heinie jokes, popular with children between the ages of 8 and 11, were found in the United States during the 1950's, and they may be still circulating. This cycle was not found in England, mainly I think because Heinie, a euphemism for rear end or bottom, is not a slang term in England: (*bum* is used.) These jokes, concerning a boy named Heinie, and his mother, present a variety of situations to make Heinie's mother look foolish. The humor is particularly appealing to the child because it is the mother who gives this name to the child, and then she puts herself into the situations that make her look foolish, perhaps a type of wishfulfillment.

Heinie gets lost and the mother asks a policeman, 'Have you seen my Heinie…' The policeman replies, "No, but I'd sure like to."

The mother goes to a shoe store and says, "I want a pair of shoes for my Heinie."

The mother buys Heinie some ice cream which he gets smeared over his face. The mother then asks the man behind the counter: "Can I have a tissue for my Heinie?"

Through some far-fetched mishap, Heinie at a fiesta gets suspended by a lasso from a balcony and the mother cries: "Oh, my Heinie is hanging over the balcony!"
(All these versions of Heinie jokes were collected by Dr. Wolfenstein, 1954, p. 83)

Similar types of jokes collected in Leeds, England, had situations in which the child has a proper name given to him by his mother, who by calling out his name, gives the child the permission to do things normally forbidden. Nickabar steals a bar of chocolate (No. 935); Shagarada entertains the milkman (No. 868); and in the United States, Johnnie Fuckerfaster plays with little girls. (No. 869)

Other jokes make other authority figures look foolish, or they give the child, through the use of the name which is given to him by his parents, a chance to mock the authorities. Mindyourownbusiness, Manners, and Trouble confront the police (No. 933); and a teacher gets smart answer to the question "What does Constantinople mean?" (No. 937).

All of the current jokes fulfill a similar function of allowing the child to reverse the tables — it's the adult who is dumb, or who gives the child a dumb name that gets him into trouble because the name has a double meaning. Puns and the duality of words and their meanings are the first type of jokes that children attempt, and Dr. Wolfenstein has estimated that children at the age of 6 and 7 tell about 3 times as many joke-riddles (conundrums and puns) as jokes in any other form. In the following three years, the percentage of riddles is a little over half. At 11 and 12 it is reduced to a third, and riddles are discarded in favor of anecdotes. (Wolfenstein, 1954, p. 94). This sort of joke, where the child's name has a dual meaning, can only be attempted by children who can and have told punning riddles and conundrums, and who can joke about the fact that their parents use their name in a loving manner as well as in an angry punishing manner. They can make the situation into an amusing one, and make their parents look silly or foolish, instead of the child feeling that way.

A second cycle that I found very popular with the children aged 8-11 in England were the wellerisms, of the form: (see Jokes VII, Nos. 606-617)

What did the big chimney say to the little chimney?
You're too young to smoke. (No. 607)

What did the big telephone say to the little telephone?
You're too young to be engaged. (No. 609)

and of this form as well: (Nos. 618-621)

Two oranges were rolling down the road. One stopped. Why…
I've run out of juice. (No. 619)

Two biscuits were rolling down the road. One got run over. What
did the other one say?
Oh crumbs! (No. 618)

All of these jokes may be found in the United States as well, but I
have evidence of only one, with a slight difference: "Why does an
orange fall out of a tree? It ran out of juice." The tree is used because
oranges are seen on trees in California, where this joke was told. (San
Diego Evening Tribune.)

From this survey of the jokes collected, it appears that most jokes
are international and very old as well, changing and adapting to each
culture and situation, but their humor remaining ever popular.

FIELDWORK

School 1, located in the center of Leeds, and of a fairly low socio-
economic structure, was my best source of jokes. My first visit to the
school yielded about 30 papers written by 8 and 9 years old entitled
"Things You Think Are Funny." This approach to collecting jokes
was the idea of the teacher and it worked quite well. The children
talked to each other and to me, telling jokes and stories, and generally
making a lot of noise. Many more jokes were told than were written
down because, as I would stop by one child, a large group would
gather, and the noise level would increase as everyone shouted out
different jokes, but they forgot to write them down, or they were too
excited to write them down. They were much more concerned with
telling the jokes than committing them to paper.

I returned to this school three more times, each time taking a group
of four children from the same classroom into the small music room to
tape record. The first four boys were chosen by the headmaster as
ones who knew and told a lot of jokes; but the last two groups, one of
four girls, and the other of two boys and two girls, were volunteers
chosen by their teacher. Almost everyone in the class volunteered,

even if they didn't know any jokes, because they got out of class for a couple of hours.

The first group was my best and most productive group, and, at the end of this marathon joke-session of two hours, I had 147 jokes, including some rambling shaggy-dog stories, on tape. The children wanted to continue in the afternoon, partly because they got out of maths, and partly because they said they knew lots more jokes. In the beginning, I thought I might have to have a joke contest to get the boys started telling jokes, but with these accomplished joke-tellers, no contest was needed. They argued with each other as to who was going to tell the first joke, and which joke should be the first one told. The tape-recorder was ignored, except for the physical necessity of handing the microphone back and forth to the speakers, and they enjoyed themselves immensely, laughing at each and every joke, even if they already knew the joke. As one boy explained, "We think they're funny just because they're funny. It's the way you tell them sometimes. Even if it's not funny you just make them *laugh*." One joke would remind another boy of another joke, and several times two would consult each other about the next joke to tell while another was telling his joke, There were very few times when they couldn't think of any jokes.

The second taping session at School 1 was with a group of four girl volunteers. The first question they asked me was whether they could tell dirty jokes, and they told quite a few, in comparison to the four boys, in a two-hour period. The boys told "rude" jokes almost as an afterthought, and at the end of the taping session. This was partly I think because they had so many other jokes to tell they didn't need to tell me "rude" jokes. For the girls, the rude jokes seemed to play a bigger part in their repertoires. Also the boys were afraid of offending me, and told me to turn off the microphone if I thought the jokes were "too smutty" for me.

Unlike the boys, the four girls had a hard time ignoring the taperecorder, and the microphone was continually turned on and off as they tried to remember jokes. They assured me that they knew "lots" of jokes, but that they needed the "boring classroom, with nothing to do" to tell their jokes. Quite a few of their jokes were riddles, and one girl had a jokemachine from a cereal box which she

went and took from her desk to test us. In comparison, the first four
boys told mainly anecdotes and stories, and if they told riddles, they
were usually ethnic riddles. At playtime, the girls went out and
gathered a few more jokes from their friends. They wrote these down
and then read them to me for the taperecorder. They knew more
parodies than the boys, several songs and poems, and I left with a total
of 80 items.

The third session of two boys and two girls was run like the first
two sessions. The girls started out telling jokes, and the boys were
fairly quiet, but by the end of the session, the two boys had told the
most jokes. One of the girls actually told very few jokes, although she
was a good and appreciative listener, making comments like "that
was good" and "that was funny" throughout the session. Again,
these four were able to ignore the taperecorder for the most part, and
they even forgot to go out for their playtime which was in the middle
of the period. I taped 108 jokes and parodies, including a lot of paper-
and-pencil jokes and tricks. Near the end of the session they also did
several imitations of their favorite singing stars, the microphone a
great aid and prop.

School 2 was a parochial school located in the suburbs of Leeds, and
of a much higher socio-economic structure than School 1. Many
children of this school were the sons and daughters of the university
professors. The first class I visited was a class of 8-9 year olds. Only the
boys were in the room working on their needlework, as often in
England; the girls were in another room working on theirs. I set the
taperecorder up on a desk, and the boys then crowded around me,
each wanting to tell a joke. Each boy gave me about one joke apiece,
but I had to tell them to slow down their speech so I could understand
what they were saying. They were very excited to have their voices
on tape and then to hear it played back. I was then taken to the girls'
section of this class, where I repeated the procedure of setting the
taperecorder up in the front of the room, and asking for those who
wanted to tell a joke. The girls were considerably shyer, and
although they all said they knew jokes, very few girls came up to tell
them. Unfortunately the situation was very formal – they were all
sitting at tables, with the teacher in the front of the room, and they
had to raise their hands and be chosen to come up and tell a joke. This

was unlike the boys, who were able to crowd around the tape recorder, and talk to each other, remembering jokes and laughing. Also, by the time I got to the girls, it was very close to their afternoon playtime, and the teacher wanted to get things put away and dismiss the children.

After the tea break, I returned with another teacher to her class of 9 and 10 year olds. Here I handed out 33 questionnaires, and while they filled them out, I went around and talked to them about what they were writing. Some were able to write jokes down without any problem, but others had to think quite a bit and ask their friends around them. The questionnaire took approximately 30-45 minutes to complete, although some finished in a much shorter period, and two weren't finished when I left. From here I went to a third class composed of 10 and 11 year olds, and the first question I received after handing out the questionnaires was from a boy: "Can we tell rude jokes?" and the immediate reply by the teacher was "You're not supposed to know jokes like that at this school." It was time for school to end, so the teacher had the children fill out the questionnaires the next day, and I picked them up from her at the close of the second day. A few rude jokes and rhymes were included.

On the average there were 2 to 3 jokes a questionnaire, but most of the children knew no parodies. Most of the jokes were joke-riddles, but this was partly because it is easier to write down riddles than long jokes.

School 3 was a very small school located down the road from School 2. The headmistress gave me permission to proceed as I liked, so I decided to tape groups of six children. She gave me the staffroom, a small room next to her office, to tape in, and she then chose at random six boys for the first group from the oldest class at the school, aged 8 and 9 years old. The boys were excited to be chosen, and to be away from their class, and though they said they knew jokes, nobody wanted to be the first to tell one. Once they started they lost some of their shyness, but they never completely forgot the taperecorder and relaxed. My second group was six girls, also chosen at random, and they were very shy. One girl told quite a few riddles, and eventually three of them got the courage to sing a song together: As I was about to take them back to their class, they asked if they could sing a song.

They ended up singing three, and then showed me the handclapping movements that went with the songs. The girls were much more interested in singing and clapping than telling jokes. The third group consisted of four boys and two girls. The two girls were very shy and didn't talk until near the end of the session, but the boys told jokes. None of the groups told very many jokes – they didn't know me, and they were leary of the tape recorder. One boy in the third group announced he was going to tell a "rude" joke, and one boy and one girl covered their ears as he talked, but they listened to the replaying of the joke without protest.

School 4, the last Leeds school, was another parochial school located in one of the distant suburbs of Leeds. The headmistress gave me permission to proceed as I liked, so I went to five classrooms to tape-record. In each I set the tape recorder up in front of the class, and the children then raised their hands if they wanted to tell a joke. This method yielded on the whole very few jokes: it was very formal with the teacher standing there, and the children having to raise their hands to tell a joke, and they were very shy as well. They said they knew jokes but very few told them. The one boy the teachers told me I should taperecord was taking a test, and was unavailable the day I was at his school. I had a range of children aged 6-7, 7-8, 8-9, and two classes of 10-11 year olds, and I collected 58 jokes.

Collection at the London Schools was set up differently, in that the London Educational Authority located two schools for me and supervised the collection of the jokes. I sent 200 questionnaires to them, and received almost all 200 back. Unfortunately, some of them had to be discarded because I couldn't read the writing. No information was sent to me on the locaton or type of each school. From School 5 I received 264 jokes from 68 questionnaires, and from School 6, 147 jokes from 90 questionnaires. The children's writing ability was better at School 5, and they told on an average of 3 to 4 jokes per child, compared to 1 to 2 jokes per child at School 6.

The procedure for taping jokes in London was the same as in Leeds and I returned the second time in 1975, except that the recording sessions were run by ITV, a television outfit, who were using the joking sessions for a documentary on humor. Three groups of six children, aged 11, both boys and girls, were recorded, and the children weren't at all inhibited by having the TV camera and taperecorder focused on them. Because of time limitations, most of the jokes were short stories or riddles.

In San Francisco, I gave a presentation on English children's jokes at a school in the suburb and played several of my English tapes to a large group of children aged 8-11. I then set the taperecorder up in front of the classroom and asked for any volunteers. Not many of the younger children told jokes, but the older ones volunteered quite a few. When it was time to go out for recess, and the teacher had left the room, several boys told a few dirty verses that they couldn't tell in front of their teacher, and several girls remained in the room to tell jokes that they were too shy to tell in front of the rest of the class.

In San Diego, one school in a middleclass area was selected. I went to three different classrooms, each time setting the taperecorder up in front of the class and having the children volunteer to tell jokes. The first classroom was of 5 and 6 year olds, and they told mainly riddles, and many more than the teacher expected. The second class had 8 and 9 year olds, and in this room each child came up individually to me while the rest of the class continued with their work. I think this method, decided upon by their teacher, was detrimental to the number of jokes the children told, since they didn't hear the other jokes told and only had my appreciative laughter to encourage them to tell more. All of these jokes collected were short riddles. In the third classroom were children aged 9-12, and there the children were allowed to crowd around me and the taperecorder. I had difficulty getting anyone to tell the first joke, so finally I played a few jokes from the previous group, and then a boy volunteered to start. After that there were many jokes told although there was still a reluctance to tell their jokes on the taperecorder. Various children, usually the girls, would volunteer to tell the joke for someone else. Those two would go off, the shy child would tell the joke, and then the second brave one would tell the joke to me for the tape-recorder. This third session was fairly short in that it was time for lunch, but I told the children I would set the tape-recorder up in the playground, and they could continue to tell jokes.

This final session proved very fruitful in that a few older girls, 11, 12 and 13, stood around for over an hour telling long involved jokes, many of them "dirty" jokes. Unfortunately, I discovered afterwards that the tape-recorder wasn't recording properly, so I returned the following week, again at lunchtime, to collect more jokes. Many of the same jokes were told again, along with some new ones, and this time a few boys also gathered around to tell jokes along with the girls.

At a snack bar next to a swimming pool at a U.S. Navy base in San Diego where I worked, I collected more jokes from a few children with whom I became friends. The children enjoyed having the tape-recorder to themselves, and one 6-year-old put on quite a monologue, including one rhyming verse she repeated several times. (No. 112) Some jokes were also received through the mail from three different children who'd seen an article in the newspaper saying I was collecting children's jokes. Two of these children wrote twice, as they remembered further jokes.

One of the advantages of taping was the enjoyment the children got out of hearing their voices on tape, and they loved hearing the same jokes over again, just to recognize the different voices. Each child was certain, though, that his voice hadn't recorded properly because it didn't sound right. Another advantage of taping as opposed to questionnaires was that the joke was much more spontaneous and natural on tape. The child could speak as he normally would, and didn't have to think about how to spell words or what word or thought came next. They talked naturally, putting in their own voice inflections, accents, and body movements. The advantage can be seen in the difference in the number of jokes collected by taping as opposed to questionnaires. The advantage of questionnaires was that many more children could be questioned at one time. With taping, the groups had to be kept small so that I could recognize individual voices on the tape, and so I could control the children and the speed of their talking.

ANALYSIS OF TEXTS AND THEMES

After dividing and placing the jokes into the twenty-five original categories, the majority of the jokes were then cross-referenced into nine final groups to discuss and analyze. These nine sections were general enough to include all the themes and ideas present in the jokes that I thought were important to the children.

1. Sex

An important theme in the jokes told is the sex theme, found in all age groups in some aspect, although the older children told the most detailed sexual jokes. My definition of sex is a broad one, based on the children's attitudes toward the jokes. Dirty or "rude" jokes are all classified under this theme, which includes actual or implied reference to the physical relationship between men and women; parts of the body, both male and female; swear words or dirty words; and bodily functions, such as going to the toilet.

The younger children find jokes concerning the toilet and the need to use it extremely funny, while the older children tell the actual "sexual" jokes. Even some of the jokes the older children tell are just excuses to describe parts of the body. All three of the older groups at School 1 in Leeds asked permission to tell dirty or rude jokes, for they were never able to tell these jokes to an adult without getting into trouble or being censored. The small groups at School 3 in Leeds told a few rude jokes, although when one boy announced he was going to tell one, another boy and a girl refused to listen and covered their ears. At School 2 in Leeds when I handed out questionnaires, one boy asked if they could write down rude ones, and even though the teacher said they shouldn't know any, I received some sexual rhymes and jokes from them. At the last school in Leeds, no sexual jokes were told by older children, I think mainly because of the taping situation, with the teacher sitting there, and because they were very shy. Only one 7-year-old boy told a joke about using the toilet, but the teacher didn't know what he was going to say. I think she was dismayed that I had recorded him telling it, for it wasn't the type of joke she wanted recorded from her class. If she had known the joke, she would have censored him, and refused him permission to tell it, or at least have refused me permission to tape it.

In San Francisco, the teacher didn't want her children to tell rude, dirty jokes because she was afraid the children would continue to tell them after I had left, and that she would get into trouble with the principal for allowing them to tell dirty jokes. At the end of the taping session when most of the children had left the classroom for recess, including the teacher, several boys told a few dirty rhymes, but most of them were at a speed that was undecipherable. At the San Diego school, no rude jokes were told during class time, but during lunch time when the tape-recorder was set outside, many rude jokes were told, mainly by the older girls. The boys didn't want to tell these jokes to me for the tape-recorder, although they knew dirty jokes.

I think what surprised me the most about the sexual jokes was the amount of sexual knowledge the jokes implied. According to one teacher at School 1 in Leeds, the children aren't viewing the adult world but live in it, and are a part of it, and this certainly seems to hold true for sex. Initially sexual jokes are a way of learning about sex, but these children seem to be far beyond just learning through the jokes. They see the innocent jokes as funny, naïve interpretations of sex. One 12-year-old girl's joke seems to sum up their attitude toward sex: "A right old-fashioned woman is one who doesn't know anything about sex, and jumps out of bed yelling to her male partner, 'eeks Henry, there's a worm in the bed.' (No. 885)

One joke told by a 12-year-old girl has a woman with her house, table, and chair named as parts of her body, and through various mishaps the lady is sexually assaulted three times by the police. (No. 880) Here the authority figures are committing the violent sexual act, and yet because they are the police, they aren't punished. The lady gets mad at them although it is implied that it is her fault, since she is dumb enough to call her possessions strange bodily names, and then goes and loses them. The woman could be a prostitute, out drumming up business, but, when she gets a policeman to respond, it is the wrong man and she protests. Also present is the idea that the adult-authority figures can do what they want without punishment. The police can break the laws: but the child, when committing the same act, would be punished and denied the same privileges.

An extremely popular joke in England has the girl named by her parents for a sexual act — Shagarada, or Fuckarada or Kissarada. In this joke the milkman offers the girl more and more milk if she'll eventually go to bed with him, and when the girl's mother comes back and calls her name, the milkman replies he's shagging her as fast as he can. (No. 868) Here, as in other non-sexual jokes, where the parents name the child a ridiculous name (Nos. 933-936) or when the parents give the child dirty or rude words as answers to innocent questions (Nos. 855, 875, 876, 937), the child boomerangs the adults' (parents') answers, or silly names, back against them. The child does things that are wrong, but because of their names and the parents' answers, the child receives permission to do wrong actions. The child is protected from punishment, at least rightful punishment, because the parents in a sense gave the permission to do it.

A similar joke is told in the United States about Johnnie Fuckerfaster, also named by his parents. He too is called by his mother when he is busy with a girl, and he calls back, "I'm fucking her as fast as I can." (No. 869)

Especially as to sex the parents have refused the child permission to enjoy it as they themselves do. Both Shagarada and Johnnie Fuckerfaster have been given names that will eventually get them into trouble, but it is their parents' fault, since they implicitly gave them sexual permission by giving them sexual names. These jokes also express wish-fulfillment, in that the children would like to be able to have sex, without fear of punishment. In other words, they would like to be like Shagarada or Johnnie Fuckerfaster and have sex. For even when Shagarada is warned not to let anyone in, especially the milkman, she still does, perhaps for the promised milk, but mainly for the advantages of the sexual act.

In two other jokes (Nos. 872, 873), a lady is taking a bath, and either the postman or milkman comes to the door. He offers to lower the price of the milk, or return the money on a package delivered, if the lady will take off the three towels she has wrapped herself in. Eventually the lady is standing naked in front of the man, whereupon the man makes some comment to the effect of, 'If I asked you to do anything you'd do it' – "So he says, if I put a penny in the slot will the bells ring?" – which is the final sexual offer. Again, it is sex at any price, and since the lady is gaining by giving in to the man, she does.

In all these jokes the imagination has created a fantastic situation where the woman or girl has sex, gets paid for it, and enjoys it as well. But there is mocking laughter present too, at the man and woman. Sex is usually a private affair between the man and woman, but with a girl called Shagarada, the sexual act becomes very open and public. You know she will eventually be sexually assaulted by many men, more than just the milkman, because her acts must match her name. The child laughs at the girl as well as at her parents who put her into this situation. With both forms of the joke about the woman and her three towels, the girls had great delight in describing how the woman first took off the middle towel, then the top one, and finally the bottom one. It is a situation that can be imagined without too much trouble, since doorbells do ring when you're just getting into the bath. The ending is what is unusual, and in this situation, the woman appears as a dumb machine, doing what the man requests for a little monetary gain.

Resentment is also clearly present in these jokes. The child, through its given name, is forced to learn about sex, whether willingly or not. This name represents the whole game of hinting about sex, and then concealing with shut doors, vague answers, and lies and fantasies. Nothing is ever what it appears, and the child turns to a willing teacher, the milkman or to whomever, for answers and for practical information.

Another joke about the milkman has the small child predicting the future. He says goodbye to his grandmother, and his grandfather, and they both die. He next says goodbye to his father, and the milkman dies. (No. 871) This joke is the logical conclusion to the Shagarada joke, and in all the jokes, the role of the milkman is consistent — the seducer who is able to offer something to the woman at home.

The consequences of seducing young females is seen in another joke (No. 870) which takes place down on the farm. The farmer's three daughters all get pregnant by three boys who spend the night at the farm. The farmer, upset at the turn of events, gives the boys two choices, either stickup their butts the fruit they have picked, or get shot. The boys choose to put the fruit up their ass, but unfortunately the third boy has chosen watermelons as his fruit. The boys are punished; the girls are not.

Finally one sexual joke (Nos. 878–879) has a little boy and little girl in bed with one another. Throughout the whole joke the little girl continually repeats, "You're not supposed to, but seeing you're my friend, I'll let you." She eventually ends up with the little boy's finger in her bellybutton, and his penis in her vagina. Appearing innocent, the little girl makes no real protest, for sexual information and freedom are much stronger urges than her parents' vague warnings against little boys. Maturing earlier than boys, little girls will often play the game of innocence to get what they want.

One joke collected by Legman (in Cannes, France, 1975 from a tourist) has a little boy and girl playing with each other, and the little boy starts tickling the little girl's bellybutton saying "Gilly Gilly." The little girl responds by saying "Lower, Lower," and the little boy says, "GILLY, GILLY" (said with low deep voice.) An American joke shows that both the little girl and boy know what sex is, but unfortunately the little girl is hampered by her age, and she promises to "give what I've got when I get it." (No. 890)

Jokes concerning parts of the body, both male and female, are quite common. One joke (No. 874) has a tramp performing acts that eventually make the woman appear sexually assaulted as well as quite foolish. The tramp drinks the lady's milk left on the doorstep, pulls her knickers down off the washing line, and pulls the hairs out of her cat, who's named Fanny. When the lady finally calls the police to complain she says, "There's a tramp, he's drunk me milk, pulled me knickers down, and pulled all the hairs off me fanny". (fanny = genitals). Again it is the woman who puts herself into the position to be sexually assaulted; she is a fool and is mocked – the wise child would never be put into that position. Legman has described the function of all such fool jokes as being " . . . intended to serve two purposes. First it exhorts the child to grow up, to learn – especially about sex and the wisdom of life – and to be a fool no more. But simultaneously, it identifies with the protracted childhood we all would love to live, and even shows it as somehow sacrosanct and above danger." (Legman, 1968, p. 189-190)

Another joke (No. 892) has three ants exploring a woman's body, and finding the three major areas of her body: the breasts, the sexual organs, and the bottom. This isn't a real joke in the sense of a story leading up to a punchline, but the child shows specific knowledge of a woman's body, and her sexual organs. A similar joke (No. 891) has three mice exploring a house and discovering a sink, a bathtub, and a toilet; and in both jokes the mouse and ant almost die when they get hit with excretion.

An explicit joke concerning a woman's seductive abilities was told by a 12-year-old girl in San Diego. The woman is having a party and comes to work walking very bow-legged – she had to curl her hair. (No. 889) Continuing along the subject of a woman's pubic hair is a trick question 12-year-old girls in San Diego ask one another: The first girl asks the second one to describe her hair. After a long description, the first girl says, "Now describe the hair on your head." The girls who asked and answered this question knew the trick, but in fact each one wanted to be the one who described her hair.

Several jokes are concerned with a man's penis, and what is done with it. A traditional "danger" joke has a man given three wishes by a fairy he helps. He wishes for a handsome face, a great body, and a dooda like his horse. Unfortunately he forgets his horse is a mare. (No. 881) An American version of this joke (No. 882) has the man himself turn into a giant weiner or penis. Another joke (No. 977) has a fellow who can't speak very well, and instead of saying bun, clock and blanket, he can only say bum, cock, and wanket. (wanket = wank = masturbate). He eventually propositions a lady on the street, supposedly unintentionally, but actually quite explicitly.

The effects of a man's overpowering curiosity and sexual urge is seen in another "danger" joke No. 888, where the man is told to not put his penis or "ukhum" in three different holes. Of course he does, but the last hole, a cow's milking machine, won't let go until it gets ten gallons. Like the previous joke where the man wants to become sexually superpotent and turns into a giant weiner, this man suffers because of his strong sexual desires, and if he survives, his sexual desires will be drained out of him.

The desire to be more sexually potent is seen in several doctor jokes. Joke No. 865 has the doctor giving a man some pills for his short willy, and it grows so long he can't control it. When he goes out he wears it like a scarf around his neck. In a second joke, the doctor recommends that the man be castrated if he wants his high voice to be lower. Unfortunately or fortunately, depending on how you look at it, he runs into a shark in the ocean who solves his problem. (No. 866) In both these jokes the man wants to change and have a better sexual image, but the end result is no better.

The penis in jokes is often called other names, just to answer children's embarrassing questions. Unfortunately the foolish answer gets the parent into trouble, as well as pain. Joke No. 883 has the penis called a teddy bear, and the daughter plays with it at night. The next morning there is blood all over, with the excuse, "Your teddy spit at me, so I bit its head off." This castration joke was also told by a child in London, except it is about the older brother and younger sister, the sister getting into the bath with her brother and inquiring about his parts. She is told it is his snake, but with the same results as before. In the American version, the father calls his penis a snake to his daughter with equally disastrous results. The penis as a snake is also found in joke No. 885, when the woman jumps out of bed exclaiming there's a worm in the bed, and in joke No. 886, when a boy asks his parents about their sexual parts and is told his father's organ is a snake, and his mum's are headlights and grass. When the boy goes into his parents' bed that night to find out what they are doing, he exclaims to his mum, "Switch your headlights on, my dad's snake's going into your grass." The child makes the adult look foolish and oh-so-innocently ruins their pleasure. Many variants of this joke exist, and two collected in the United States use a car and garage, and train and cave.

In a final and frankly incestuous joke (No. 884) a girl asks her father what it is, and he says "It's just something you can play with." But, when the girl sneaks in at night to play with it, she is admonished by her father that "his prick ain't bloody for you, it's your mom's."

Knickers (underpants) are an important motif, and traditionally little girls are warned by their mothers to never let anyone see their underwear, especially males. Joke No. 897 has the little girl eventually following her mother's warning exactly. A man or group of boys offers to pay the little girl if she'll climb up a lamp post so he can see what color her knickers are. The girl does this, getting paid more and more, until her mom absolutely forbids her to show her knickers. She returns with more money and when her mom starts yelling at her, she says, "I know mum, so I took them off." The girl is never told why she shouldn't show her knickers, and so by following her mom's advice, she shows what her knickers are suppose to hide. A "knock knock" joke also has this warning about not showing knickers. "Knock knock, who's there? Nicholas. Nicholas who? Knickerless girls shouldn't climb trees." (or ride bicycles) (Nos. 583, 584)

Popular knicker joke in England (No. 893) has men, either a bus conductor, Irishmen, or fellows, throwing 10 pence pieces down on the street, watching the women pick them up to see what color their knickers are. The joke plays on the color of the knickers as related to football teams (soccer), and the woman with no knickers on must support Arsenal. The girls know they aren't suppose to show their knickers, so they have adult authority-figures setting up situations whereby the lady has to show her knickers, but for gain.

This theme of selling one's body for gain, either in actual sexual acts, or by showing various parts of the body, is recurrent in these jokes. A symbolic joke, complete with walking up the garden path, has a woman claiming to a man that everytime a train comes by, she falls out of bed. He doesn't believe her, so she takes him to her room where both of them get into bed. When her husband returns and inquires why this strange man is in bed with his wife, he answers, "You'll never believe it, but we're waiting for a train." The answer fits the joke situation, but more than that, it's a classic answer for a man caught in bed with someone else's wife. The man is quite innocent: he has been asked there by the woman, but he came quite willingly, and got into bed with her, so he's as much to blame as the woman. (No. 898)

Back to the motif of the need to use the toilet, a popular joke (No. 896) has a woman refused passage on a bus because she is carrying a parrot. She puts the parrot in her knickers and gets on the bus, but when the bus conductor says "It's a nice day", the parrot answers and says, "It's pissing down here" or "It's wet down here." The visual image created is extremely vivid, and the children found the joke very funny. The idea that an adult wets her pants, something that children are always accused of, is quite a reversal. The woman had to do something with the parrot if she wanted to ride the bus, and where could be a better hiding place than one's knickers – she would just appear pregnant. It would be a parrot who is used, one who can talk and can accuse the woman of wetting her pants, something that is usually known only to that person. In some ways this is a form of retaliation, for a parent will often tell friends that his son or daughter wets his bed or pants, embarrassing and shaming him in front of others and telling a secret that shouldn't be told. Why not reverse the situation and embarrass the adult, especially when the adult is supposed to be old enough to know better?

English children told quite a few jokes about the toilet. Farting appears in two rhymes, both about boys and the results of the fart

(Nos. 89, 90); going to the toilet in a variety of places (Nos. 91, 923, 926, 927); confronting the teacher with a demand to use the toilet (Nos. 920, 921). When going to the toilet an Englishman, Irishman, and Scotsman confront a ghost (one version of No. 809); and another when a Scotsman, Pakistani, and Englishman meet a ghost, only the Englishman stays, is granted his wish, and he asks for toilet paper. (No. 819)

Some parodies, verses, and joke-riddles imply sexual relations of some kind. Parodies of Mother Goose rhymes are extremely popular, such as Mary had a little lamb, and Jack and Jill. Jill forgets to take the pill and now she has a daughter, and the verse is no longer an innocent rhyme of two children going up the hill to fetch a pail of water. (No. 46) Dundes and Hickerson (1962) have collected many of these sexual nursery rhyme parodies in the United States, many of them referring to Jill as a prostitute. Little Miss Muffet was also attacked sexually, not by the spider, but by Little Boy Blue (No. 48). "Mary had a little lamb, she also had a bear, I've often seen her little lamb, but I've never seen her bare" is probably the most common. (Nos. 53, 54). Implying homosexuality is a rhyme about Georgie Best, "who wears frilly knickers and a see-through bra." (Nos. 63-65).

Many of the joke-riddles refer again to the use of the toilet: "When I was a wee wee tot" (No. 88); "What's the definition of agony? A woman (or drunk) standing outside a toilet with a bent penny" (No. 307); and "Knock knock, who's there? Ipe, Ipe who? Do you?" (Nos. 562, 563) Some jokes relate to the toilet theme; what some think is a ghost is actually someone trying to go the bathroom, who sits so long he becomes a skeleton (Nos. 826, 827); or from the shit left under the bed in the pisspot; 3 flies or 2 mice float around in the pan singing. (Nos. 807, 808)

Motifs of body parts are also found throughout all the categories, such as "What's the definition of agony? A fly going down a razor blade using his balls as brakes: (No. 308, 309); "What's the definition of blockbuster? Square tits" (No. 316); a verse about willy's (Nos. 56, 76); and cocks. (No. 143) Foreigners are mocked for being unable to speak the language, and yet the foreigner wins when he learns three words to tell his new English wife: "Take off ze—bra baby." (No. 828). The doctor also plays a part in mocking adult wishes for bigger breasts, a bigger penis, or more hair on one's head. (Nos. 864-867) A frankly implied sexual act is the joke about the pub named the Queen's Legs. Two men are asked why they are waiting outside the pub and they reply: "We're waiting for the Queen's Legs to open so we can get a drink." (No. 981)

A few jokes have the motif of rape, but rape of special people — nuns, those who are supposedly immune to sexual desires and fantasies. Joke No. 912 has two nuns raped as they're going down the road, and one says "What are we going to tell Mother Superior when we tell her we've been raped twice? But we've only been raped once. But we're going back again aren't we?" Or the man who interviews a monk and the monk explains how during the war the Americans, Germans, and English raped everyone except Sister Matilde. When asked why they didn't rape her he said, "Sister Matilde doesn't like that sort of thing." (No. 913) Both of these jokes imply the child's distrust of adults, for they are hypocritical, and, although they are figures of authority, they still do things they profess they are against or have given up. One of the jokes about Sister Matilde was told by a child in a parochial school. The implied criticism is that the child is forbidden to do such acts, and the adult says they are nasty and bad, but underneath they still perform the same forbidden acts.

The last motif included under sex is logically that of pregnant women and babies. An ancient series of jokes tells about a pregnant woman, who has twins, but they can't or won't come out. In modern forms, the doctor makes the woman swallow a series of objects, such as a settee (couch, rocking chair), a hat, a banjo, a feather, a lighted cigar, and a song book, and after swallowing all these things, one baby is born. Upon cutting the mother open, they find the other baby singing "you got my brother but ya didn't get me, doda doda day." (Nos. 852-854). It seems like an incredible fantasy, that a woman would be able to swallow all these objects, and still the baby is alive inside, thinking and plotting how to stay inside. One theory in psychology talks about the birth trauma being the first and major trauma of a person's life. This is one facet of Sigmund Freud's psychoanalytic theory, which states that the birth trauma is the prototype of all later anxieties. This joke portrays this wish to stay inside the mother, or to return to the womb where it is safe, warm and protected. Then the child sets up home inside his mother's stomach with all the things he needs to be comfortable. The American version of this joke is more violent, and expresses the danger in this desire to return to the mother's womb. The pregnant mother learns she is going to have a lawyer and a rock singer, and when the husband is told this, he stabs his wife, trying to kill the rock singer, but instead kills the lawyer baby.

In modern terms, the child of today knows that a baby comes from the mother's abdomen and not from under the gooseberry bush, or the cabbage patch or the stork. The joke is reality-oriented in that it uses real information, but for a new-born baby to have the cunning and skill of these babies, plus the woman swallowing these objects, sends the joke back into fantasyland. Another joke has a pregnant woman wanting lots of children, and all of them "right polite", but the babies won't come out. When the doctor opens her up, there are all these babies saying "After you, no after you." (No. 861) Again the unborn baby is given intelligence and the ability to speak. This joke is open mockery of the parent's desire for their children to be polite at all times, even when it is difficult for the children. Like these babies, the parents place too much emphasis on politeness, and therefore you have the extreme case of the children being polite before they are born, and so polite they won't be born. Perhaps this is a desire the children think their parents have: "We wish you were more polite: or we wish you weren't born, you're such a trouble."

Another joke has the pregnant woman able to talk to her children in her belly: the girl asks for a doll and a pram, and the boy asks for a real gun. (No. 862) When asked why he wanted a gun, the boy answers "To shoot that great big hairy monster that comes in my window every day." In Oedipal terms, here is the boy, not even born yet, wanting to shoot and kill his father (and father's penis) for disturbing him, and implicitly for bothering his mother, when he himself is inside her.

Modern concepts are again shown in several jokes where the child asks where the baby comes from. In joke No. 856, the mother responds to her son's questions that his dad gave her the baby, and the boy goes to his father and says, "I don't feel you'd better give Mummy any more babies. And his Daddy said why? Because she's just eaten it." This is one way children think babies get into their mothers "stomachs," and this corresponds to the joke where the mother is able to swallow impossible objects. I think the children think this is a stupid answer, but typical of what their parents might tell them, instead of telling them the truth, When this joke was told, all the children laughed, partly at the image created, and partly at the idea that a child would believe a baby could be swallowed, since they are aware of the real way a baby is formed. Joke No. 858 has the father giving his son a ridiculous story about a bench inside his mother's stomach, and the father using a long pole to knock babies off, one at a time. Five babies all at once were explained as the bench being knocked over because the father was in a hurry. Again, the child telling this joke told it as a ridiculous lie parents tell their children to explain about babies. A last joke has the boy asking his father about life, and his father says "he'll tell him about the birds and bees." The boy responds, "I don't want to know about the bees, I want to know about the birds," (bird = chick = girl) (No. 857) The boy knows exactly what he needs and wants to know, and is prepared when his father starts to give him foolish and vague answers. Sex education starts at a much earlier age nowadays, and children can no longer be fobbed off with traditional stories and fantasies, and as their jokes show, they are aware of the truth anyway.

2. Adult Authority Figures

One premise I held before going into the field to collect jokes was that the children would tell jokes and parodies mocking and laughing at the adult authority-figures. These could be a variety of figures in the child's life, but mainly the teacher, the policeman, and the parents. In addition, authority-figures appear in the jokes which I will discuss. They are: the doctor; church officials (vicar, priest, nun); and those under a prison warden, either in a criminal prison, concentration camp, or lunatic asylum.

A. Police: The police motifs are divided into two groups; the helpful policeman, and mocking the police. The helpful motifs include: a joke-riddle (No. 221) about the police meeting the Beverly Sisters; seven news-flashes (Nos. 784, 910, 1039-1043) concerning a 2 ft. man and 12 ft. man who escaped, eight watches were stolen, 500 wigs were stolen, a box of wigs fell off the back of a lorry, a lady's toilet was broken, a pregnant Irish woman was arrested for carrying a dope, and a clergyman was arrested for speeding. The police help a lady look for her husband missing in their jungle garden for several days (No. 1017); the policeman is turned to in fear and hysterics in an old joke where a man hears God and the Devil sharing out souls in the graveyard (No. 773); and the police find a gorilla missing from the zoo. (No. 1145)

I thought there would be more mocking police motifs, but the ones present reduce the police to: pennys (No. 321) – "What would you do if coppers were surrounding you? Pick 'em up and spend them"; a pickle (No. 489); fuzz (No. 260); or else make them appear foolish, for example: a policeman stops a drunk Irishman, and first the Irishman refuses to comply with the policeman's questions for the logical reason that he is drunk (No. 774); or upon being asked to blow in a bag for a breath analyser, the Irishman responds with "Why, are your chips cold?" (chips = french fries) (No. 775); a policeman asks some boys their names, and all he gets is "shut up and mind your own business" (No. 933); a boy responds to the policeman's question with a truthful but seemingly mocking answer (No. 979); a policeman asks a tramp if he's had a bath that morning and he answers "Why, is there one missing?" (No. 990); and a traffic warden has a yellow band around her head so nobody can park on her. (No. 435)

Actually, in all the jokes concerning policemen, the policeman is made to look foolish in some manner. In the first set of jokes, the policeman is handling ridiculous problems, such as combing the area for a fallen box of wigs, or looking high and low for a 2 ft. and a 12 ft. man who have escaped, or looking into a lady's broken toilet. Even the situation in the graveyard makes him appear stupid, for the man who first hears the two men in the graveyard convinces the policeman he should come and hear and see for himself, instead of the policeman immediately testing the man to see if he had been drinking.

In the second set, all the people that the policeman questions respond with silly answers, or the truth; but both mock the policeman's foolish questions and desire for personal information.

The joke-riddle about picking up the coppers and spending them, or turning him into a pickle, reduces the policeman to a non-human being, or into a much smaller than normal object which can then be successfully handled. The child ridicules his own fear of the police and also the policeman himself at the same time, for he is no bigger than a penny or a pickle, and although the child might respect him (he picks him up instead of stepping on him), he doesn't fear him.

B. *Teachers:* The teacher motifs are also split into two groups: dislike of the teacher, and mocking of the teacher. This first motif is found mainly in parodies of Glory Glory Alleluya (Nos. 16-23); parodies of the Bonfire song (No. 26); a limerick which concerns hitting the teacher back after the child has been smacked (No. 128); a song about the end of school term, when it is hoped the school falls down (Nos. 70-74); a song about going to school with hand grenades (No. 35); a joke about playing hookey and not coming to school (No. 941); and a joke about a dream where both the child and the teacher have to count all their sins before they are admitted into Heaven, and the teacher has more sins. (No. 1005).

The second motif about teachers includes silly but logical answers to foolish questions, such as "What would you have if you had 10 apples and the boy next to you took 6 apples from you? A thump-up, Miss" (No. 325); or "How far is Africa? Well, it can't be far away cause he goes home to his dinner." (No. 744) Perhaps the most popular such joke has the teacher asking the child to go home to find out the answer to a question. The boy asks members of his family, and they respond with words that correspond to what they are doing and not to the question, and the child dutifully reports these silly answers back to the teacher. (No. 937) Thus, if he gets into trouble, it isn't his fault, but the fault of his family who gave him the answers. Another joke has the teacher yelling "Order, children, order" and one child says, 'I will have jelly and custard." (No. 1070) The child responds literally to the teacher's question, even though he knows what the teacher really wants. One boy thinks his teacher loves him because she puts kisses by his sums. (No. 1052)

The last few jokes concern the need and use of the toilet. Although the children are by this age usually past the bed-wetting stage, having to ask permission from the teacher to go to the toilet, or having specific times when they must use it, can still present problems of control for the child. Several jokes (Nos. 920, 921) have the child losing control, as when he must recite the alphabet and leaves out the 'p' since it's gone down his leg; and a Leeds joke where the child protests that he can't swim when refused permission to go to the toilet. (No. 915) Several jokes show the child's mocking compliance to his teacher's or parents' demand for polite words referring to the need to use the toilet. (Nos. 914, 919) Children don't think these polite words for the basic functions of life are useful or needed, so their jokes ridicule these words and phrases.

In only one joke does the teacher get the better of the students. Four college boys arrive late for an exam with the excuse that their car had a flat tire. Instead of getting mad the professor asks each one, for their test, to write down which tire was flat. (No. 939) This is an old Middle Eastern "wise sage" story modernized.

Like the policeman, the teacher is scoffed and laughed at, and his authority undermined by silly answers to what the child considers foolish questions. Going to school seems foolish and useless, so the child finds reasons not to go, and hopes the school will fall down. When the teacher punishes the child by hitting him, the child retaliates and hits back, and in this manner he can get out his frustrations and anger in fantasy in a reasonable manner. At school the child is punished if he is too cheeky and too much of a smart-aleck, but through these jokes the child can answer as smartly as he desires, especially when he tells the teacher to shut up – something his mother has said to him.

C. *Parents:* Again, as with the police and teachers, parents give silly answers to questions their children pose. These questions could be what certain swear-words mean (Nos. 855, 875, 876); what Constantinople means (No. 937); where babies come from (Nos. 856-859); what the sexual organs are (Nos. 883-887); why a girl shouldn't show her knickers or underwear (No. 897); or polite euphemisms for the need to "use the toilet." (No. 914) The child gets into trouble (sexual, stealing) because the parent has given him a strange name (Nos. 868, 935, 936), but the child also tries to help the parent out of trouble (Nos. 834, 947, 948). Normal interaction with the parents is also present; in trouble with them (Nos. 942-945);

following their demands and requests (Nos. 862, 930, 938, 949); and in a joke collected from an older informant from her childhood in New York City about a mother and her two sons Ikey and Mikey living in a tenement. The mother gets locked out, and yells up to Ikey, "Throw me my key", so he picks up his brother and throws him out of the window. (No. 946) In a special series of jokes, the cruel joke cycle, the child commits various acts, or is subjected to various cruel punishments by his mother (Nos. 1110-1117)

The emotions shown in these jokes are very close to real children's emotions. The child loves his parents and tries to follow their instructions, but inevitably, because of false information or lack of understanding, the child gets in trouble, or gets his parents in trouble. The child does try hard to do things properly as the parents wish. A lot of the trouble springs from the parents unwillingness to explain things properly or truthfully to the child, either because they think the child is too young to know and understand, or because they just don't take the time. As discussed earlier, the child is refused permission to do what his parents do, and so he creates joke situations in which his desires are satisfied. The joke about saying whisper, insteading of saying "I want to piss," (No. 914) can be imagined as a real situation, however horrible. It would serve the parents (father) right if his son actually did piss in his ear, since he is following both his mother's and father's instructions. This can be a major problem – to decide whose instructions to follow, and if he does both, or neither, or just one and not the other, he is in trouble. The child feels resentment and anger when no matter what he does, and however closely he follows the parents' rules and instructions, he still gets into trouble and is punished.

Joke No. 944 presents the situation where the son is told to tell the truth always, like Winston Churchill's son. Churchill's son didn't get a whipping when he told the truth, but when the boy does tell the truth, he still gets a whipping.

The cannibalistic joke where the boys cuts off his own bottom rather than tell his mother he lost the money and risk punishment (No. 930), seems strange, but then children do fear getting punished. If there is something they can do to prevent the punishment, they will probably do it, at least in fantasy. The man trying to smuggle his own child in through customs (No. 948), or smuggling him in without paying his fare (No. 834), shows the child's idea and fear that perhaps he is in the way and a nuisance. He is a person not to be proud of, but hidden, out of the way. This is especially shown when the father would rather have his son thrown overboard than pay his fare. Even when his only son is dying, the father is still more concerned about the yellow ping pong ball. (No. 949)

As mentioned earlier, the Oedipus complex is portrayed quite clearly in joke No. 862, where the unborn son, inside his mother, wants a real gun to shoot the big hairy monster (his father's penis) who comes in his window every morning, bothering him and his mother. The child also throws balls of nose-snot at his dad (Nos. 2,3), showing complete contempt for him and his role as father. Sibling rivalry can be seen in joke No. 856 where the son tells his father he better not give his mother any more babies since she's just swallowed the last one (wish fulfillment?) and in the Ikey-Mikey joke, where the brother throws his brother out of the window at his mother's request, mistaking (accidentally?) Mikey for 'my key.' (No. 946)

Other motifs like brothers and sisters fighting (No. 943), mother washing son (No. 930), buying fish and chips (No. 936), or waiting for the bus (No. 935), make these activities appear quite normal, but the undercurrents portray the problems of family living, and of children interacting with their parents — sometimes on an equal basis, and at other times as parent/child, and the confusion resulting when the proper roles are unknown, mistaken and confused, or played at the wrong time. G. Legman writes:

From my own earliest recollections: *A little boy is sent to get meat from the butcher, but on the way loses the money his mother has given him, by playing dice. He goes down an alley, "slices off a piece of his ass," and brings it home. His mother cooks it and the family eats it. This happens several times. Finally he has no ass left, and has to come back with neither money nor meat. He tells his mother he has lost the money playing dice, and she goes to spank him, "but she can't — because he hasn't got any ass!"* (Atlantic City, N.J. 1928, told by a little boy of my own age: about ten. I should perhaps add that my own father was a butcher and very severe with me, which probably explains why I remember this story so clearly, and the implied threat it involved for me.) This strange cannibalistic story, authentically told by one child to another decades before Portnoy's slice-of-liver food-defiling, well emphasizes the "protective" intention of the self-castration theme — namely: "I castrate myself so that others cannot do so!"

D. Doctors: The doctor plays a unique role in that all people regard him as an authority on medicine and health, and blindly follow his instructions and rules. The doctor is usually seen as quite helpful, kind and wise, saving people and aiding them in their troubles, but not always. The doctor in jokes plays two roles. One of them appears in the wellerism doctor jokes where neither the patient nor the doctor is taken very seriously. (Nos. 622-644) When a patient complains he "feels like a dog", the doctor tells him "Get down", or when the patient says "People ignore me", the doctor says "Next please". All the situations are imaginary, although a mental patient could conceivably feel like some of these patients. These jokes are told as ridiculing the patient, who imagines he has various illnesses, none of them real, and mocking the doctor as well, who takes the patients' word about their symptoms quite literally, and who thinks he is all-powerful and can cure anyone of anything.

In another type of doctor joke the doctor unsuccessfully attempts to cure real problems and illnesses, one very common being the pregnant lady whose babies won't come out. (Nos. 852-854) The poor lady either must swallow a variety of strange objects, or lots of water and pills. In another joke, three pregnant ladies are given red, blue, and iron pills, and each one gives birth to a child, one a red baby, one a blue baby, and one an iron robot. (No. 860) Other jokes concern the sexual organs. In joke No. 863 a man wants more hair for his head, and a lady wants bigger busters, but the cures get reversed. Another man wants a bigger willy, but it grows too long (No. 865); and in three similar jokes, a man wants his finger or his nose to grow, both growing an inch everytime 'pardon' is said. (No. 867) (Motif D1376.1). When a man complains his voice is too high, the doctor suggests he should cut off his penis or testicles, but a shark does the job instead. (No. 866) One poor man has troubles with worms, and is cured with a sandwich and a cream bun. (No. 863)

In these jokes, the humor rises from the doctor's unsatisfactory cure, which is anything but normal and ordinary. Worms are given human attributes of speech and after a week of a sandwich and cream bun being stuck up the man's bum, only a sandwich is placed there. When the worm demands the cream bun, he is hit over the head with a golf stick. This joke creates a vivid and amusing picture, but it is based on fantasy and not on reality. Neither are the cures for the short finger or nosed based on reality, where the word "pardon" has magical qualities of growth. Unfortunately the men run into Arabs or Jews who say "a thousand pardons". Again, with the pregnant women, there is no way a woman could physically swallow a rocking chair, or all of the other required objects, but the descriptive picture of this woman's abdomen being opened to find a baby playing a banjo and singing, is vivid.

It is evident that the doctor's great curative powers are being scoffed and laughed at. Although his cures work they either go too far, or work in reverse, or only work part way, and are never completely successful, except for the worm who is hit over the head. The doctor's authority and fearful power are successfully brought down to size. By imagining these crazy situations, a child's fear of the doctor and what he can do (especially shots and pills) can be allayed.

E. *Church officials*: This section of jokes can also be divided into several sets of motifs. The authority of the church and the vicar or preacher is ridiculed, and is brought down to the level of his followers. In joke No. 903, the vicar is reminded that God is above all, especially in an airplane; the poor vicar is knocked down accidentally by a car (No. 906); a man swears at church and when warned by the preacher that God will punish him, he still persists, and God sends down a thunderbolt, but it hits the preacher instead (No. 907); a priest warns a boy not to say God dammit, and yet the priest eventually ends up yelling 'God dammit' when the wheel of the boy's wagon falls off and hits him (908); a priest brags about his ability with his holy hands, but a boy says he has the same ability with a bottle of acid (No. 909); and after hearing a sermon a man tells the preacher he's got every word of it in a book at home, and after getting angry the man sends the preacher a copy of the English dictionary. (No. 911)

The dignity of church officials is shaken by the view of a vicar walking on his hands for Palm Sunday (No. 477); and the sight of nuns tumbling downstairs, black white — black white, is quite incongruous with the quiet dignity and authority of a nun. (No. 254)

The church official is also seen as a normal person, with the same problems as everyone else, and, behind the stateliness of office and clothes, is a quite ordinary person. The nun is especially attacked in this way, and is seen as enjoying sex and rape (Nos. 912, 913), or as liable to death as other people. (No. 253). The vicar can also kill people, bringing a machine-gun to church "to make the people holy" (No. 476). He can be close to death himself when three out of four engines of an airplane fail, although all he complains about is being up in the airplane all night if the fourth engine fails as well. (No. 904) Jesus also appears in these jokes; in one a boy is called Jesus and is sent to buy some fish and chips, but ends up in church being the first served for communion (No. 936), and in another a Pakistani brags that Jesus was born in a stable (No. 842). A final joke has a Christian, a Moslem, and a Jew discuss how much money they give to charity, and the Jew gets the best deal out of God. He throws all his money up in the air, and all that God wants he takes, and all that comes down belongs to him. (No. 803)

Like other authority figures, the vicar or preacher is invested with a lot of power, in some ways considered supernatural power from God. Fear of Heaven and Hell can be an actual emotion, and several jokes portray the horrible Hell (No. 1006) or the problems of getting into Heaven (Nos. 804, 835, 1005), or the actual fear of the Devil (Nos. 773, 777). By laughing at church officials, and seeing them as real or ordinary people, the fear they inspire can be controlled.

F. Prisoners: Another type of adult authority is that of the prison warden over his prisoners, in the last stage of punishment before death. The prison in these jokes is either a criminal prison, a German concentration camp, or a lunatic asylum, and the prisoner is forced without choice to follow the rules of the prison. Seven jokes (Nos. 793-798, 930) take place in a German concentration camp. The action concerns either someone being up against the firing-squad with that person being given a last request, or else different ethnic groups (Scottish, English, Irish, and Jewish) are pitted against each other.

The Jew is always placed in the position of receiving the worst of the punishment, and receives the full hatred of the Germans. Although other groups are shot and punished, the Jew is the real target. One boy started his joke by saying, "Well, you know Germans hate Jews." I wondered why this motif still existed in the jokes, but the Jew takes the brunt of many ethnic jokes. Perhaps by retaining this actual emotion in their jokes, the English children can justify and rationalize their own prejudices against the Jews, though meanwhile hating Hitler too. Parodies of "Whistle while you work" are still sung about Hitler, who is a twerp, and half balmy, like his army, which is the other side of the picture. (No. 25) Hitler and his actions have had a huge influence on the Western world, and he has obviously been caught in the imagination of the children and their jokes.

Other jokes are told about the problems of living in a prison. Joke No. 817 has three men being gassed to death for their crimes. Each one, (either a Scotsman, Englishman, and Irishman, or an American, Irishman, and Canadian) is given a last request and the Englishman and Canadian survive by asking for and playing a piano, because "Tunes help you breathe more easily." (An advertisement.) In joke No. 1002 the warden gives three fellows a test, and if they pass it they can go free. Only one passes the test of determining which bird can't fly because "everyone knows Penguins are chocolate biscuits." In both of these jokes, prison life is something to escape, in whatever manner possible, but those who do survive and escape do so by knowing trick answers. The prison is just one more authority to scoff, beat, and keep out of the way of, and if by chance you get caught, all means are fair to extricate oneself. The child can identify with the clever one who escapes with clever answers, for his is equally clever. The authority is mocked by clever or by silly answers, and the prisoner is able to fool the warden and escape.

The people in the lunatic asylum are not to be envied, but the clever looney is able to escape. The same bird test is given to three nuts, one escaping when he knew the right answer. A free-association test is also given to a nut, but all he can answer is tits and nipples. (No. 999) On the whole, though, the nut is seen as illogical and irrational, and perchance he gets the right answer, as in joke No. 998, where a test is given and one nut gets the right answer by using his kidneys. But it is by luck, and illogical. In joke No. 1000, one nut appears quite sane as he reads a book, but his craziness is revealed when he says he couldn't read if another nut who thinks he is a light bulb got down from the ceiling where he is hanging. When a looney fellow sees a farmer putting manure on his rhubarb field, he is confused, for he puts custard on his. (No. 1001) When the prisoner does get out, he shouts "I'm free, I'm free", but a little girl puts him in place by replying, "So what, I'm four." (No. 1003)

With all these looney jokes, the characters are not what they appear; under a mask of sanity they are crazy, or under a mask of craziness they are quite sane. The fear present is that a child might be or might become as crazy as the looneys, and therefore be locked up under the authority of a warden. The clever looney has a chance to escape, but usually once looney always looney, and anyone with the stigma of being different or odd has a hard time of it to lose that stigma and blend in again. Even if craziness is a mask, once this mask is donned, it is very difficult to take it off again and fit in with the rest of the society. In some ways nuts have an advantage, like fools and "morons," because they can do whatever they want. Crazy people have a reputation for doing strange things, and their strange actions are regarded as acceptable within the boundaries of their mode of existence.

3. Transportation

A motif found throughout the jokes is that of some form of transportation. Cars, bicycles, lorries and trucks, trains and ships, are all mentioned several times. Buses are very popular, including waiting for buses and getting on and riding buses. Other actions involve planes and rockets and odd space-ships are also found.

The plane is seen in relation to modern problems and fears — bombs, engine trouble, and crashing. One joke told by an older informant was about a statistician who had figured out the odds for a plane having one bomb on it. Since the odds for a plane carrying two bombs on it are so much higher he carried a bomb with him on the plane. Ethnic relationships and stereotypes are shown in several jokes where the plane is going to crash and people have to jump. Joke No.

820 has a Jew and an Englishman jumping (or an Englishman and Welshman) and asking God to save them, and He does; but when the Chinese man jumps he asks God to shave him, and he ends up in a barber shop. Another joke (No. 823) had the pilot asking people to jump to save the plane and the rest of the people. The Englishman and Scotsman always jump, but the punchline varies; an American pushes a Mexican out, an Englishman pushes the Irishman out, and a German throws out the pilot. Joke No. 811 has an Englishman, Scotsman, and Irishman arguing about who the cow in the field belongs to, and one of these conversations takes place in a plane. The Scotsman wins the argument, since the cow has bagpipes. National pride in one's country is found in joke No. 821, where either a Scotsman, Englishman and Chinese man, or a Scotsman, Irishman and Chinese man are in a plane, and as the Irish, English, and Scots men see their countries, they either jump out of the plane, or upon landing run off to their country. The poor Chinese man can't see his country, so he drops a china plate and "sees" his bonny China. Engine trouble in joke No. 904, has a vicar (or an Irishman or Polack) appearing very dumb and complaining that they would be up in the air all night if engine 4 fails as engines 1,2 and 3 have failed. A London child told about a pilot who calmly tells his passengers the plane is on fire. (No. 968)

Some interesting actions are associated with buses; violence as well as implied sex. Joke riddle No. 292 asks "What is red and upside down in the gutter? A dead bus", and joke No. 718 asks "How do you kill a Jew? You roll a ha'penny under a bus". A TV couple complain about the noise from all the buses that go by, so Stanley digs a big hole in front of his house that is guaranteed to stop the buses. (No. 1009) Sex appears again with knickers: joke No. 893 has the bus conductor throwing down 10p pieces so he can see the color of the ladies' knickers as they bend down, and joke No. 896 has the woman sticking her parrot down her knickers so both of them can ride the bus. The last few jokes about buses involve waiting in line for the bus to come (Nos. 405, 935); trying to get on a full bus (Nos. 969-971); a man getting on a bus with a lemon behind his ear – a lemonade (No. 972); and a joke-riddle about when a bus isn't a bus. (No. 497)

Modernization and parodying of nursery rhymes in the three kings of Orient driving taxis, cars, prams and scooters. (No. 13) The fancy super-car, the E-type Jag, has been transferred to various objects; a carrot, a mole, and a fag. (No. 358). An older motif of witches has been modernized to contemplating vacuum sweepers instead of brooms to ride, but being rejected because they are too heavy (No. 432), and new spacecraft from outer space appear, like the 6-foot raspberry pudding pie (No. 917). Ever-popular is the drunk, driving his car and being stopped by the police (Nos. 774, 775). In England, the traffic light speaks to the cars or lorries or drivers, telling them not to look because it is changing (No. 223) and in London a big train tells a little train it's too young to smoke. (No. 608). A Paky driver leaves his train asleep at the junction (No. 844); a man has trouble getting a ride from a car driver who can't make up his mind (No. 974); a small man gets a free ride in a car pushed by a big man (No. 952); a man runs out of gas in the middle of the desert (No. 956); and another man gets his car running on Bee Pee. (B.P. = British Petrol) (No. 975)

4. Characters

This section discusses the various characters that appear throughout the jokes, and that are not found in other sections. These include: the waiter, skinheads, queers, tramps and drunks, and couples.

A. Waiters: Waiters appear in several quick pun jokes (Nos. 1023-1036). Nine of these are complaints about the soup served. In another a man demands a crocodile sandwich; another is a complaint about the size of the chicken. A man deliberately misunderstands the waitress' question about the condition of his steak, and two are about the condition of some food – hot dogs and rice. These jokes are quick to tell, and they portray the problems of eating out in a restaurant, with poor service and poor food, but especially they emphasize the advantages of home cooking and cheaper prices.

B. Skinheads: Only two English jokes were told about skinheads or bubbleboys, but they sum up the image of the skinhead, who is rough, nasty, and tough, wearing levis and jacket, riding motorbikes, and beating up people for no reason, if it suits the skinheads. In the first joke, the boys trick/threaten a poor Irish fellow into buying the next round of drinks (No. 993), and in the second for no reason, they beat up a fellow, who, out of fear, doesn't fight back or protect himself. He retaliates though by running over their motorbikes with his car. (No. 994) Both jokes show the general dislike and fear of running into these gangs, and the general lack of control over them. A Hell's Angel appears in the joke with the queer (No. 996), and the queer tries to imitate the tough behaviour the Hell's Angel uses to get a drink at the pub.

C. *Queers*: Queers (queer = homosexual) are definitely stamped with the stigma of being different, odd, and not to be envied. Two jokes show the problems that one queer had getting a drink; and no matter what he did, he couldn't forget his role as a queer, and the bartender couldn't ignore it either. (Nos. 995, 996) Even using his supposedly tough dog Pinkie, or emulating the behaviour of the Hell's Angel failed to get him a drink. A third joke was a pantomine of a queer washing his eyes, by taking them out of his head to wash them. (No. 997) The definition of success is two pouffs (homosexuals) with a pram (No. 311), and both Donny Osmond and Georgie Best are seen as pouffs. (Nos. 63-67) The queer is laughed at, but people also feel sorry for him, for he can't help himself. No matter how funny he appears, you laugh but keep your distance, for his queerness might rub off. Because of this, the queer appears as a lonely person, unable to talk to people, and even unable to buy a drink because he's different.

D. *Tramps and Drunks*: Tramps, drunks, and Irishmen are almost synonomous in most of these jokes. All three commit similar acts, such as: stealing food (Nos. 773, 989, 991); begging for food and shelter (Nos. 874, 987, 988); finding food (No. 992), or sex (No. 899); finding and drinking alcohol (Nos. 776, 777, 981-986); and getting stopped by the police (Nos. 774, 775, 990).

Irishmen are seen as quite stupid, and they drink a lot, and are dumb enough to get drunk and act foolish. Both the drunk and tramp are seen as outcasts of society. The tramp is dependent on others for food and shelter, and the drunk relies on others to take care of him when he is drunk. Neither are reliable characters, and they are the most apt to get into trouble with the police. When the drunk Irishman confronts the police, he's so drunk he can't really answer his questions, but gives 'smart' cheeky answers. The tramp, when begging for food and shelter, is quite clever, and when caught can also give smart cheeky answers.

Why these characters are portrayed so often I'm not sure, except that both the drunk and tramp are free to roam, and this type of freedom must be enviable and desirable. The married drunk and Irishman have their wives to confront when they return from their wanderings, which can't be that desirable, but these characters are able to bring a laugh. Perhaps this is because their actions are typical of their roles and are expected from them. If they didn't act in these stereotyped manners, they wouldn't be funny, but pathetic or horrible.

The tramp who, with 25p. (approx. 50c) gets a bed and sex with the manager's wife, while leaving his fleas with the manager, creates a humorous picture, and he comes out on top. In real life he would be thrown into jail. One laughs at the picture created, knowing it isn't real, but somehow hoping it could be true anyway. The tramp who eats the dead dog because he's so hungry, is a pathetic creature, but when his friend re-eats it when he throws it up because he only likes warm food, he is disgusting. Again though, it fits the image of a tramp and one expects such behaviour from him. Or the poor drunk man who falls down the stairs, breaks his hip-flask and cuts his bum, but is so drunk he puts the plaster (plasters = band-aids) on the mirror instead of himself, is also a funny character. One feels sorry for him, but instead one laughs at the picture of the plasters on the mirror and the man thinking he has repaired himself. Perhaps people just like to laugh at others who are worse off than themselves.

E. Couples: The themes portrayed in the couples jokes are typical of real married life, such as envy and competing with the neighbors (No. 1010); nagging wives (Nos. 1011, 1012); unfaithful husbands and wives as murderers (No. 1014); stingy husbands and unfaithful wives (No. 1013); arguments and complaining (Nos. 1009, 1015); missing husbands (No. 1017); and ordinary married life, complete with old-fashioned ideas. (Nos. 1016, 1018-1022); Children are great observers of their family life, and the family life of neighbors and friends. Although they may not have witnessed all these motifs first-hand, most are very popular in the news media, either real or fictional. Evolving around the unhappy wife or the unhappy husband, these jokes portray the turmoil present between most couples. Unfortunately, the jokes relate only the problems of married life, and show nothing about the happy life of a family. That is the nature of jokes however, to make something that is serious or painful appear funny so that one can laugh and survive.

5. Animals

The animal motif section is the largest of all the subsections of motifs, and includes: A. Dogs; B. Cats; C. Birds; D. Rodents; E. Farm Animals; G. Elephants; H. Wild Animals; I. Insects; and J. Fish. The outstanding characteristic of all these motifs is the human attributes given to the animals, such as speech and thinking-power; human actions, like the use of the toilet, and playing cards and wearing clothes; and sexual powers.

The dog is a popular animal and he is seen playing cards (No. 1123); wearing boots (No. 1122); running errands and chasing girl dogs (No. 1124); being clever but not too clever (No. 1121), as well as just being a nuisance (Nos. 628, 1100, 1120); fighting (No. 487); fetching objects (No. 950); being compared to a hot-dog (No. 337); or just being a dog. (Nos. 215, 398, 629, 992, 995, 1126-1128).

Cats appear several times performing normal actions of cats, getting killed 'just like that' (No. 55) or bringing bad luck. (No. 328)

Budgies and various birds are also popular. My most favorite joke and one of the best-told is about a man who buys a budgie, and continually has to buy his budgie new playmates because it kills them all! (No.1130) Another well-told joke is about a man who buys a brand-new budgie, and he keeps buying it everything to make it happy, but it finally dies – he never bought it food. (No. 1131) A similar joke was told by an American boy. The child buys a bird, but when he goes back to buy birdseed, he can't pronounce it correctly, and the pet-store man won't sell him any food until he says it right. The boy returns every day until he finally asks the man if he wants to buy a dead bird. (No. 1132) A lot of joke-riddles are told about various birds, the most popular being the classic "Why did the chicken cross the road? – To get to the other side." (No. 442), and in London, "Why do birds fly south? – It's too far to walk." (No. 427) Ducks and chickens, especially to be stolen and eaten, appear a lot, and the penguin as a chocolate biscuit rescues several men from prisons. (No. 1002) The parrot appears in the lady's knickers while riding the bus (No. 896), swearing at church (Nos. 1133, 1136), and with an old woman and a wizard. (Nos. 1134, 1135)

All sorts of wild animals are in the joke-riddles, where they are compared to humans and to objects. For example, "Why can't you play cards in the jungle? – Too many cheetahs" (No. 424); or "What do the monkeys put toast under? – A gorilla" (No. 169); or "Why does a giraffe have such a long neck? – Because he didn't want to smell his feet." (No. 466). The zebra and skunk are ever-popular in "What is black and white and red all over?" (Nos. 255-257) Three long versions of the same shaggy dog story, two of these involving gorillas, were told, and they all end up with the punchline "Tag, you're it" (of Tag). Here the gorillas aren't mean and nasty but want to play games (Nos. 1018-1020). In another joke a gorilla escapes from the zoo, but the man treats the animal as a companion and they visit the zoo and plan on going to Sea World. (Sea World – marine amusement park). (No. 1145)

Insects of all sorts also have human attributes, the favorite being two flies playing football in a saucer, waiting to go to the cup to play. (No. 1118), or "what goes 99 clump? – A centipede with a wooden leg." (No. 360)

Very few jokes about the elephant were told, for the elephant joke cycle is no longer popular. However, a popular joke in London is "two elephants fell off a cliff. Boom boom." (No. 717) Jokes about farm animals occur quite a few times, mainly the cow, such as "Why does a cow have bells? Because its horns don't work" (No. 467); "Where do you find prehistoric cows? – In a mooseum" (No. 380); and "What goes oom oom? – A cow walking backwards." (No. 244). The ownership of a cow in a field is contested by an Englishman, Irishman, and Scotsman, and the Scotsman wins since the cow has bagpipes (No. 811); while a well-endowed bull jumps over a fence every morning greeting the cows with "Hiya, I'm Billy Bigballs" (No. 1138). Lambs appear in almost all of the parodies of "Mary had a little lamb," appearing either with cats or bears. (Nos. 51-58). Horses mainly occur in the joke-riddles and catches, but an amusing joke tells how a man gets another man to help him put a horse in a bathtub, just so he can tell his wife he already knows it's there. (No. 951). Horse muck is used by tramps to get food from large houses, but the second tramp is always offered fresh warm horse muck instead of the piece he has (Nos. 987, 988) An interesting but astute view of pigs is seen in a joke-riddle: "What happens when pigs fly — The price of bacon and sausages goes up." (No. 373), and a Paki's smell (or Englishman or Polack) is worse than a pig. (No. 815)

Rodents, such as rats, hamsters, a mole, and mice, appear in the jokes. Three mice go exploring in a house, discovering all the modern conveniences (No. 891); and a man asks the health society to rid his house of rats, but when they come to investigate, both rats and fish come out — the house is damp as well. (No. 965) Fish appear a lot, mainly in the joke-riddles where fish are related to famous people or fish, such as "What is green and swims in the ocean? — Moby Pickle" (No. 277), or "What fish scares other fish? — Jack the Kipper." (No. 338)

Animals are also seen as friendly, even the wild animals, and the only fight/attack is between a lion and a hyena (No. 1144); and in case you are surrounded by 6 elephants, 2 giraffes, 4 lions, 6 tigers, and 3 monkeys, and wanted to get away, all you have to do is stop the merry-go-round and get off. (No. 401)

Pets, such as dogs and cats, are often very good friends to children, so what would be better than a magical world where all animals talk and act like people?

6. Supernatural Creatures

Supernatural motifs are found throughout all the categories; the ghost, either actual (Nos. 806, 819, 826, 827), or false (Nos. 807-810) is the most common and popular, and joke-riddles about skeletons and ghost are also common. (Nos. 220, 226-228, 312-314). The most popular one was "Why didn't the skeleton jump off the cliff? — Because he didn't have any guts." (No. 459) Creatures such as Dracula, Frankenstein, Wolfman, werewolves, and vampires are mentioned several times (Nos. 186, 242, 376, 402, 555, 916, 980), a creature from outer space (No. 917), and a 'big hideous fellow' who murders a couple (No. 1022) also appear. The devil makes his appearance a few times (Nos. 773, 777), and a fairy grants three wishes to his benefactor. (Nos. 881, 882) Witches occur (No. 432), a wizard (No. 1135), a gnome (No. 1018), a giant (No. 812), and a three-headed monster. (Nos. 396, 976-978).

On the whole, though, supernatural components are lacking, compared to the number of jokes collected. These jokes tend toward reality-oriented situations and characters. Even ghosts are real boys, picking their noses, or a constipated man who sat so long on the toilet he's become a skeleton. Dracula and Wolfman are both related to natural human actions: buying oranges, and needing to use the toilet. A real ghost, the ghost of Aunt Mabel, is beaten by the rational logic of Davy Crockett; and the skeleton has human attributes of guts. Supernatural motifs don't fit into the world of the child, unless he moulds them to modern situations and actions, like ordinary people.

It was mentioned earlier that moron jokes, current in the United States in the 1950's, were never present in England as about morons, but concerning ordinary people. The moron is like the supernatural creature, and can't always fit into the fairly rational reality-oriented world of the joke. The moron is unknown to the child as an actual character. It is much easier to visualize a man doing the foolish deeds of the moron, or a strange and unfamiliar character performing natural human actions.

Although the moron has dropped out of the joke repertoire of the older child, the fear of odd or different people that the child could possibly be like, is still present. The younger child tells the joke-riddles about the moron/man who performs odd acts, while the older child tells jokes about the prisoner, the lunatics in the looney asylum, and the queer. All of these characters are seen as distinctly odd and different from the normal population, and have committed strange undesirable actions that get them defined as odd and different. These characters aren't admired, but are seen as foolish. If there are three in a joke, usually the third one (as in folktales) by clever, logically-based, yet irrational answers, gets the better of the rational authority figure.

Throughout all the jokes, the preference is away from characters who aren't real or known to the child, toward characters that they can imagine, and who commit actions that they themselves can commit, or fear that they might commit. If the character is supernatural, he is seen doing human things, or having human attributes. Most popular are real people, although odd. These characters seem to represent a fear of the child's about being locked up for similar actions and deeds, either in a prison or a lunatic asylum.

7. Death, Violence, and Killing

Death, violence, and killing are motifs that appear in most of the categories, from innocent short rhymes, to joke-riddles, and real jokes. Sometimes this motif is incidental to the joke plot; at other times is a major theme of the joke. When I first formed the category, I didn't subdivide the motifs, but the number of them forced me to try and split them into violence, killing, and death. A lot of the jokes overlap all three categories, but the final result of the action has determined what section it was placed in.

A. Violence: One of the largest groups of jokes in this section involved the teacher and child hitting each other, as in the parody of Glory Glory Alleluya, where the teacher hits the child with a ruler and a shoe; and, in two versions, the child hits the teacher back with a rotten tangerine. (Nos. 16-23) In a song about the end of term, the teacher is threatened with boxed ears and being blown up with dynamite (No. 70); in a limerick, the teacher's whacking machine breaks and hits the teacher instead (No. 128); and when a teacher asks a silly question, the replay is a threat of a fight. (No. 325)

Fighting or hitting is a popular form of violence, and appears in a parody of "Mary had a little pig" which gets kicked (No. 57); Paddy on the railway gets kicked up the bum (No. 99); two potatoes fight who can't see eye to eye (No. 479); an Irishman has to learn Kung Fu to keep two Englishmen from continually beating him up (No. 790); Nic, Mac, Paddy, and Wac all beat up on the new man (No. 818); 8 bubbleboys beat up an innocent man (No. 994); a man buying a coat misunderstands the question "do you want a belt?" (No. 1098); a boy is walloped by a man who had just slipped on the same piece of dog shit the boy slipped on (No. 1100); a ghost is offered a second black eye (No. 1054); a boy is spanked by his father for telling the truth (No. 944); and a poor hyena is continually beat up by a lion. (No. 1144). The threat of violence is also present, such as a child being threatened with a spanking unless his grades improve (No. 942); the difference between a glass bra is smash and grab (No. 305); a boy threatens a bash if someone touches his lolly, in a knock-knock joke (No. 554); and a ghost who is actually a cat threatens to tear a mouse's body apart. (No. 810) The violence of hitting one's head on the wall is tolerated because of the lovely feeling when you quit. (No. 640)

Sexual violence comes in the form of rape (Nos. 912, 913), and a little girl who plays with her daddy's teddy-bear and bites its head off when it spits at her. (No. 883)

Other forms of violence include a man thrown down the stairs (No. 59); three men who have to jump out of a plane but are saved (No. 820); a woman who falls out of a plane but her husband doesn't complain (No. 1012); several cruel jokes where the mother is violent toward her child, her husband or the dentist (Nos. 1110, 1113–1115, 1117); and two jokes about dogs that are a nuisance, and are thrown down the road, or thrown on a fire. (Nos. 1120, 1121)

B. Killing: As in the previous section, the killing motif is sometimes incidental to the plot, and at other times it is the major theme, Who and what gets killed varies tremendously, from animals such as cats and lambs as in "Mary had a little lamb" parodies, (Nos. 51–58); to elephants who are shot with blue elephant guns (Nos. 709, 710), or else they fall off cliffs (No. 717); to biscuits which get run over. (No. 618) A variety of people also get killed, and these include teachers and prefects (No. 26); nuns (No. 253); a priest (No. 907); the Osmonds (No. 517); various ethnic groups such as Jews (No. 718), the English, Irish and Scottish (Nos. 812, 814), and others such as Americans and Canadians (No. 817); prisoners (No. 1004); babies (No. 856); a young Army boy (No. 949); a drunk killed by a train (No. 986); a boy by his brother (No. 946); and a couple named Hill who are killed and then are brought back to life with the song, "the Hills are alive with the sound of music." (No. 1022)

Various people are also seen as killers, such as a vicar wanting to make his people holy with a machine gun (No. 476); the Germans, at concentration camps (Nos. 793–798, 830, 1003); various people trying to save their own lives in a crashing plane, such as an Englishman, an American, or a German (No. 823); an unborn child wants to kill his father (No. 862); a wife poisoning her husband (No. 1014); a man tarring the street (No. 1008); a man in the army killing the cook to save the regiment (No. 1053); and Wolfman running around London killing people. (No. 916).

C. *Death*: Death occurs in a variety of ways. Some die 'just like that' (Nos. 55, 521); or they go into a safe and say 'shut that door' (No. 520). A dead bus is described as red and upside down in the gutter (No. 292), and when Donny Osmond died he asked for help. (No. 518) Poor Thiney dies when Fattey rolls over on him (Nos. 93, 94); an Irishman blows himself up trying to throw a hand grenade (No. 787); and six men die trying to dig an Irishman's grave in the sea (No. 739) Suicide is a popular form of death, and Popeye blows himself up with gas (No. 28); Tarzan jumps off the cliff (Nos. 204, 205); a Scotsman, Englishman, and a Chinese all jump out of a plane when they see their countries (No. 821); a Jew jumps off the Eiffel Tower when he thinks he sees a 10p piece at the bottom (No. 802); a Pakistani falls down a big hole in the mountains (No. 832); an Indian chief dies after taking bigger and bigger pills for constipation (No. 925); and Blackmen smuggling themselves into England in coffins are prepared for death by suffocation (No. 836)

Violence can occur in all facets of life, as these children have realized; even a poor biscuit with the human attributes of speech can get run down by a car. Oranges are also compared to cars, as when an orange stops rolling because it has run out of juice/petrol. Cars can also hit people, such as the priest; and the other forms of transportation, such as buses, trains, and airplanes, are also seen as possible paths to death. These jokes are well-related to reality, where the most common violent death occurs in car crashes, and lately, in plane crashes. Transportation has become more and more popular and necessary, so that other-people's deaths occuring in this manner are now almost considered the price to pay for increased convenience and speed.

Forcing people to do what others want runs throughout the jokes; the extreme example being the German concentration camp, where the prisoners are given no choice between life and death. The vicar is also prepared to use violent means, and the Englishman (or German or American) forces people to jump off the plane, either to save the plane or to save himself by helping someone else out the plane door.

Almost anyone can be a killer, and you see family members killing one another, usually for the wrongs that the killer thinks have been inflicted upon himself. As in real life, almost anyone can be killed, or be subject to violence. Death is the expected fate of everyone, young or old.

A child learns early that his fists are often the best way to solve problems, or at least the quickest and perhaps the easiest. Instead of tolerating abuse, one hits back to shut the person up, but one can't react that way in real life to adult authority figures. In jokes the child hits back, or does violent things to his teachers and parents, and in this way, through wish fulfillment, he can rid himself of some of the frustration and violence he feels when he can't react to the teacher's or parent's scoldings or whipping. Kung Fu, the Oriental art of self defense, has become very popular, especially through the television programs. There the hero gracefully and courageously defends himself against all foes, and he is quite an ideal figure in the eyes of the children, to follow and try to imitate.

Even if the child usually experiences no extreme form of violence or of death himself, the new media are strikingly full of articles about killings and violence, and television programs often show death and violence. But many of these motifs can also come from the child's experience or imagination; car crashes and accidents; fighting, especially within the family and at school; problems at school, perhaps being too cheeky and talking back to the teacher; and cruelty to animals. Often the violence or death is presented as a merited punishment or frankly as a thrill, instead of as a danger.

Sexual violence in the jokes is seen as the fault of the parent who didn't answer the child's questions truthfully, both about where babies come from and what the sexual organs are, how they work, and how they are used; or the violence may be actually desired, by the nuns who get raped. The little girl playing with her father's penis can also be seen as the traditional Freudian urge all little girls are supposed to have of wanting sex with their fathers. Her biting off the head of his penis is her frustrated attempt to retaliate and get revenge for his refusal of her.

Death can also result from one's own greed, or foolishness, or stupidity, as to the Pakistani, the Jew and the Irishman. In that way, they are seen as deserving death. Death is a common end during war, so the young Army boy who died, although not deserving it should have known of the possibilities of death. Killing others to save yourself is also seen as fairly just and allowable, for your own life and existence are necessary and must be protected. Death also results because the person just can't help it, as when Fattey rolled over and smashed Thinney, or the Indian chief who eventually had a big fart, but blew himself up.

Stereotypes are often portrayed: the Pakistani who falls down the hole in the mountain was so pig-headed and conceited, that he fell, but he also talked and bragged a lot, which finished him off the second time. The Jew's desire for money is even greater than desire for life, as he jumps off the Eiffel Tower for a 10p piece, and found out too late it was only a dustbin. Blackmen are seen as fatalistic, and willing even to die, just to get into England. Immigration and smuggling of aliens is a very current problem in England, but this joke views the men as really desperate to get into the country, to the point of suffocation. Again, the Irishman is portrayed as stupid and inept in the joke about trying to throw a hand grenade, but he can't count, and so blows himself up. Inter-ethnic stereotypes are shown in the plane joke, when the American throws the Mexican out to save himself; the Englishman throws out the Irishman, and the German throws out the pilot. They aren't like the other stupid people who jumped to save others, but are very selfish; and, as far as they are concerned, they are getting rid of unneeded or unwanted people.

Attitudes toward death, killing, and violence on the whole, then, seem fairly tolerant. People are seen as justified in committing these actions, or else other people deserve to die. Only in the joke about the skinheads, is their action seen as unnecessary, as they beat up an innocent man, but he retaliates and returns violence for violence as he runs over their motorbikes with his car. The Christian ethic of turning the other cheek is lost, and one must return violence for violence. Often violence is the only way to have any effect, as with the skinheads, or because you would lose face if you didn't fight back and act like a man. Proving one is a man, brave and courageous, and one of the gang, becomes a motivation to follow the crowd and do what they do, no matter what. Outsiders are mocked and laughed at, and are subject to violence that an insider can dish out, but doesn't receive. So, the child learns how to fight and how to protect himself. Violence has become the way to react in a world of increasing frustration and anxiety. At any rate, that is what the child is learning.

Finally, death is ridiculed, as in the joke about the couple named Hill, who are murdered, but who come miraculously alive with music. Children know death is permanent, but they can always hope it isn't. It is almost as if they are tempting death to come and get them, for they too will come alive with music. The joke, though, mocks these inner desires, and the couple is seen as innocent and as a bit foolish. Unfortunately, death is just too permanent for the child, and he wants to change it, in whatever manner possible.

8. Television Programs, Football (Soccer), Mock Stars, Stars, Brand Products

I was surprised to find relatively few references to real people, television programs, and stars in these jokes. I divided this group into five subsections: A. Football songs and stars (soccer); B. Stars – pop, movie, and real people; C. Mock Stars; D. Television programs and stars; and E. Brand products.

A. Football Songs and Stars: The most popular character in this section was Georgie Best, a football player on the Manchester United team. He is very good-looking, wears flashy clothes, and is popular with the girls. The verses about Georgie Best have him wearing women's clothing, either a see-through bra, or a padded bra, frilly knickers, 2 pink ribbons, and walking like a woman or a wally. (Nos. 63–65) Various football teams are mentioned in a knickers (panties) joke, the punchline always being no knickers meant Arsenal. (No. 893) Teams are also compared to each other (No. 1037), or Leeds United is declared the greatest team in the land. (No. 69)

B. Stars: Five real people who have no association with movies or records are mentioned in these jokes: Prince Charles is mentioned in two joke-riddles, but the riddles' answers are not dependent on his name being in the joke –anyone's name could have been used (Nos. 302, 465). Ted Heath has split lips and laughing shoulders (No. 103) Hitler, who is found in a parody of "Whistle while you work" (No. 25). Mark Spitz, in a joke-riddle (No. 456) Evil Knieval, who is also in a joke-riddle. (No. 284)

Pop stars included rhymes and joke riddles about Donny Osmond, Garry Glitter, Chuck Berry, David Bowie, David Cassidy, the Beatles, and Cliff Richard; Donny Osmond being the most popular. Movie stars included Betty Grable and Shirley Temple, and characters were Dracula, Wolfman, King Kong, Cinderella, and Winnie the Pooh. Note that none of these movie stars and characters are recent or current.

C. Mock Stars: I include these motifs in this section because the child had to know the real person if he was to understand the mock star and what he did. All of these motifs were found in the joke-riddles, and they included: Gooey Armstrong (No. 184); Alexander or Peter the Grape (Nos. 288, 289); Jack the Kipper (No. 338); Billy the Squid (No. 367); Moby Pickle (No. 277); Jonathan Livingston Pickle (No. 275); and Marshall Dill (No. 489)

D. Televison Programs: This subsection is the largest, and while most motifs refer to a specific program, several jokes refer to TV or the BBC and ITV, as in a parody of "While Shepherds Watch." (No. 7) Doctor Who is the most popular, and is found in a knock-knock joke. (No. 547); Batman is referred to in a variety of jokes (Nos. 478, 937); and Robin Day once (No. 524). Two popular stars with their catch-phrases are Larry Grayson and "shut that door" and Tommy Cooper with 'just like that'. Coronation Street is mentioned once (No. 1009); "This is your life" (No. 522); and Popeye the Sailor man appears (No. 28). Tarzan is also very popular (Nos. 204, 205, 377, 698). Others include Donald Duck and Mickey Mouse (Nos. 548, 580, 581); Kojak (No. 172); Laurel and Hardy (No. 216); and Smoky the Bear. (No. 437)

E. Brand Products: Brand products are included, since a knowledge of what the products are, is needed to understand the jokes. Some of these are Avon (No. 553); Weetabix (No. 384); Sago rice pudding (No. 387); Marmite (No. 577); Guinness beer (Nos. 182, 729); Wellington boots (Nos. 734, 778); treacle pudding (No. 779); Tunes (No. 817); Bird's Eye Fish Fingers (No. 979); Stork margarine and Penguin Chocolate Biscuits (No. 1002); Robertson's marmalade (No. 1013); milkduds (No. 185); coca-cola and 7-Up (No. 211); Betty Crocker (Nos. 418, 538); Ronald McDonald (No. 591); and the Kodak Instamatic Camera (No. 172).

Anyone who is in the popular eye, either through the news media (radio, television, newspapers, magazines) or makes records or movies, is apt to be caught in the imagination of children and found in their jokes. The character has something – some appeal – that makes him stick in their mind, and almost all of these characters are popular and good people, except for Hitler, Jack the Kipper, Dracula, and Wolfman, who, although bad and feared, are also admired. Actions that make these people stand out as courageous, brave, or daring, can make them popular; or how they talk or think, or even how they dress and walk, can make them admirable. Products are chosen whose names can have dual meanings, their advertising has given them a catchphrase that is easily remembered. The ads create a good picture in the children's minds, or they are common products and seen every day. The children are seen as a valuable market by the advertisers and are manipulated as such.

9. Ethnic Groups

The ethnic jokes, actually *anti*-ethnic jokes – cover many peoples and many stereotypes. The three main types of such jokes told by the English children are the Irish and Jewish joke-riddles and jokes, and the Scottish, English, and Irishman jokes. Other groups found in the joke-riddles are the Chinese, the Eskimo, the Indian, and the Mexican. In the jokes (anecdotes) sections, the other groups mentioned are Americans, Canadians, French, Germans, Pakistanis, Arabs, and the Blacks. The American children mainly told aggressive, anti-ethnic joke-riddles and jokes about Polacks, although they also mention Italians, French, Germans and Russians.

As mentioned in the historical trends section, clusters of joke motifs can make up the ethnic stereotype. More often than not, an alleged national or ethnic trait is ridiculed. The children are definite about what the Jew and Irishman and others are supposed to be in the jokes. The Jew is defined as 'mean', the Irishman 'thick', the Englishman 'posh' the Scotsman 'stingy and crafty', and the Italian 'soft'.

Joke-riddles concerning the Jew are mainly concerned with his presumed greed for 'money at any price,' sometimes with his being quite clever, and other times very stupid, and his stinginess or meanness. These motifs as well as others concerning Jews in German concentration camps and the Germans' hatred of the Jews; also being made fun of; and their dislike of Christianity, appear in the jokes proper. A Jew is willing to jump under a bus for a penny (No. 718); or jump off the Eiffel tower for a penny (No. 802); you can get a Jew mad by putting him in a round room and telling him there's a penny in the corner (No. 719); you can get a Jew in a telephone box by throwing in a ha'penny, and yelling gas to get him out (No. 723) Jews are also willing to cheat and steal money or riches; and two Jews steal the Golden Gates of Heaven (No. 804); or they cheat charity and God of their donations by throwing their money up in the air and all that comes back down is theirs to keep (No. 803)... Synagogues are built round so that the Jew can't hide in the corner when the collection comes round (No. 724); and they will even sell flies to Arabs or Pakistanis to make money (No. 841). Stinginess is indicated by bog-rolls (toilet-paper) up on the washing line (No. 720); their dustbins or gardens have padlocks on them (No. 721); the chimney has a parking meter on it during Christmas (No. 722); their sugarbowls have forks in them (No. 725); and the largest book in the world is the Jewish book of savings. (No. 726).

The German concentration camp shows the Jew as clever in putting off his execution by asking to sing a song (No. 794); trying to avoid trouble (No. 798); and being pitted against other prisoners, such as Englishmen, Irishmen, and Scotsmen – the Jew always getting the worst punishment. (Nos. 795-797)

The Jew as a figure of fun to mock is portrayed in several jokes; in one a Pakistani asks him an innocent question, but he's sure he's making fun of the name Jew (No. 799); or a Chinese waiter misunderstands the question "Do you have any Chinese Jews?" and thinks the person is asking for a special brand of juice (No. 800); a knock-knock joke gets someone to admit they are a Jew (No. 559); and the cure of a short nose or finger is the word pardon, but the man runs into a Jew who says "a thousand pardons." (No. 867)

The Jew's dislike of Christianity is found in the joke where a Jewish man, a Christian and a Methodist get together to discuss religion, and the Jew thinks he's seeing miracles, but only proves to the other two that he's very stupid. (No. 801) A final joke takes place in Northern Ireland, where a priest asks three children, a Catholic, a Protestant, and a Jew, who the most famous person in the world is, and the

Jewish boy correctly answers St. Patrick, for he knows "business is business". (No. 805)

The Irish jokes are the most popular ethnic joke to tell in England, and they all revolve around a few stereotyped ideas; the Irishman's presumed drunkness, stupidity, and dirtiness; he is also crafty in some instances, and patriotic. Two drunken Irishmen pinch a bag of apples and are mistaken for the Devil and God in the graveyard (No. 773); a drunken Irishman mistakes his wife for the devil (No. 777); another is stopped by the police and gives foolish answers to all questions (Nos. 774, 775); an Irishman is sent by his wife to get some beer, but he foolishly puts it in his trilby hat) and then dumps it out (No. 776); and an Irishman will go on the roof when you tell him the beer is on the house. (No. 740) In America these would now all be told of the equally mythical "Polack".

The stupid Irishman is perhaps the most popular motif, and he commits all kinds of dumb, foolish acts. He usually survives – he's too dumb to die. Some of these include: opening a tin of treacle-pudding and then standing himself in the boiling water for 20 minutes (No. 779); being confused by a card that has printed on both sides 'Please turn over' (No. 783); blowing himself up tyring to throw a hand grenade since he can't count (No. 787); Paddy doing a great somersault act off the top of a scaffolding all because Murphy dropped a hammer on his feet (No. 789); trying to learn Kung Fu to keep himself from being beaten up by two Englishmen, but it takes so long to say all the necessary ritual words before he strikes that he still gets beaten up (No. 790); six men drown trying to dig an Irishman's grave at sea (No. 739); needing the words 'Open other end' on the bottom of a Guinness bottle (No. 729); driving a 2-ton truck over the edge of a cliff to test the air brakes (No. 730); being able to brainwash him by putting water in his Wellingtons (No. 734); breaking his leg by falling out of a tree as he's trying to sweep up leaves (No. 785); moving the wall up and down to paint it, the painter and ladder staying in one place (Nos. 735, 736); a pregnant Irishwoman is arrested for carrying a dope (No. 784); an Irishman gets tricked and threatened into buying the next round of beer for twelve skinheads (No. 993); and one of the shortest books in the world is the Irish book of knowledge. (No. 742).

The dirtiness motif is shown in a joke where three Irishmen shit all over the floor, and flies sing and float around on a matchbox in it: (one version of No. 807). Cleverness is shown against the Germans in the same way as the Jew; as a last request he asks to sing a song and he sings 1,000,000 green bottles standing on the wall. (No. 793)

Looking at the English, Irish, Scottish jokes, again the Irishman is seen as stupid. When confronting a ghost, usually the Scotsman and Irishman run out, and the Englishman is either the brave one who discovers the real ghost, or is clever enough to not go alone but gets the other two to come with him. The Scotsman is the brave one several times, and once the Irishman is the courageous one. (Nos. 806-10) When confronting a giant, the Englishman comes out on top, and in a second version the Irishman does; both by spitting on the ground and asking the giant to swim in it. This can be seen as the dirty Irishman motif, or the clever Englishman (or clever Irishman as well.) (No. 812) The three also contest the ownership of the cow, and there the Scotsman wins, since the cow has bagpipes. (No. 811) When needing to be brown to cross a bridge, the Irishman loses out because he only painted his face and arms brown, and not the rest of his body. (No. 813) Again, when the three try to cross a bridge, they must give the bridgeman some gold, and the Irishman gives him a golden wonder crisp (potato chip) (No. 816) Gassing kills the Scotsman and Irishman, but the Englishman survives by playing the piano, since Tunes help you to breathe more easily. (One version of No. 817.) The Irishman survives when the lady all three love asks them to go over the cliff, the one not dying winning her; but when it's the Irishman's turn, he says 'Ladies first,' and so she dies. (No. 814, London version-Englishman wins).

The Irishman, Englishman, and Scotsman are patriotic as is shown in several jokes; one when they see their country and jump out of the plane or run off to their country (No. 821); or when the plane is crashing and people are asked to jump, usually these three volunteer to jump out, although in one version the Englishman saves himself and throws out an Irishman. (No. 823) A final joke in this series has an Irishman and American having a riddle contest, the Irishman telling a riddle the American doesn't know, but then he admits he doesn't know the answer either. (No. 840)

Continuing with the Englishman, he is usually seen as quite clever, being able to come out on top. When a Scotsman, Frenchman, and Englishman all ask for lolly's of a certain color but don't get that color, the Englishman responds by giving the shopkeeper a different color of money than is wanted — less than the proper amount (No. 824) When both an Englishman and Frenchman confront a ghost, the Frenchman runs off and is never seen again, but the Englishman at least goes to Scotland Yard (No. 827) When he needs to get on an all Black ship, he is able to (No. 829); he confronts the Germans and cleverly answers their 'no' answer (No. 830); and when he's with a conceited bragging Pakistani, he is able, by asking one question, to make the Pakistani refall down the hole in the moutain. (No. 832) The Englishman is also seen as a little 'thick', as when he asks a French lady if she wants to ride in his new car, and when she says *oui oui* (French for yes) he says not in his car. (No. 825); or when the English lady marries a foreigner, either a French or Italian man, and tells him to go out and learn some English words, he comes back with "take off ze—bra baby." (No. 828) The Englishman tries to be clever and changes the code word for farting to include shitting as well, but the two Muslims don't understand him and so he shits all over the tent. (No. 831) The Scotsman, seen alone, is stingy with his money, and is willing to let his child drown rather than pay his fare (No. 834). The Scotsman and Englishman also appear with a Black man, all trying to get into heaven; the two are given easy words to spell, but the Black man is even discriminated against in heaven. (No. 835).

Other jokes about Black men have them trying to smuggle into England in coffins (No. 836); compare them to Guinness (No. 182), to an oil slick (No. 837), to a chocolate drop (Nos. 265, 276), and to Africa (No. 744); or the Black man is used by a white lady to make her husband jealous (No. 1013); and Tarzan plays nought and crosses on his bum (No. 97). The Americans also appears in other jokes, such as when he's with a Canadian and Irishman getting gassed and he asks for a big cigar as a last request, but the Canadian is smart and asks for the piano to play tunes (No. 817). The American is also seen as the braggart: everything is bigger and better in the United States, but the Englishman is eventually able to show him something either bigger or faster (Nos. 838, 839). In the riddle contest with the Irishman, the

American brags he knows every riddle there is (No. 840). In connection with the American there is the Mexican, whom the American pushes out of the plane; and the Mexican is also found in two idiot tests. (Nos. 646, 647, 823)

The Arab, Muslim and Pakistani are all seen as dirty and capable of eating anything; in one joke they eat flies, and the Jew catches on quick and tries to sell flies to them (No. 841). The Pakistani also brags about taking all the houses so that Jesus was born in a stable. (No. 842); he runs from a ghost (No. 819); and his smell is worse than a pig (No. 815). Several jokes appear about Indians, but these include both American Indians and East Indian Indians. American Indian jokes include a catch-question on how to turn someone into an Indian (No. 656); a joke-riddle about a squaw and a squawker (No. 233); and an Indian chief who can't fart (No. 925). One joke was told about Eskimos — a husband gets locked out of his igloo and must burn his way in (No. 1015). The other Indian jokes are about an Indian faker who sits on pins (No. 843); a West Indian who leaves his train asleep at the junction (No. 844); and an Indian gives the doctors a cure for a short man by saying 'a thousand pardons' (No. 867)

Several jokes were also told about Italians, another stereotype similar to the Irish and the Polack jokes but with an additional characteristic: Italians lack courage. One of the shortest books in the world is the Italian book of heroes. (No. 742)

A final ethnic group found in the English jokes is the Chinese, and this stereotype mainly plays on the Chinese lack of ability to speak English properly. When a plane is crashing and everyone must jump, the Chinese man asks God to shave him and he lands in a barber shop. (No. 820) A Chinese man goes to the dentist at tooth-thirty (No. 355); the Chinese get their children's names from throwing knives and forks up in the air and listening to the sound they make as they fall (No. 399); and the Chinese man in the hospital almost loses his life when the Englishman stands on his air pipe and he can't speak English to tell him to get off it (No. 846). The Chinese are also found in a simple knock-knock joke (No. 543); a Chinese painter gets lost after painting a room all yellow (No. 962); and when the Chinese man can't see China, he drops a plate of china to see. (No. 821)

The Polish jokes the American children told revolve around two characteristics: Polacks are dirty, and they are stupid. The dirty motif is probably the most popular and is shown in several ways. A Polack carries a piece of shit in his pocket for identification (No. 750), for spare parts (No. 751), or because two heads are better than one (head = toilet) (No. 752); he pees or spits in the wind for a shower (Nos. 753, 754); you can tell a Polack's house because his sewer has a diving board (No. 755); you can break up a Polish party by flushing the punch-bowl (No. 764); and a Polack buys 12 pairs of socks, one for each month. (No. 847)

The stupidity motif is portrayed in a variety of ways. A Polish motorcyclist uses training wheels (No. 748); he cleans the water out of his boat by cutting a hole in the bottom of the boat (No. 749); or you sink his boat by putting it in water (No. 759); the Polish national fish drowned (No. 763); and the Polack has 43 holes in his head from learning how to eat with a fork. (No. 768)

Usually the Polack appears by himself, but in two jokes he appears with other ethnic groups. The American astronauts are going to Mars, the Russians are going to Venus, and the Polacks will go to the Sun, at night. (No. 850) When the Englishman and Frenchman go into a pig-sty, they come out saying phew phew, but when the Polack goes in, the pig comes out. (This motif has also been attributed to a Paky, and an Irishman) (No. 815)

Only two other ethnic jokes were told by the American children. One has an Italian and an Englishman living next door to each other, and each owns a horse which both share the same field. After much experimentation, the two men decide there is no way to tell the white horse from the black. (No. 833) The other joke has a German calling up the Russian and telling him to come over. The Russian replies "I'm rushing, I'm rushing." (No. 845)

The Jewish stereotype and joke cycle exists in the United States, but none of the children I talked to told any of these jokes. The closest to this stereotype is a combination joke – a Jewish Polack broke all the windows because he wanted to go window shopping. (No. 770)

One of the reasons why so few ethnic jokes were told by the American children was that their teachers did not allow them to tell this type of joke, and the majority of the Polish jokes were collected at lunch time at the San Diego school when there was no teacher around and when I assured the children I wanted to hear their Polish jokes.

Where do the children learn these stereotypes; why are they perpetuated, and are they thought of as accurate views of the ethnic groups? According to Dundes:

> In the United States, as elsewhere, individuals acquire stereotypes from folklore. Most of our conceptions of the French or of the Jew come not from extended personal acquaintance or contact with representatives of these groups but rather from the proverbs, songs, jokes, and other forms of folklore we have heard all our lives. The stereotypes may or may not be accurate character analyses, that is, they may or may not be in accord with actual, empirically verifiable personality traits. The point is, rather, that the folk stereotypes exist and more importantly that countless people make judgements on the basis of them. There is probably no other area of folklore where the element of belief is more critical and potentially dangerous, not only to self but to others. (Dundes, 1970, p.180)

From the comments the children made, I believe that Dundes' hypothesis is correct – the stereotypes are learned through their jokes. As two English boys said, "We have nothing against the Irish; my father and his father are Irish. They're just *supposed to be stupid*." In this case, the stereotype is not particularly dangerous, in that the boys realize the ideas portrayed in the jokes belong just to the joke and not to reality.

Although Jews are supposed to be mean and stingy, the part of the stereotype portrayed in jokes that I consider potentially dangerous is the German concentration camp motif. By this time, the war, although never forgotten, should have diminished in people's memories, and the idea that Germans hate Jews should be forgotten. The only reason I can see they keep this idea in current popularity and circulation is to rationalize their own resentment and prejudice against the Jew, which is still present in reality; or to hide their prejudice behind the Germans' hatred. Although by far the largest number of Jewish jokes were about their meanness, a number of jokes are told that mock and make fun of the name Jew. This stereotype seems much more serious than the Irish stereotype, who appears as stupid and foolish, but also loveable. In only two jokes does the Irish stereotype turn more real and aggressive, when the Englishman throws the Irishman out of the plane, or when two Englishmen beat up the Irishman for no reason.

In contrast, the Polish stereotype in the United States is a much nastier image, and the Polack is compared to shit and has other dirty habits. As far as I know, no German concentration camp jokes are told in the United States. This might be explained as follows: the Polack is more resented in the United States than the Jew, because the Jew has integrated into so many areas, and is no longer as visible. The Polack is a newer immigrant group and is threatening jobs and positions traditionally held by other groups. In England, the Irish, although at times immigrants, are considered members of Great Britain, and are not a visible ethnic group, and therefore are acceptable. The Jew, integrating into many areas and occupations, is resented, for he is an outsider to the British country and culture, and is threatening jobs that could be held by the British. Additionally, many war refugees fled to England, which was another threat to the over-populated country.

Although some of these stereotypes are potentially dangerous to the group and individual, members of the stereotyped groups often tell the same jokes about themselves. Often a joke is acceptable if it is told by a member of that group (esoteric factor of folklore) but if told by an outsider it would be offensive.

What about some of the other stereotypes shown, such as the Pakistani/Arab, and the Blackman? Both of these groups are presently in the news, trying either to immigrate or smuggle into England, and then trying to fit into the culture itself. Much resentment is felt toward them, and even with the few jokes told about either group, some of this resentment and conflict seems to be present. The Pakistani/Arab is seen as something so non-human or so poor and dirty that he will eat a fly, and perhaps this is the way to handle the resentment, by treating him as non-human. He is also seen as conceited and pig-headed, thinking he knows all, but he gets his just due by falling down a hole, and when he opens his mouth again – he hasn't learned yet – it is fatal; plus his smell is compared to that of a pig, and the pig is cleaner.

The Blackman is also compared to objects (zebra-crossing, oil slick, etc.) and when he smuggles into England it's in coffins, prepared for suffocation and death. This could be the resentment and wish that the Blacks should die. Two curious jokes have the white man needing to be black to 1) board a ship, and 2) cross a bridge. The white man can easily make himself black, with shoe polish or paint or whatever, but the Blackman can't make himself white, which may suggest that the Blackman could never successfully enter the white man's culture and be accepted as white – he would always be black. Even in heaven, the Golden Gates are shut on the Blackman, which suggests the Englishman's wish that the doors of England be closed to the Blackman, and all immigrants.

The Chinese stereotype portrays the difficulty of fitting into the English culture successfully, for the language is perhaps one of the most telling signs of a foreigner – he just can't learn 'proper' English. Even the American can't speak 'English,' and so his culture and values (everything is bigger and better in the States) are put down by the 'superior' Englishman. Unfortunately the American culture can't be defeated as easily as in the jokes, and so a 'final solution' is found, the American with his big cigar is gassed to death "for committing crimes and all that."

Whether the ideas present in these jokes are from actual fact or not, people still make judgements on the basis of them, and perpetuate the idea that foreigners are trying to get into one's country, and that they are potentially dangerous, changing the culture and language. With these types of jokes in circulation, I think the foreigner's ultimate acceptance and acculturation, if ever, might be made more difficult. Even if none of the children know any Pakistanis or Blacks, they will think they know them through these jokes, and are apt to feel prejudices without knowing why or where they learned them. This is especially true when the children learn the jokes from adults, as they often do, for then they learn the prejudices but can't see the reasons for them, and accept them as real beliefs. On the other hand, the presence of these ethnic jokes might also signify a gradual acceptance – a joking acceptance to be sure – of the foreigners and their presence in the country.

Stereotypes such as these give the person an outlet for aggression and a means of feeling superior over someone else. (Dundes, 1970, p.

202) In this way, I think they are beneficial, in that jokes are just jokes, and usually told in fun, and are accepted as humorous. The person can get out the frustration, resentment, and aggression he feels towards these groups by fairly harmless means. Again, it is a question of how seriously the stereotypes in the jokes are taken; for some of the children, the Irish jokes weren't serious and were not told as real truth. The danger comes when the jokes are believed as truth and are not questioned, and some of the ideas can be substantiated by real facts, such as that Pakistanis and Blacks are really trying to get into the country illegally. The study of stereotypes and prejudices then becomes important, for by airing and discussing them, they can be exposed for what they really are.

COMPARISONS

Several comparisons can be made in this large collection of material; older children (10-13) vs. younger children (6-9); boys vs. girls; and American children vs. English children.

The majority of the jokes, especially in Leeds, England, were told by the older children. Although age is not a pre-requisite of good joke-telling – for several children aged 8 and 9 were good joke-tellers too – the older children have had more experience telling jokes and have had a chance to develop a larger repertoire.

Experience and larger repertoires are only part of the age factor. The older child is more aware of life. Girls around 10 or 11 may have started menstruating, developing breasts, and becoming aware of boys; and boys are also approaching puberty. Sex becomes interesting, and the children's earlier delight in jokes about the toilet and the rear-end or bum changes to an interest in the opposite sex and the sexual organs. Greater independence and freedom is striven for, from the parents as well as from other adult authority figures, and one sign of a person's supposed independence is mockery and laughter at those people he thinks are suppressing him. Fear of these figures is lessened as well by jeering and mocking. The police, religious figures, and even prisons and wardens are cut down to a controllable size. The 10 to 13 year old is learning to question. He has been taught

Darwin's theory of evolution, which leaves out God and the story of the Creation. The powerful control the religious official once had over the soul of a child is weakened, and has become less important in our culture. Only the really bad go to hell; and heaven takes on aspects of earth, choosing its members by color and not by standards of good and evil.

Awareness of themselves as individuals also leads to awareness of other people. The older children told most of the ethnic jokes, I think because they are more aware of these people forming distinct groups. They become aware of adult ideas and emotions, especially towards various ethnic groups, as well as current events and problems, such as immigration or the smuggling of various ethnic groups into England. New jokes are learned that are more apt to be adult jokes, and these jokes are no longer non-specific, but are aimed at a particular person or role, pointing out inefficiencies, or ridiculing alleged traits. The ethnic jokes usually pick a national or ethnic trait the group is supposed to have and then make fun of it. The Irish jokes are extremely popular in England, and the Polish jokes in the United States, and there is no way the children can ignore these types of jokes, especially with the number of these jokes currently in circulation. Both the teller and hearer can feel superior to the group that is mocked, and can be aggressive in a harmless manner (usually).

Why boys tell more of these ethnic jokes than girls is perhaps related to the commonly expressed idea that men are more aggressive than women and that men need to let their aggression out by making someone else feel inferior while boosting their own egos. Perhaps this is a learned trait, but it is certainly culturally supported. The difference between the older boys and girls in the number of ethnic jokes told tends to disappear with the younger children. This may be because the younger males haven't yet fully developed their expected roles as aggressive, hard, and demanding, the bread-earners of the family. Or that the girl hasn't yet learned her expected role. But by the age of 11 to 12, at the beginning of puberty, the boy is expected to don his male role and act masculine; while the girl is expected to act feminine, or be soft, yielding, weak, and non-violent. These ideas are slowly changing, as woman's liberation is showing the woman that she doesn't have to be submissive. Even in sex, the female can be more demanding, and is more apt to know about sex before marriage. She is expected now to know more, and is old-fashioned if she doesn't. Although females are changing slowly, to be verbally aggressive is still difficult for most females, and this shows in the difference in the number of jokes told by the older boys and girls.

Violence/death/killing motifs increase in the jokes as the child grows older, and this I think is part of his growing awareness of the world and people around him, especially of odd characters like the drunk, tramp, skinhead, and queer, all who may be associated with violence in some way. Even parents, couples, and family fighting are found in the jokes, as the children begin to see their parents as individual with problems. Neighborhood fighting and quarrelling is also observed and accepted as a fact of life. Aggression isn't viewed with such horror, but as one way of facing problems, either by aggressively solving your problems, or by fighting when you're in a tight corner. Anyone can be a killer, if the need arises, and the older children seem to have a fairly realistic view of killing and death; it exists and occurs, in almost any form or place or person, either accidentally or on purpose.

As the child grows older, he is under more and more pressure to perform as his teachers and parents want him to, and he is taught to be an adult, but is not treated as one. Resentment and pent-up aggression build up, and violence in some form is a natural outlet. If the child doesn't physically fight, he can tell aggressive jokes. Boys tend to use this mode, of aggressive jokes, to release this pressure. Girls, not expected to be aggressive, don't tell as many jokes, and there are fewer good girl joke-tellers. But the girls, or anyone listening can profit from the jokes as much as the tellers, with an added advantage: the listener isn't telling the jokes, and is therefore safe from punishment. Girls tend to release their tension and aggression through other forms, such as songs, jump-rope rhymes, and singing and clapping games.

The predominance of the older children in categories 3 — transportation; 5 — animals; 6 — the supernatural; and 8 — TV products/stars; comes from the larger repertoires these children have. The younger children are more apt to tell joke-riddles, and these involve very little detail or emphasis on any particular point. With the real joke or anecdote, details must be added to make the story believable, and the child learns a number of these motifs to expand his story. Animals, of all types, shapes, and sizes, are much more popular than television characters and stars, and this might be because animals are alive, and can easily be changed into talking and thinking type people, who have character and personality, and therefore can be manipulated as people. Television people and stars, although useful, have no real personality to the child because they are too distant, and in some ways are harder to imagine than a dog who plays cards or wears boots.

Considering the remaining categories of motifs, one large difference remains between the boys and girls, both with the younger and older children, in the animals category. The boys tell many more jokes with animal motifs. This might be explained that boys can imagine animals more easily performing various actions in a variety of situations, whereas the girls are more reality-oriented. The boys also led in the supernatural category. I thought the girls would have told more jokes concerning the supernatural, because they are usually more apt to believe in ghost and spirits. Most of these motifs show a funny or mocking view of the ghost, and this might be the boys' way of handling the supernatural and not really believing it exists. The ghost and skeletons that appear perform very unsupernatural acts, like using the toilet, a very human act, which takes away the scariness and mystery of the creature.

Sex for the younger children, is mainly concerned with the bodily functions and use of the toilet. The doctor as a curer of illness, but also vulnerable, appears, as does the teacher. The teacher is probably the easiest person to mock, in that the child has the most exposure to the teacher, and it is expected as well. Violence begins early, especially in the home fighting situation with brothers and sister, and at school fighting with friends and enemies. The younger child isn't as specific in his violence/death/killing motifs as the older ones. Two biscuits walk in the street and one gets run over, or Tommy Cooper dies 'just like that', but nothing is found like the description of the poor Irishman getting beat up by the two Englishmen, or the skinheads beating up an innocent man, such as were told by the older children. The younger child's views of violence and of aggression aren't as broad or as experienced as the older child, and often violence and aggression can be ignored. Ethnic jokes, although certainly not as numerous as with the older child, are beginning to be told, and become more popular as the child grows older. The dumb Irishman or the stupid Polack are both popular characters.

Viewing the section of parodies, rhymes and songs, the older children no longer dominate, and these are mainly told by the younger children. They are often associated with games that the older children once played but no longer do. Parodies can also be seen as the first sign of the child's attempt at independence, by mocking the nursery rhymes his parents have taught him. (Opie's, 1959, p. 89-90) Although a variety of types of parodies exist, the majority of the parodies collected were of two sorts; the simple change of single words (Mother Goose rhymes), and the substitution of a subject as incongruous as possible with the original while closely preserving the style, meter, sentiment, and phraseology (On Top of Spaghetti). True riddles and wellerisms were also very popular with the 6-9 year olds, being easy to remember and easy to tell. The joke-riddles, though, were by far the most popular with all age groups and in all geographical areas. Knock-knock jokes were also very popular with all the children. The only category of jokes that really belongs almost solely to the older children is tricks and catches. These involved being able to fool the other child and make him believe in what the teller is doing. For a younger child, this is more difficult to do, in that he is apt to start laughing, or give the trick away. Although not many elephant jokes were told, the majority of them were told by girls, when aged 12 and 13, who remembered telling them when they were that age in 1962 and 1963.

A final comparison can be made between English and American children. This comparison is more difficult to make in that jokes were mainly collected in only two areas in California, and not the rest of the country; and the majority of the jokes collected were from English children — seven schools were visited in England as opposed to only two in California. A difference can be seen, though, as to who volunteered to tell jokes. In England the boys were the better joke-tellers and they volunteered more often to tell them. In the United States and particularly at the school in San Diego, the older girls volunteered more often, and at lunch time when anyone could tell a joke, the girls stood around and told jokes, especially sexual jokes. The boys needed encouragement from the audience, and often they couldn't be persuaded to tell them, especially the 'rude' (sexual) ones. This held true in England as well, where the girls asked if they could tell rude jokes and proceeded to do so. The boys knew rude jokes, but told them only upon assurance from me that it was alright. The four boys from Leeds who were expert joke-tellers told rude sexual jokes almost as an after-thought — they had so many others to tell. At the San Diego school, children would know a joke but they wouldn't want to tell it for the tape recorder, so they would tell it to a friend — almost always one of several girls — who would then tell it to me and the tape recorder. San Diego was the only place I observed this sharing of jokes, although in San Francisco several girls wouldn't tell their jokes until the class was dismissed and no one was around (especially the boys and the teacher), and until they had encouraged each other to tell their jokes. In England, the girls on the whole were fairly shy and knew fewer jokes than the boys. When one boy would tell a joke, two others would whisper together about a joke they wanted to tell next. The girls' becoming more aggressive and telling more jokes in the United States might be an indication that Woman's Liberation is beginning to have an effect on the young girls, and that the movement has had less effect in England, where traditional values still hold.

Concerning content matter, the main difference can be seen in the ethnic jokes. Where the English children told Irish, Jewish, and English, Irish, and Scottish jokes, the American children told Polish jokes. In both cultures, the majority of these ethnic jokes were told by the older boys, although many more ethnic jokes covering many different groups were told in England. The lack of ethnic jokes told by the American children can be partly explained by their teacher's orders not to tell ethnic jokes.

Looking at the sexual and doctor jokes, the English children led in the number told, although for both groups the boys and girls were fairly evenly divided as to the number of jokes told. Some of the jokes were the same or variants from England to the United States, such as the pregnant lady (Nos. 852, 853); the girl and her underwear or knickers (No. 897); the little boy and his parents (Nos. 886, 887); Shagarada and Johnnie Fuckerfaster (Nos. 868, 869); and the good fairy. (Nos. 881, 882). As previously mentioned, the girls were more eager or less shy about telling their sexual jokes, and were just surprised that I was willing to listen to them and to put them on the tape recorder. Jokes concerning the use of the toilet are missing from the American children's repertoires, as represented here, and only two were told, Nos. 922 and 928. This lack of toilet jokes by the American children is perhaps because the younger children told almost no real jokes, and stayed with the joke-riddles and knock-knock jokes.

This same difference is seen in the number of American jokes told about death/violence/killing. The most aggressive jokes are No. 853 — the husband shoots his wife to kill the unborn rock-singer baby; No. 870 — 3 boys must stick fruit up their butts in preference to being shot; No. 888 — the man sticks his penis in 3 holes, the last being a cow's milking machine; and No. 946 — Mikey is thrown out the window by his brother Ikey. All of the Polack jokes can also be viewed as aggressive, especially in the contempt they show for the Polish people. Almost all of these aggressive jokes were told by the older children, and the non-specific aggressive jokes like the two biscuits rolling down the road and one getting run over, that were told by the younger English children, are missing.

Missing also from the American children's repertoires are parodies, and rhymes and songs. This is partly because I didn't emphasize that I wanted to collect parodies. Also the majority of the parodies collected in England were from the questionnaires, which were not used in the United States. The majority of the American jokes collected were joke-riddles, which were also the most popular and numerous jokes collected in England. Almost every true joke or anecdote collected in the United States came from a child aged 10 to 14; the younger children stayed with the joke-riddles and knock-knock jokes.

The major differences, then, between the American children and English children can be seen in who wanted to volunteer to tell jokes, and which ethnic groups were picked on. The difference in the number of jokes collected in each area precludes more detailed comparisons, but the number of similar or identical jokes told by the two groups of children indicate that the interests and problems of children as shown in their jokes are the same in England as in the United States.

FUNCTIONS

Earlier were examined some of the main themes present in the jokes collected, such as sex, adult authority figures, characters, etc. In some ways the themes are difficult to separate from the various functions the jokes fulfill. Sex or stereotypes are often present in the jokes, but sex or stereotypes as a function of aggression, anxiety, or rebellion, also exist. This chapter will attempt to expand the outlook beyond set themes, to general functions that may hold for a variety of themes and jokes.

I think one of the main functions of the jokes and parodies is that they are a means of the children's expression and communication. They represent modern folklore, continually changing and being updated, but surviving as a function and mode of expression. As the children themselves said, "We tell them anywhere," at school, at home, to friends, to parents, to anyone and everyone. Jokes are told to show off, to amuse and entertain others, to impress, perhaps with one's special knowledge, and those who can tell jokes get a reputation as 'good joke-tellers', which gives them a certain status, and respect from their peers. Parents are also proud of their 'funny, clever' child, and have them 'perform' before their friends.

A sense of humor is considered an important attribute. Being a good sport when a joke or trick is played on you is also important. When jokes are told, a person is expected to tell a few jokes himself, or at least laugh and appreciate the jokes told if he wants to get along with the others. A respected person is the one who can laugh at his own expense and pretend it doesn't matter when things go wrong and he goofs, or his joke flops. To have this type of control and laughter is a hard thing to do, but it is a necessary lesson if the child is to continue communicating with his peers.

Jokes can also function to separate the insiders from the outsiders. Esoteric jokes are told about the outsider, that are known and understood by the insider. It is therefore important for the child to belong, to know the same jokes and have the same knowledge the others do, or at least pretend he understands, or else he is placed in a position to be ridiculed. When families move, the child learns quickly the slang terms, the names and rules of the games, and the jokes in the new area, so that he appears the same as everyone else. He is slow to introduce his own ideas and lore from his last area, but first must learn the rules of the group, and gain acceptance; and then he is free to introduce new ideas without getting jeered at, rejected and ignored.

Other possible functions of folklore/jokes have been suggested by Brunvand as: ". . . education, entertainment, protest, release for anxieties and frustrations, channelling aggression, satire, and perhaps even attempts to modify other parts of culture as typical functions of folklore." (Brunvand, 1972, p. 6) Looking at the material collected, I would say that all these functions are present in the children's jokes. For the child, the most important function, besides being able to communicate with all his friends on an equal basis, is that of entertainment. Jokes are liked because they are funny, or good; they create vivid pictorial images, and they make you laugh or they make your friends laugh. When the child is bored, a joke can relieve the tedium, especially in the classroom or schoolyard, two popular areas for telling jokes. And also, a reputation of being funny and clever is a valuable acquisition.

Jokes can also be seen as a form of education, in that the child's imagination, guessing powers, and memory are tested and expanded. Riddles — either joke-riddles or true riddles — stimulate the child to think logically and imaginatively, to find the correct answers; while to remember the joke to retell it again increases the powers of his memory. Once joke and riddling contests and sessions start, the child must quickly recall the joke, organize it in his mind, and tell it with all the smoothness and verbal skill he can muster, if it is to be acceptable and if he is to compete with the others. The aim is to give a good show, and convince everyone of your story, and its truth. This type of situation trains his mind to think quickly, and gives him verbal skills that are tremendously important for any person to have and use.

Each person develops his own style of talking (and writing), and these jokes give the child a chance to try a variety of styles and forms, before finding the mode he best communicates in. For some, jokes are never a means to work with people; but for others, this early training in public speaking continues throughout their life. The lessons they learned in getting and keeping an audience's interest and attention in what one is saying, being able to trick or convince them into believing what he wants, and being able to entertain and amuse others, are valuable and necessary lessons, gained in the painless manner of telling jokes and riddles.

Protest, channelling of aggression and satire appear in many of the jokes. This appears as the mocking of various figures, especially the adult authority figures in the child's life; the parents, teachers and police mainly, although other figures appear as well. "The discovery of a phrase which can be understood as both respectable and indecent makes it possible to express rebellion against forbidding authorities by a mocking compliance." (Wolfenstein, 1954, p. 160-161) By using these phrases and jokes, the child protests and rebels against too many restrictions placed on him because he is a child. The frustrations associated with these growing pains often are released by some form of aggression, perhaps physical (fighting) or verbal (jokes) or even sexual (rape – physical or verbal).

The joke can have all these forms of aggression and still the child can be safe and unguilty. ". . . the joke becomes a harmless aggression – an aggression which hurts no one, but which provides a transitory gain for the ego of the joker." (Dundes & Abrahams, 1969, p. 228) As a harmless aggression, and because the teller is still considered a child, the joke is acceptable to adults (at least most jokes are acceptable), even if the adults are made to look foolish and silly, but not too foolish. The jokes that are usually unacceptable to parents and adults are explicit sexual jokes. Aggression and protest against the parents are often against their non-truthful answers to questions, especially about sex. The parent is afraid to answer the child's questions, and does not want the child to know about sex, because he would then be admitting his child is an adult or is becoming one.

Another cause of rebellion and protest against the parents is the continual reminder "You're too young to do that" and "Wait until you're older," as is found in the wellerisms which have chimneys, telephones, and candles telling the little one it's too young to smoke or to be engaged or to go out. The joke makes a mockery of this type of answer in that no candle or telephone or chimney is too young to be used, and on the contrary, the younger one is often the better one. This is a defense against the parents' rules and negative answers. Adults are seen as not-that-great, and the adult role isn't as admired and in fact can have disadvantages, like growing old. This is implied in the joke on the candle, for a candle that goes out is dead. Therefore the child is better off young and alive.

Teachers and police as upholders of education and law, are traditional figures to rebel against. Teachers are eventually left behind, but police will always be there forcing you to obey laws and rules. The child, being full of new modern ideas, feels that the teachers and police stand in the way of his progress, both physical and mental.

Aggression is also directed at various ethnic groups, and this is based on stereotypes of widespread assumptions. Here, a person can feel superior to another group, boosting his own ego at the expense of theirs. Various opinions exist as to the potential power of these types of jokes and ethnic slurs to hurt and harm the people involved, and to be real forms of aggression. They can be harmful if they are accepted as true views of the ethnic or national character. Then they have the power to continue prejudice and hatred against various groups. Members of the attacked group often tell the jokes themselves, though, and these can then function as "... harmless outlets for possible resentment against derogatory stereotypes." (Brunvand, 1972, p. 15) Stereotypes, as they exist in the jokes, are continued and reinforced; although not all stereotypes are bad. On the whole the group is mocked and demeaned. But when the stereotype is remembered as a function of the joke — humorous but unreal — and is considered as a harmless aggression, with possible advantages to both sides, then the ethnic jokes can perhaps be worthwhile.

The position of the child as too young and confined, and the position of the ethnic group, are both seen as roles to mock and protest and rebel against. Both positions are made acceptable or at least tolerable by the use of jokes that can release pent-up aggression and frustration in a harmless manner. A child and an ethnic group member learn a joking acceptance of their own group's character, plus that they can put other people into the same positions by making fun of their role, or power and authority, or lack of it.

Another role to escape and rebel against is one's social/economic position. The joke about the Blacks trying to smuggle into England shows this desire to improve their status and position in the class and money structure. The jokes about the German concentration camps show the Jews caught in a position, both ethnic as well as social and economic, from which they cannot escape. This is perhaps a more realistic or perhaps pessimistic view of the world: that one is stuck in a social/economic position from which there is no escape. Even the Blacks are prepared to die before they make it, and they are still caught. Some of the characters seem quite content with their role. The drunks and tramps continue to drink and rummage for food, although if given a chance, the tramp might go on to better things, but he seems quite capable of weaselling food and shelter out of people by various tricks, and yet he still keeps his freedom and way of life. Drinking must already be an escape for the drunk who can't handle reality without the haze of alcohol to aid him, so he is not likely to change. Each socio-economic class has its advantages, but the poor man who complains because his neighbor bought a bigger car and yacht than his, is very typical of a person trying to escape his given role, and appear richer and better than he is. In the end, he is still defeated by a man who has greater wealth.

The money motif doesn't appear too often in the jokes except that Jews are shown as greedy and not wanting to spend money (Nos. 720-727, 802-805); a tramp has 25p for which he gets a bed and sex (No. 899); a pound note is eventually grabbed from the ghost by the clever Englishman (No. 806); Shagarada sells her body for milk (No. 868); and two other ladies sell their bodies for a decrease in the postman's bill (Nos. 872, 873). By hanging on to his money, the Jew is preserving his social/economic role, for even if he is Jewish, and not socially acceptable to some people, he still has his money, which makes him independent. The tramp gains momentarily a higher status – he sleeps in a hotel, in a bed, with the manager's wife – but the rise in status only lasts one night, and then he is back to being an ordinary tramp. The Englishman doesn't gain in status by grabbing the money, but he does confirm the role he already plays, of being clever and not being scared of ghosts and other things he can't see. In contrast, the Irishman, who is low on the totem pole, also confirms his low position by being afraid of the ghost and running away. Shagarada, if a virgin, gains the status of womanhood, and increased sexual knowledge, and she does earn a lot of milk! But socially and economically she hasn't moved. In conclusion then, the socio-economic role is seen as escape from one level to a higher level if possible, but, on the whole, change is seen as impossible, or the gains are short-lived.

A final role the child can find himself, in, and from which he tries to escape, is the role of ignorance. Schools, supposedly there to teach, don't teach about life or the things a child is interested in, and so the schools and teachers are mocked. When the child goes to his parents for information, he is again turned away by foolish or nonsensical answers that he knows are false, but he has nothing else. He is then forced to go to his peers for knowledge and information. They are in the same position as he, and so this information can be just as unreliable, biased or untrue, as that which his parents or teachers give him. His quest for knowledge is directed towards three areas: intellectual, sexual, and physical. The poor Irishman who is beat up by the two Englishmen seeks to learn Kung Fu, a highly technical and skillful physical weapon, to help himself; while rhymes about the end of the school term talk about reading, writing, French, and math. But the most important area is sexual knowledge. Since he usually doesn't get this information from his parents, the child experiments, sometimes with disastrous results, as when the little girl bites her father's penis because it spit at her. Shagarada gains in sexual knowledge by going against her parents wishes, and both the little boy and girl learn the difference between the bellybutton, finger, and sexual organs.

Another function of joking, described in psychological terms, is the release of anxieties and frustrations, which has been referred to already in relation to the other functions. Children have many problems deriving from just being a child and trying to grow up, but being continually pushed back into the child's role of innocence and of ignorance. Anxieties of everyday living are attempted to be made livable, by mocking and parodying the situations that children can't handle, or aren't allowed to handle. The ability to laugh at one's own failures and frustrations helps to get over them, and to continue on to new situations. Hopefully, through the jokes the child will be more prepared to meet these new situations, people, and actions.

As the child grows older, he is frustrated in many ways, especially in his sexual and aggressive tendencies (he isn't allowed sex, and he isn't allowed to fight). He also learns he can't express these ideas directly without first being punished, and then later feeling ashamed and guilty. He therefore develops a joke façade to cover up these real desires, emotions, and thoughts in acceptable forms, acceptable to others as well as to himself. Jokes that are considered 'clever', and therefore hearable, are the ones that hide the real impulses behind symbolic terms; but those that don't succeed in this are just considered 'stupid' and unacceptable. (Legman, 1968, p. 13-14) Jokes and riddles are often remembered because they are clever and acceptable, and the dangerous hostile or sexual impulses have been well hidden below the surface of the joke.

A final point concerning function is to be considered. Are the children or any person who tells jokes aware of any of these functions? For the children, the main function they are aware of is amusement. Only jokes that they consider 'funny' will be told and remembered. But what is funny? The children in the present research couldn't explain this, except that the jokes made them laugh, which is the surface function of jokes. The themes and internal functions considered aren't explicit, and the children can't explain them and are, most likely, unaware of them. However, the children seem to gain from telling the jokes for the reasons given. This lack of knowledge why a person likes the jokes or how they function for that person, can be explained by the safety-valve theory:

> The veil of nonsense is so opaque that the serious nature of the underlying rationale of the humor is effectively concealed. This is as it should be, or rather as it always is. The release, the safety-valve function of oral humor, would be less effective if one knew what he was saying or was laughing at. This veiling from

consciousness is one way of duping society into the casual acceptance of argument. As an escape from the psychological pressures of the human condition we must translate or transmute reality into an unrecognizable form. (Dundes & Abrahams, 1969, p. 228)

The child releases aggression, frustrations, anxieties, and rebellion through the jokes, and, because he is unaware of this, these are safely and harmlessly released. The child thus gains in entertainment and amusement and he doesn't have to explode in other ways, such as fighting, killing, or possibly even committing suicide when the pressures become too great. This safety-valve function works for both the teller of and listener to the joke, They can both share the release of their problems safely and harmlessly, without guilt or shame, boosting their egos, and making life appear, at least for a moment, as amusing and fun to live. The person who is in trouble is the one who can't or doesn't tell jokes, or can't enjoy other peoples jokes — he lacks a sense of humor which can help him slide past life's disasters, laughing. See the introduction to Legman's *No Laughing Matter* (1975) p. 44-47 which develops this same idea much further and in similar terms.

CONCLUSIONS

Within the limited bounds of this research, I feel I have satisfied some of my own curiosity as to children's humor — what kinds of jokes children tell, and some of the reasons why they tell their jokes. Many of the assumptions came from my own background and childhood, because I faced the same problems these children are facing. Through their jokes I feel I understand my upbringing a little better, and how and why I react the way I do to certain problems, anxieties, tensions, and impulses. I developed a sense of humor as I was growing up. I think this is one of the most important attributes a person can have, and especially valuable to a child learning to accept his environment and the adult world.

Through his jokes and humor, the child is prepared for the adult role he is so anxious to fill, for he learns to accept things with a grain of salt, that salt being the humorous or funny side of any situation and problem. He learns to laugh at himself as well as at others, at his difficulties in growing up, in curbing his desires and impulses within his cultural bounds, and easing the friction of everyday living. In other words, he learns to accept himself and others, and if he does feel aggression he can release it through hostile jokes relatively harmlessly. Even if the jokes are based on fantasy, the undercurrent ideas and themes are real. The child can then logically and more realistically face these problems; and by mocking the situation or person, he can learn to see both sides of the problem. He hopefully gains guidance and help in solving the actual problems or situations as they come up.

Since "man is the only animal who laughs," I think the study of a culture's humor is highly important if one wants to understand that culture and its people. I feel that I now know English children and American children much better after studying their jokes and parodies, for the themes and ideas present have shown the children's deep concerns and their thoughts about many areas of their lives, but especially about certain topics that every person must face at some time — aggression, sex, authority figures, and ethnic stereotypes. In that these themes are vital to most Western cultures, I feel that I know children in general better, as these problems are faced by all children; and even though the texts of the jokes may vary, the underlying themes and functions remain the same. If a child is to grow up and take his adult role, he has to determine his attitudes toward precisely these topics. Through his jokes, he has an easier time accepting such ideas as the prevalence of violence and of dying, which can be a shocking idea and very frightening. But jokes mock death, and all kinds of things get killed, even biscuits, and so death becomes a more acceptable idea. Sex is a major problem for most kids, and again through jokes the child tries to lose his fears, and accept sex for what it is. Cultural values differ towards these topics, and therefore the jokes I collected in England represent just the Englishman's solutions; each culture will have its own. This is most obvious for stereotypes, which can be the same for two cultures about a third group, but they can also vary. The two cultures may also have stereotypes about each other which will make those jokes unique for that group.

What is similar about jokes of children from the two cultures is their unawareness of the functions and even the themes of their jokes. For the children, the entertainment and amusement function is the most important, and if a joke is funny, it is acceptable, But jokes continue to circulate, and new ones are evolved or made up continuously. Some of these must be important for the individual and his group and must fulfill some function. Communication is definitely a function of humor, as well as amusement and education, and as a release of tension and anxiety. With a pessimistic view of the world that sees all things as bad, and never getting better, humor is certainly needed to make life livable, or at least tolerable. Even with an optimistic view, life is just that bit more nice and fun with humor, and it makes things go easier. Children realize early that too much seriousness isn't good. They learn jokes that help them to comprehend the world and other people, especially the ones they must live with. Jokes help them learn to like themselves and the person they will be, for they have learned to laugh.

CHILDREN'S
HUMOUR

QUESTIONNAIRE: JOKES, PARODIES, RHYMES

NAME: _____ AGE_____ MALE/FEMALE

1. Do you have any favourite jokes you like to tell? Write them down. Extra paper is available if needed.

2. When and where do you tell these jokes? During school, playtime, after school in the yard or playground, at home, in the streets, weekends?

3. To whom do you tell these jokes? Just to your friends, just to parents and/or teachers, to everyone, just to girls, or just to boys?

4. Where or from whom did you learn these jokes?

5. Why do you like these jokes, why do you tell them?

6. Do you know any parodies (your version of songs and rhymes), like 'Glory, Glory Alleluya, Teachers hit me with a ruler', or 'The boy stood on the burning deck'; or any other rhymes? Extra paper is available if needed.

7. When and where do you tell these parodies or rhymes? During school, playtime, after school in the yard or playground, at home, in the streets, weekends?

8. To whom do you tell these parodies or rhymes? Just to your friends, just to parents and/or teachers, to everyone, just to girls, or just to boys?

9. Where or from whom did you learn these parodies or rhymes?

10. Why do you like these parodies or rhymes, why do you tell them?

TEXTS OF THE JOKES

KEY TO ABBREVIATIONS

Locations:
CA: California
CO: Colorado
Eng: England
IN: Indiana
L: London
Ld: Leeds
NJ: New Jersey
NY: New York
OR: Oregon
SD: San Diego, Cal.
SF: San Francisco
US: United States

Sex:
g: girl
b: boy

Form of Joke Reference:
Location: sex, age, year-date collected.
For example: L:g.12.74
London: girl, age 12, collected 1974

I. PARODIES

1. The boy stood on the burning deck,
   Playing a game of cricket
   The ball rolled up his trouser leg,
   And stopped his middle wicket

   Ld:g.13.73 (Eng:b.8.74)

2. The boy stood on the burning deck
   Picking his nose like mad, ,
   He rolled them into tiny balls
   And flicked them at his dad.

   Ld:b.10.73 (Eng:g.8.74, 2-g.9.74)

3. The boy stood on the burning deck,
   Washing himself like mad
   He got the soap and rolled it up
   And flicked it at his dad.

   L:b.10.74 (Eng:b.10.74)

4. A man stood on a burning deck
   A pocket full of crackers
   One flew up his trouser leg
   And paralysed his nakas

   (English def. nakas = knackers = norakers = testicles)
   Ld:b.10.73 (Eng:g.10.74)

5. A boy stood on the burning deck
   His heart was all ablaze
   A spark went up his trouser leg
   And sent him down the river.

   Ld:b.9.73

6. A boy stood on the burning deck,
   His leg was all a quiver
   He gave a cough and his leg fell off
   And floated down the river.

   L:g.9.74

7. While shepherds wash their socks by night,
   All watching ITV
   The angel of the Lord came down
   And switched to BBC.

   (BBC = British Broadcasting Corp;
   ITV = Independent TV)
   L:b.11.74 (Eng:b.9.74, 4–b.10.74)

8. While Shepherds wash their socks by night,
   All seated round the tub
   A bar of sunlight soap came down
   And they began to scrub.

   L:b.10.74 (Eng:g.10.74, b.10.74, b.11.74)

9. While shepherds watch their flocks by night,
   And eating fish and chips
   The angel of the Lord came down
   And charged them two and six.

   (chips = french fries)
   L:b.11.74 (Eng:b.11.74, b.9.74)

10. While shepherds cooked their turnip tops,
    A boiling in the pot
    The angel of the Lord came down
    And ate the blooming lot.

    L:b.10.74

11. While shepherds watch their flocks by night
    The earthly angel sing with great big rings.

    L:b.9.74

12. Randolph the red-nosed cowboy, had a very shiny gun
    And if you ever saw it, you would turn around and run.
    All of the other cowboys, used laugh and call him names,
    They never let poor Randolph, play any cowboy games.
    Then one foggy Christmas eve, Santa came to say,
    Randolph with your gun so bright,
        won't you shoot my wife tonight?
    Then all the other cowboys didn't laugh and call him names,
    They let poor Randolph, play in all their cowboy games.

    NJ:b.8.65

13. We three kings from onat ar (Orient are)
    One in a takie, one in a car,
    One on a scooter bibin' his hooter
    Following yonder star.
    Oh star of wonder, star of light,
        Charlie caught his pants a light
    Still they burning following yonder star.

    L:b.10.74

14. Good King Wenceslas looked out on the feast of Stephen,
    Turned his britches inside out to stop his ? from freezing.

    L:g.11.74

15. On top of spaghetti, all covered with cheese
    I lost my poor meatball, when somebody sneezed.
    It rolled on the table, and on to the floor
    And then my poor meatball, rolled outside the door.

    It rolled out in the garden, and under a bush
    And then my poor meatball, was covered in slush.
    So if you have spaghetti, all covered in cheese
    Hold on to your meatball, cause somebody might sneeze.

    Ld:g.13.73

16. Glory, glory alleluya, teachers hit me with a ruler
    The ruler broke in two, so she hit me with a shoe
    And I went home black and blue.

    Ld:g.9.73 (Eng:g.8.73, 3–g.10.73)

17. Glory, glory alleluya, teacher hit me with the ruler
    The ruler broke in half so she kicked me up the ass
    And made me black and blue. bom bom

    L:g.9.74 (Eng:b.10.74, b.9.74)

18. Glory, glory alleluya, teacher hit me with a ruler
    The ruler broke in 2, and she hit me with a shoe
    The shoe broke in 3 and she hit me with a tree
    The tree broke in 4 so she hit me with a door
    The door broke in 5 so she hit me with a knife
    The knife broke in 6 so she hit me with the sticks

The sticks broke in 7 so she sent me up to heaven
Heaven broke in 8 so she hit with the gate
The gate broke in 9 so she hit me with the line
The line broke in 10 so she hit me with the hen,
And I never went back to school.

Ld:g.13.73

19. Glory, glory alleluya, the teacher hit me with the ruler
The ruler broke in half and we all began to laugh
And we never came to school again.

L:b.8.74 (Eng:4-b.8.74, b.9.74, 3-b.10.74, b.11.74, 2-g.8.74, 4-g.9.74, 2-g.11.74)

20. Glory, glory alleluya, teacher hit me with the ruler
I hit her back up the bum, and then we had a lot of fun.

(English def. bum = rear end or arse)
L:g.8.74 (Eng:g.8.74, g.9.74, g.10.74)

21. Glory, glory alleluya, the teacher hit me with the ruler
I hit her on the beam, with a rotten tangerine
And there ain't no teacher anymore.

Ld:g.10.73

22. Glory, glory alleluya,
Teacher hit me with a ruler
She opened the door,
And I shot her with a 44 (or 22)
And I didn't go to school no more.

SD:b.10.75

23. Glory, glory alleluya, my teacher hit me with the ruler
The ruler snapped in half and the teacher fell in the bath
And saints go marching on.

L:g.9.74

24. Glory, glory alleluya, It is 4 4
Go to school and learn some more.

L:b.7.74 (Eng:g.8.74)

25. Just whistle while you work
    Hitler is a twirp
    He is balmey, Like 'is army
    Whistle while you work.

    Ld:g.10.73 (Eng:b.8.73, b.10.73,
    2-g.10.73)

26. Build a bonfire, put the teachers on the top
    Put the prefects in the middle
    And burn the blumming lot.

    (Prefects = older schoolchild in charge of discipline, mainly at
    dinnertime, in the classroom, and playground. Can't punish the children
    themselves, but can send them to the teacher.)
    Ld:b.10.73 (Eng:g.8.73, b.10.73)

27. Yankey Doodle came to town riding on a pony
    He stuck a feather in his nose, and called it mack-a-roney.

    Ld:b.8.73 (Eng:b.8.73)

28. Popos the sailor man, he lived in a caravan
    He turned on the gas, and blew off 'iss ass,
    And there's the end of Popos the sailor man.

    Ld:g.8.73

29. I am the mustard man, I wear a frying pan
    I walk with a wobble, and talk with a gobble
    I don't wear a shirt, my name is Bux Buirt
    Oh, I am the mustard man.

    Ld:g.8.73

30. There was an old man who lived in a van
    And carried a pan all over.

    Ld:b.9.73

31. There was an old man who lived in a van
    And he went to bed with a pan.

    Ld:g.9.73

32. My old man's a dustman, He wears a dustman's hat.
     He took me round the corner to see a football match.
     Fate passed to Skeing, Seing passed to Fate
     Fate took a long shot and kicked the goalee flat.
     They put him on a stretcher, They put him on a bed
     They rubbed his bum with a bath of rum
     And then he was dead.

     L:b.10.74

33. My old mans a dustbin, he wears a dustmans hat
     He has long baggy trousers
     So what do you think of that?

     L:b.10.74 (Eng:g.10.74, b.9.74)

34. Happy Birthday to you
     You belong in the zoo.
     You look like a monkey,
     And you are one too.

     OR:g.7.57

35. Heigh ho, heigh ho, off to school we go
     With razor blades and hand grenades, heigh ho, heigh ho
     Heigh ho, heigh ho, heigh ho, off to the lakes we go,
     With fishing hooks and playboy books heigh ho, heigh ho
     Heigh ho, heigh ho, heigh ho, off to home we go,
     With hot dog buns and 22 guns, heigh ho, heigh ho,
     Heigh ho, heigh ho, heigh ho, off to school we go,
     With a bottle of wine and a kick in the behind
     Heigh ho, heigh ho.

     (sung to tune 'Heigh Ho')
     SD:b.10.75

36. Humpty Dumpty sat on a wall but the wall was too tall
     So he had a small fall and rolled like a ball and
     All the kings horses and all the kings men shouted
     Bravo brave Humpty, now do that again.

     Ld:b.9.73 (Eng:g.8.73)

37.   Humpty Dumpty sat on a wall, Humpty slipped off the wall,
      All the Kings men got flatted under and never were near him
          again.

      Ld:b.9.73

38.   Humy Dumy sat on a wall, Humy Dumy eat Barnes,
      Where do you think he put it down
      'is mother parlor's.

      Ld:b.10.73

39.   Humpty Dumpty sat on a wall, eating two bananas
      Where do you think he put the skin down
      The King's pyjamas.

      Ld:b.10.73

40.   Humpty Dumpty sat in a chair, while the barber cut his hair.
      Cut it long, cut it short, cut it with a knive and fork.

      (Ld:g.8.73)

41.   Humpy dumy sat on a wall, Humpy dumy had a great fall
      All the king's horses and all the king's men
      Had scrambled eggs for breakfast again.

      Ld:b.10.73 (Eng:b.8.73, b.10.74)

42.   Its raining, its pouring the old man is snoring
      He went to bed and bumped his head, and couldn't get up in
          the morning.
      The doctor came and pulled the chain and out came a
          chutter train.

      Ld:g.9.73

43.   Jack and Jill went up the hill to get a bucket of popcorns
      But bad old Jack he lit a match and bang went all the
          popcorns.

      Ld:b.8.73 (Eng:b.9.73)

44. Jack and Jill went up to get a bag of cheese.
    Jack fell down and broke 'is crown and the bag of cheese fell
       down
    The mice went cheese cheese, this is my dinner for today.
    Ld:b.8.73

45. Jack and Jill went up the hill to get a bag of cheese.
    Jack fell down and broke his crown, and a mouse came eating
       his knees
    And when Jill came the mouse ran away
    So Jill got her brush and waddles her brush till the
       mouse got dizzy.
    Ld:b.9.73

46. Jack and Jill went up the hill to fetch a pail of water
    Jill forgot to take the pill, and now she's got a daughter.
    Ld:b.13.73

47. Old Mother Hubbard, went to the cubboard, to get her poor
       doggie a bone.
    When she turned round, the dog came around, and gave her a
       bone of his own.
    Ld:g.13.73

48. Little Miss Muffet, sat on her tuffet, knickers all
       tattered and torn
    It wasn't the spider that sat down beside her, it was Little
       Boy Blue with the horn.
    Ld:g.13.73 (Eng:b.13.73)

49. Little Jack Horner sat in a corner
    Eating his Christmas pie
    He put in his thumb to pull out a plum
    And the juice squirted right in his eye.
    Ld:b.10.73 (Eng:b.11.73, g.9.73)

50. Little Jill Horner sat in a corner watching a T.V. show.
    She spent so long sitting that the scarf she was knitting,
    Grew longer than scarves ought to grow.
    Ld:g.8.73

51. Mary had a little lamb, her father shot it dead
    And now it goes to school with her, between 2 slices of
    bread.

    Ld:g.13.73

52. Mary had a little lamb, its fleece was white as snow
    But when it fell in the river, she found it very low.

    L:b.10.74

53. Mary had a little bear, the best that you could find
    And everywhere that Mary went, the bear was right behind.

    L:b.10.74

54. Mary had a little lamb, she also had a bear;
    The lamb saw Mary but never saw her bare.

    Ld:g.9.73 (Eng:b.10.73, b.12.73)

55. Mary had a little lamb, she also had a cat
    Tommy Cooper came along and killed it 'just like that'.
      bom bom

    (Tommy Cooper = British TV comedian, catch phrase is 'just like that')
    L:g.8.74 (Eng:b.10.73, g.10.73, g.11.73, g.8.74, g.9.74, b.8.74, b.10.74)

56. Mary had a little lamb she thought it rather silly
    So she threw it by the left leg and caught it by the –
    Willy is a watch dog sitting on the grass,
    Along came a bumble bee and stung he up the –
    Ask no question, tell no lies,
    Have you ever seen a Chinese man doing up his –
    Flies are a nuisance, bugs are worse,
    This is the end of my little verse.

    L:g.9.74 (See No. 76 and 77)

57. Mary had a little pig, it wouldn't stop a grunting
    She took it up the garden path, and kicked its little runting.

    Ld:g.13.73

58. Mary had a little lamb, she also had a pig
    Everytime the pig went 'ooik' the lamb said Pardon.

    L:g.10.74

59. There was a man who wanted to say his prayers,
    so I took him by the left leg and threw him down the stairs.

    Ld:b.10.73

60. Hey diddle diddle, the cow jumped over
    The little cup laughed to see cow flattened the cat.

    L:g.10.74

61. Little boy blue come blow your horn,
    The sheep in the meadow, the cows in the corn
    Christmas is coming, the goose is getting fat
    Pray put a penny in the old mans hat.

    L:g.10.74

62. Roses are red, violets are blue,
    my dog is pregnant, thanks to you.

    SD:b.11.75

63. Georgie Best, Super Star
    Wears frilly knickers, and see-through bra.

    (Georgie Best = ex-football player on Manchester United. Very good
    looking and appealing to the girls)
    Ld:g.10.73 (Eng:g.8.73, b.10.73)

64. Georgie Best Super star
    He wears two pink ribbons and a padded bra.

    Ld:b.9.73

65. Georgie Best, Super Star
    Walks like a woman, and wears a bra.

    Ld:g.10.73 (Eng:b.9.73)

66. We are ace, we are tough; Donny Osmond isn't a puff
        (pouff)
    With a nick nack Paddy Wack, give the dog a bone
    Why won't Donny come to Leeds.

    (pouff = homosexual)
    Ld:g.10.73

67. We are ace, we are tough, Donny Osmond is a pouff
    David Cassidy cannot sing, Garry Glitter is our King

    Ld:b.10.73

68. Glory, glory Donny Osmond
    Glory, glory David Cassidy
    Glory, glory, David Bowie
    They're the greatest fellas in all the land.

    (Donny Osmond & the Osmond Brothers,
    David Cassidy, Garry Glitter & David Bowie = all pop singers)
    Ld:g.10.73

69. Glory, glory Leeds United
    Glory, glory Leeds United
    Glory, glory Leeds United
    They're the greatest football team in all the land.

    (English football team = soccer)
    Ld:g.10.73

70. We broke up, we broke up, we don't care
        if the school blows up
    No more English, no more French, no more sitting on the old
        school bench.
    If the teacher interferes, pick her up and box her ears.
    If she thinks this is not right, blow her up with dynamite.
    Come to our park, come to our park, its a life of misery
    There's a sign post, round the corner,
        saying welcome unto thee.
    Don't believe it, don't believe it, cause its all a pack lies
        If it wasn't for the teachers,
        life would be like Paradise. (sung)

    Ld:b.12.73 (Eng:b.9.73, b.11.74, g.10.74)

71. We break up, we break down,
    We don't care if the school falls down.
    No more English, no more sums
    No more teachers smacking our bums.

    Ld:b.10.73 (Eng:2-b. 9.73, b.10.73, g.10.73)

72. No more pencils, no more books, no more teacher's dirty
        looks.

    SD:b.10.67

73. Reading, writing, arithmetic,
     Put them all together and they make me sick.

     Ld:g.11.73

74. All the teachers at our school go to Church on Sunday
     To pray to God to give them strength to whack the kids
         on Monday.

     Ld:g.9.73

75. Custard custard snot and pie
     All mixed up with a dead dogs eye
     Stir it stir till its gets thick
     And then drink it down with a hot cup of sick.

     Ld:b.9.73

76. Lulu had a baby, she called it sunny Jim
     She took it to the swimming baths
     To see if it could swim.
     It sank to the bottom and floated to the top
     Lulu got excited and grabbed it by the cock —
     les and mussels two and six a jar if
     You do not like them stick them up your as—
     k no questions tell no lies
     have you ever seen a policeman doing up his
     flies are a nuisance, fleas are even worse
     And that is the end of Lulus dirty verse.

     Ld:g.10.73 (See no. 56)

77. Three Irish men, three Irish men were digging in a ditch.
     One called the other a dirty son of a
     Peter Aterfy had a dog, a faithful dog was he
     Lend it to Murfy to bear her company
     Taught it how to jump, jumped up a ladies dress
         and bit her in the
     Countryboy countryboy was setting on a rock,
     Along come a bumblebee and stung him in the
     Couchtale general five cent a glass
     If you don't like it shove it up your

Ask me no questions, I'll tell you no lies,
These are the words of old mother wise.

SF:b.11.74

78. I had a little dog that sat on the log,
It never done as its told so I hit with a rock
I took it to the vet and it fell on 'is head and
What a naughty dog it was to fall on its head and
Then I went home and gave it some food and then
I left it with it.

L:g.8.74

79. Oh dear what can the matter be, three old lady's locked in the
lavatory.
They will be there from Monday to Saturday,
nobody knows they'll be there.

Ld:g.11.73

80. You're daft, you're potty, you're made of treacle toffee.

(treacle = dark or light syrup, usually dark syrup like molasses)
Ld:g.10.73

81. You're daft, you're barmy, you ought to join the army.

Ld:g.10.73

82. I'm Shirley Temple, I wear my skirts up there
Two big dimples, and curly hair
I'm Shirley Temple, I wear my skirts up there.

L:g.10.74

83. I have a boy-friend Tony, he comes from Macaroni
With two black toes and a pimple on his nose
That is how my story goes.
I want to kiss kiss you in the park park
I want to love love you all the time time.

L:g.8.74 (Eng:g.9.74)

84. Ding dong the bells shall ring for Cinderella and her king.

L:g.10.74

85. Yellow is the colour of my true loves teeth in the morning
    when she rise.
    Blue is the colour of my true loves nose in the morning
    when she rises.
    White is the colour of my true loves lips in the morning
    when she rises.

    L:g.11.74

II. SONGS AND RHYMES

86. We only girls of Hepworths, we work by night and day,
    And we have no color in our cheeks, it disappeared
    out of sight
    Mr. Cable says we're lazy, and lazy we might be
    But if it wasn't for the girls in the trousers room
    Where would all Hepworth's be
    Down in the sewer, shovelling up the shit. (sung)

    (Hepworth's = men's chain clothing store)
    Ld:g.12.73

87. Pancake Tuesday is a very fine day,
    If we don't get a holiday
    We'll all run away.

    Ld:g.10.73 (Eng:g.10.73)

88. When I was a wee wee tot,
    They took me from my wee wee cot
    They put me on my wee wee pot
    To see if I would wee or not
    When they found that I could not,
    They put me in my wee wee cot
    And there I did wee wee alot.

    Ld:g.12.73

89. 10, 20, 30 40, 50 or more,
    Peter done a fart at the grocery store

The poor old man couldn't hold his breath
So he did another one and killed the rest.

L:b.8.74 (Eng:b.74, b.9.74)

90. Little boy Brown went to town riding on a donkey
He did a fart in the cart
And made the wheels go wonkey.

L:b.10.74

91. John done it number two, lost a teeth
        where his tongue pokes through
John done it number two.

L:g.9.74

92. Sambo had an aunty, an aunty very poor
Auntie said to Sambo, go and scrub the floor.
Sambo didn't want to, went upstairs to bed.
Slipped down the banister, and landed on his head.

Ld:g.10.73 (Eng:g.9.73, 2-g.10.73)

93. Fattey and Thiney went to bed.
Fattey rolled over
and Thiney was dead.

Ld:b. 9.73 (Eng: 2-g.9.73)

94. Fatty and Skinny went swimming
Fatty jumped in and the water jumped out.

L:b.10.74

95. 2 little sausages sizzling in a pan,
One went pop and the other went bang.

L:b.8.74 (Eng:b.8.74)

96. Twist me turn me show me the elth
I looked in the water and there saw — MY-SELF.

L:g.9.74 (Eng:g.9.74, 2-b.10.74)

97. Tarzan in the jungle have lots of fun
Playing noughs and crosses on the black man's bum.

L:b.8.74 (Eng:b.8.74)

98.   It was raining one day in Spain, I sat in a chair
      And tore my hair and never sat there again.

      L:g.10.74 (Eng:g.10.74)

99.   Paddy on the railway having lots of fun
      Along came an engine and kicked Paddy up the bum.

      L:b.8.74 (Eng:b.8.74)

100. I saw a man love in up a dog, I see papa on the moon
      Tom Tom you look like a cow.

      L:b.10.74

101. I tried to help a pussycat, I did I did I did
      I tried to help a pussycat, but it ran and hid

      L:g.10.74

102. Martin Chivers had the shivers by two great rivers
      When he got home for tea he had two large livers.

      L:b.11.74

103. Ted Heath has split lips and laughing shoulders.

      L:b.11.74

104. I have three in my coffee, I have three in my tea
      I have three in my hot mike. That is all for me.

      L:b.9.74

105. Silence in the jungle, Silence in the court,
      You're a big fat monkey, if you're first to talk.

      L:b.9.74

106. Two little monkeys jumping on a bed
      One fell off and hurt his head
      One called the doctor, doctor said,
      No more monkeys jumping on bed.

      SD:b.7.75

107. Two little monkeys, teasing Mr. Alligator
      Can't catch me.
      Along comes Mr. Alligator, cross as can be
      Snap, then there was one.
      (repeat, one little monkey . . .)

      SD:b.7.75

108.   Once there was a dark dark planet
      On the dark dark planet there is a dark dark state
      On the dark dark state, there's a dark dark city
      On the dark dark city, there's a dark dark street
      On the dark dark street, there's a dark dark house
      On the dark dark house, there's a dark dark stairs
      On the dark dark stairs, there's a dark dark closet
      On the dark dark closet, there's a dark dark cupboard
      On the dark dark cupboard, there's a little green
        jelly bean.

      SF:g.10.74

109.   When I die, bury me
      Hang my balls on Cherry Street
      If they fall, catch them all,
      Take them to City Hall
      If they say they do smell
      Tell them to go to hell.

      SF:b.11.74

110.   One great day in the middle of the night
      Two dead boys got up to fight
      Back to back they faced each other
      Drew their swords and shot each other
      A deaf policeman heard the noise
      And saved the lives of the two dead boys.
      If you don't think this story's true
      Ask the blind man, he saw it too.

      SF:b.11.74

111.   When you get married, and you have twins
      Don't come to me for safety pins.

      Ld:b.13.74

112.   See my pinkie, see my finger,
      See my thumb, see my fist, you better run.

      SD:g.6.75

113. A little seed best fits a little soil
     A little trade best fits a little toil
     As my small jar best fits my little oil.

     L:g.9.74

114. About my sister – My sister is bad, my sister is good,
     My sister is always sad. And my sister said
     That and that is the end of my joke.

     Ld:b.8.73

115. My Mom – My mommy is good, my mommy is bad,
     My mommy is very very sad.
     Sometimes she is good, sometimes she is bad,
     She sometimes laughs, sometimes smiles,
     But never sulks at us.

     Ld:g.8.73

116. My dad – My dad is funny, my dad is a bunny,
     My dad is a silly bunny.
     We can not stop him to be no bunny
     But we play with him a lot.

     Ld:g.9.73

117. A funny thing happened. A mouse said to a lion to get him a
     bag of cheese, but a funny thing happened, the lion brought a
     deer.

     Ld:g.8.73

118. There was a mouse that lived in a house and he longed for a
     piece of cheese and when he got it he dropped it and he was
     sad as can be.

     Ld:g.9.73

119. Billy-boy Billy-boy where are you riding to?
     I'm riding old Dobbin to Banbury Fair, I won't be long.
     What will you bring me back?
     One girdle to keep your fat belly in.

     L:b.11.74

120. Goosey goosey gander, where do you wander Upstairs, downstairs in the ladys chamber.

Ld:b.10.73

121. Little John Horner, sat in a corner
Eating Christmas pie
He put in his thumb, and pulled out a plum
And said what a good boy I am.

Ld:g.10.73

122. Little Jack 'aner sater in a corner eating his Christmas pie
Put in his thumb, pulled out a plum,
and said what a clever boy am I.

L:g.8.74

123. A dillar a dollar, a ten o'clock scholar,
What makes you come so soon, you used to come
at ten o'clock but now you come at noon.

Ld:g.8.73

124. Jack and Jill went up the hill
To fetch a pail of water
Jack fell down and Jill came down after him.

Ld:g.9.73

125. Little Miss Muffet, sat on a tuffet
Eatin' an apple pie.
Down came a spider and sat down beside her
And frightened little Miss Muffet away.

Ld:g.8.73

126. Glory, glory alleluya, glory glory alleluya
Glory, glory alleluya, when the saints go marchin' in.

Ld:g.9.73

127. Little Tommy Tuker sang for his supper
What shall we give him, brown bread and butter.

Ld:g.9.73

III. LIMERICKS

128. There was a young teacher called Bean
      Who invented a whacking machine
      On the 99th stroke, the rotten thing broke
      And hit Silas Green on the bean.

      Ld:b.8.73 (Eng:b.10.73)

129. There was a lady from China
      Who traveled on a boat called Liner
      She slipped on the deck and twisted her neck
      And couldn't see behind her.

      L:g.10.74

130. Doctor Foster went to Gloucester in a shower of rain
      He stepped in a puddle right up to the middle
          and never came back again.

      Ld:b.9.73 (Eng:g.8.73)

131. Doctor Foster went to Gloucester eating his pies.
      Doctor Foster sat on the pie and said
          what a good boy am I.

      Ld:g.8.73

132. There was an old man from Glosom
      Who took out his false teeth to wash them
      His wife said Jack, if you don't put them back
      I'll put them in the spin dryer and squash them.

      L:g.10.74

133. There was a young lady from Gloucester
      Whose parents thought they had lost her
      One night from the fridge they heard bang bang
      They opened it up and saw her
      But the trouble was now to defrost her.

      L:b.10.74

134. Doctor McKenee is a very fat man
     He washed his face in a frying pan.
     He washed his hair with a leg of the chair
     And he's watchin' the door with his foot in the air.

     Ld:g.8.73

135. There was a young man from France
     Who invented a new sort of tank
     He said it'd float, just like a boat
     But the first time he tried it it sank.

     Ld:b.12.73

136. There was a man from ibra,
     He tried to swallow a piano
     He lost a key and found it with me
     And beat me up in an hour.

     L:b.10.74

137. There was an old woman from Kent
     Whose nose was remarkable bent
     One day they suppose she followed her nose
     And nobody knows where she went.

     L:b.10.74

138. There was an old man from Leeds
     He swallowed a packet of seeds
     In less than an hour, he found he was a flower
     Surrounded with weeds.

     L:b.10.74

139. There was an old man called Mark.
     Who was rather scared of the dark
     One night he went out and gave a great shout
     What a sportun' man was he.

     Ld:g.8.73

140. There was a young cannibal called Ned,
     Who used to eat only onions in bed
     His mother said son, its not very funny
     Why don't you eat people instead.

     Ld:b.12.73

141.   There was a young man called Paul
        Who grew extremely tall
        One night in bed he stretched out his leg
        And turned out the light in the hall.

    Ld:g.10.73 (Eng:b.9.73, 2-b.10.73, 2-g.10.73)

142.   There was an old man from Peru
        Who thought he was eating a shoe,
        Woke up in the night, had a terrible fright,
        And found it was perfectly true.

    Ld:b.8.73 (Eng:b.10.73)

143.   There was a mechanical rocket
        The rocket went bang, his balls went twang
        And he found his cock in his pocket.

    Ld:b.13.73

144.   There was a young man called Rotor
        Who decided to fly to Calcutter
        He started with a bang, a clash and a clang
        And the furthest he got was the gutter.

    Ld:b.12.73 (Eng:b.10.73)

145.   there was a young man from Surrey
        Who was in a terrible hurry
        He tripped over a stone, and broke his leg bone
        And that was the end of the man from Surrey.

    Ld:b.9.73

146.   There was a young man from Syme
        Up a clock tower started to climb
        He shouted oh vex, but I've broken my specs
        And I'm anxious to know the right time.

    Ld:b.9.73

147.   Way down south were bananas grow,
            a grasshopper stood on an elephant's toe
        The elephant said with tears in his eyes,
            why don't you go and pick on someone your own size.

    Ld:b.12.73

IV. TRUE RIDDLES

148. What's black and white and red all over?
A newspaper

Ld:g.8.73 (Eng:g.8.73, g.10.73, b.10.73, b.11.73, b.11.75, US:g.8.58, g.10.75, b.12.74)

149. What is the smallest room in the world?
A mushroom

Ld:g.10.73

150. What room has no doors or windows, no furniture?
Mushroom

L:b.10.74

151. What house has no door?
An egg.

OR:g.8.58

152. What goes up and never comes down?
Your age

Ld:g.8.73 (Eng: 2-g.8.73, b.8.73, 2-g.10.74)

153. What goes up when the rain comes down?
Your umbrella

Ld:g.9.73 (Eng:g.10.74)

154. What has teeth but no mouth?
A comb

Ld:g.8.73

155. What can run but can't walk?
A river

Ld:g.8.73

156. Well, what can you put in the water that will never get wet?
Shadow, your shadow

Ld:g.12.73 (Eng:b.11.73)

157. What bow can you never tie?
      A rainbow

      Ld:b.8.73

158. What sings but has no voice?
      A kettle

      Ld:g.8.73

159. What has hands but no arms?
      Gloves

      Ld:g.8.73

160. What do you use today, and make tomorrow?
      A bed

      Ld:g.8.73

161. What stands still and goes?
      A clock

      L:g.10.74 (Eng:g.9.74)

162. What can you hold without touching?
      Breath

      L:g.9.74

163. What's small at the top and big at the bottom?
      A mountain.

      SD:b.10.75

164. Well, there was a farmer, his lion, a bundle of hay and a goat.
      And they all wanted to get across the river. Now, if he left the
      goat with the lion and took the hay first the lion would eat the
      goat, and if he left the hay there the goat would eat the hay.
      So what could he do, how could he take them across? Well, if
      he took the goat across, the lion wouldn't eat the hay, would
      he? And so he took the goat across, came back took the hay,
      brought the goat back, took the lion, and then he came back
      and took the goat back.

      Ld:g.12.73

165. Are you a turtle? If not, you are asked 4 riddles, seemingly obscene, but the answers are straightforward. Person gets embarrassed to answer, but when he hears the answer, he's even more embarrassed. Once you are a turtle, you answer, 'You bet your sweet ass I am.' If person fails to say this, then he owes the questioner a beverage of his choice.

    a. What does a man do standing up, a lady sitting down, and a dog on 3 legs?
       Shake hands.

    b. What goes in hard and dry and comes out soft and wet and gooey?
       Bubble gum.

    c. What sticks out of a man's pyjamas, has hair around it, and is long enough to stick a man's hat on?
       His head.

    d. What is it that's hard, and long and leaks?
       A fountain pen.

NJ:g.12.62

V. RIDDLES

166. What do cannibals play at parties?
    Swallow my leader.

    Ld:b.9.73

167. What do cannibals eat?
    Baked beings on toast.

    Ld:g.12.73

168. What do vampires do every night at 10.30?
    Take a coffin break.

    SD:b.8.75

169. How does a monkey cook toast?
    He puts it under the gorilla.

    L:b.11.74 (Eng:b.12.73)

170. What do spooks eat?
      Spookeghetti.

   Ld:b.9.73

171. What do you get when a bird flies into a lawn mower?
      Shredded tweet.

   (Shredded wheat = breakfast cereal)
   SF:b.11.74 (Eng:g.10.73)

172. What do you get when you got a bald-headed detective with
      a camera?
      A Kojak instamatic.

   (Kojak = bald-headed detective on TV series played by Telly Savalas)
   L:b.11.75

173. What do you take off last when you go to bed?
      Your feet off the floor.

   SF:g.9.74

174. What do you put on the table and you cut it but you don't
      eat?
      A deck of cards.

   SD:b.7.75

175. If cowskins make good shoes, what do banana skins make?
      Good slippers.

   Ld:g.10.73

176. What do you get if you mix a sheep and a leopard together?
      You get a shepard.

   Ld:b.8.73 (Eng:b.9.73)

177. What do you get when you mix a sheep and a kangaroo
      together?
      A wooly jumper.

   (jumper = sweater)
   Ld:b.8.73 (Eng:b.8.73, g.12.73, b.10.74, b.11.75)

178. What do you get when you cross a kangaroo and zebra?
      We get a jumping zebracross.

   (zebracross = crosswalk)
   LD:b.10.73

179. What do you get if you cross a giraffe with a hedgehog?
      A twenty foot tooth brush.

      L:b.11.74

180. What do you get if you cross Peter Williams and Paul
      Carthy?
      An elephant.

      (2 boys in their class – Peter Williams is thin with big ears. Paul Carthy is
      fat and broad)
      LD:g.13.73

181. What do you call an kqqer (Jumper) and a shirt?
      A jump-shirt

      Ld:b.8.73

182. What do you call a black man with white hair?
      A guinness.

      (guinness = dark Irish beer)
      Ld:b.9.73

183. What do you call a judge with no thumbs?
      Justick fingers.

      Ld:g.12.73

184. What do you call a trumpet player that's got bubble lips?
      Gooey Armstrong.

      Ld:b.13.73

185. What do you call a cow that doesn't give milk?
      A milk dud.

      (milk dud = type of chocolate caramel candy or sweet)
      SD:g.10.75

186. What do you call a dentist who offers to clean your
      werewolves teeth?
      Crazy man, crazy.

      SD:g.8.75

187. What do you call a skeleton when sleeping on?
      A bed of lazy bones.

      Ld:g.9.73 (Eng:b.9.74)

188. You've heard of Aborigine tribes and things like that, but what do you call a loo in a zoo?
A zooloo.

(Loo= bathroom, toilet)
Ld:g.9.73

189. What do you call a camel with 3 humps?
Humphrey.

SF:g.10.74 (Eng:b.10.73)

190. What do you call a lazy bull?
A bulldozer.

Ld:g.10.73 (Eng:b.10.74)

191. What do you call a cat who's been, who hasn't been brushed regularly, looks very tatty, and is just eaten a duck?
A duck-filled tatty puss.

Ld:b.8.73 (duck-billed platypus)

192. What do you call a duck playing in the rain?
Quackers.

L:b.10.74

193. There were 3 ducks in a box. What were they called?
A box of crackers (quackers).

Ld:g.9.73 (US:b.11.75)

194. What do you call a alphabet drinking water?
Cheers.

L:b.8.74

195. What do you call a bear with curly hair?
The hair bear bunch.

L:b.8.74 (Eng:b.8.74)

196. What do you call a boy with curly hair?
Fuzzy.

L:b.8.74

197. What do you call a boy with big ears?
A monkey.

L:b.8.74

198. What does a spud turn into?
   A potato.
   L:b.9.74

199. What else does yellow mean?
   To call out in pain.
   Ld:g.12.73

200. A butcher's 6 foot tall and he wears a 5-8 shoe. What does he weigh?
   He weighs meat.
   SD:g.10.75 (Eng.b.8.73)

201. What does a male centipede say to a female centipede?
   What a lovely pair of legs, legs, legs, etc.
   Ld:b.12.73

202. What does an envelope say when you lick it?
   Nothing. It just shuts up.
   SD:b.12.75

203. What did the duck say to the mailman?
   Nice ducky.
   L:g.8.74

204. What did Tarzan say when he jumped off the cliff?
   Goodbye to Jane, Goodbye to Jane.
   L:g.9.74 (Eng:g.9.74, b.7.74)

205. What did Tarzan say when he climbed up the cliff?
   Hello, Hello I'm back again.
   L:b.8.74

206. What did Tarzan say when he fell off a cliff?
   a A a A.
   L:g.9.74

207. What did the safari man say when they saw a zebra crossing a road?
   Look Joe, its a zebra crossing.
   L:b.10.74 (zebra = traffic crosswalk)

208. What did the dragon say to the cock?
     I have not a cock.

     L:b.8.74

209. What did Adam say to Eve?
     Where is your bellybutton?

     SF:g.11.74

210. What did the bird say to the worm?
     You're tasty.

     SF:g.11.74

211. What did the coca-cola say to the diet 7-Up?
     They're in the refrigerator.
     Cool man, cool

     SF:g.10.74

212. What did the bullet say to the other bullet?
     I'm having a BB.

     SF:g.10.74

213. Did ya hear about the 22 shell that married the shot gun shell?
     They had a little BB.

     SF:b.11.74

214 What did the football say to the football players?
     I get a kick out of you.

     SD:b.10.75

215. What did the boy say when his dog ran away?
     Dog gone.

     SD:b.12.75

216. What did the cannibal say when he met Laurel and Hardy?
     Meal on wheels.

     L:b.11.75

217. What did the cat do when he was not fed?
     He stole the refrigerator.

     SF:g.11.74

218. Why did Humpty Dumpty have a great fall?
He made up for a rotten summer.

SD:b.8.75

219. What did the tree say to the leaf?
Leave off.

L:g.9.74

220. What did the skeleton say to the lavatory?
You won't get nuthing out of me.

L:b.8.74

221. What did the policeman say when he met the Beverly sisters?
Hello, hello, hello.

LD:g.10.73

222. What did the lady octopus say to the man octopus?
I want to shake your hand, hand, hand, hand, hand, hand, hand, hand,

LD:g.10.73

223. What did the traffic light say to lorry?
Don't look I'm changing.

Ld:g.10.73 (Eng:g.10.73, g.12.73, g.8.74, 3-g.10.74, 3-b.10.74, b.11.74, g.11.75)

224. What did the 500 pound mouse say to the cat?
Here kitty, kitty, kitty.

SD:b.10.75

225. What did the salad say to the cucumber?
Lettuce get married.

Ld:g.12.73

226. What did the ghost say on guard duty if he hears a noise?
Who ghost's there.

Ld:b.9.73

227. There were two skeletons walking down the road and they met a man.

What do you think he did?
Jumped out of his skin and joined them.

Ld:g.10.73

228. There was a skeleton sitting outside a ballroom crying, and a
witch came up to him and said what are you crying for?
And the skeleton said because, I have no body to dance with.

Ld:b.10.73 (Eng:2-b.10.74)

229. What did the Olympic runner say when he ran out of fags?
I'm fagged out.

(fag = cigarette) Ld:b.9.73

230. What did 2 horses want in the theatre?
A couple of stalls.

Ld:g.12.73

231. What did the beaver say to the tree?
Its been nice gnawing you.

Ld:g.12.73

232. What did the left arm say to the right arm?
Shake hands.

Ld:g.10.73

233. This boy said to another boy, If an Indian woman is called a
squaw, What is an Indian baby called?
A squawker.

Ld:b.8.73

234. What's the longest word in the dictionary?
Elastic, it stretches.

Ld:g.10.73

235. What is a zebra?
A horse that has escaped from jail.

SD:g.10.75

236. What's a volcano?
A mountain with hiccups.

SD:b.7.75

237. What's the surest way to double a pound?
Fold it in half.

Ld:g.10.73

238. What is sometimes a secret and is sometimes not?
Love.

SF:g.11.74

239. What is so surprising about coffins?
People are dying to get into them.

Ld:b.9.73

240. What is more useful after it's been broken?
An egg.

SD:b.12.75

241. What's a polite ghost?
One who spooks only when he's spooken to.

Ld:g.12.73 (Eng:g.8.73)

242. What's the best way to talk to Frankenstein?
Long distance.

SD:b.9.75 (US:b.8.75)

243. What is the biggest kind of mouse?
A hippopotamouse.

Ld:g.8.73 (Eng:g.12.73)

244. What's worser than a giraffe with a sore throat?
A hippopotamus with chubbier lips.

SD:b.8.75

245. What is the hardest key to turn?
A donkey.

L:g.8.74 (Eng:g.10.74)

246. Do you know 4 keys that won't open the door?
Monkeys, turkeys, donkeys and hankies.

SD:g.8.75

247. What's the sea never grows?
BBC.

Ld:b.8.73

248. What's tall and says eef eif of muf?
      A backward giant. (fee fie fo fum)

      Ld:g.12.73

249. What goes oom oom?
      A cow walking backwards.

      SF:b.11.74

250. What's long and lights up in the dark?
      A glowworm.

      Ld:b.8.73

251. What's black, sits in a tree, and is dangerous?
      A crow with a machine-gun.

      Ld:g.12.73

252. What's black and white, black and white, and black and white?
      Three penguins rolling down a hill.

      Ld:b.8.73

253. What is black and white with red in the black?
      A nun getting stabbed in the back.

      Ld:g.8.73 (Eng:g.9.73)

254. What's black and white, black and white, black and white, and black and white?
      A nun falling down the stairs.

      SF:b.10.74 (Eng:g.9.74, 3-g.10.74, US:g.11.61)

255. What's black and white and red all over?
      An embarrassed zebra.

      NJ:g.11.61 (US:g.10.75, b.10.75)

256. What's black and white and red?
      A zebra with blood-shot eye-balls.

      SD:b.10.75

257. What's black and white and red all over?
      A skunk with diaper rash.

      SF:g.10.74. (US:g.10.75)

258. What's black and white and red all over?
     A sun-burned penguin.

     L:b.11.75 (Eng:b.11.75)

259. What is black and white and red all over?
     A penguin on a meat hook.

     (originally, a newspaper)
     SD:b.18.75

260. What's black and white and has fuzz in it?
     Police car with a policeman in it.

     (fuzz = police)
     SF:g.10.74

261. What is black and black and white?
     A bird

     Ld:b.10.73

262. What's blue and can fly?
     A blue bird.

     Ld:b.11.73

263. What goes black white black white?
     Black and white mistril.

     L:g.9.74

264. What is white when its dirty and black when its clean?
     A blackboard.

     L:b.10.74

265. What is black and red and green?
     A bus full of black men going over a cliff.

     L:b.9.74

266. What goes black white black white?
     A zebra crossing.

     (= traffic crosswalk)
     L:g.10.74 (Eng:g.9.74)

267. What's a black man falling from an upstairs window?
     A chocolate drop.

     L:g.9.74 (Eng:b.11.73, b.11.75)

268. What is green and hair all over and goes up and down?
     A gooseberry in a lift.

     (gooseberry = green berry, tart, and fuzzy when fresh)
     Ld:b.10.73 (Eng:g.8.73, b.10.73, b.12.73, b.9.74)

269. What's red and goes up and down?
     A raspberry in a lift.

     L:b.11.75

270. What's purple and hairy and goes up in a lift?
     A hairy grape.

     Ld:b.10.73

271. What's green and hairy with yellow dots?
     I don't know, but it's crawling up your back.

     Ld:g.11.73

272. What's got 3 eyes, no legs, 5 arms, 2 hands, uh 3 legs (you said
     no legs) oh well, and 1 nose?
     I don't know, but there's one crawling on your back.

     Ld:b.12.73

273. What has 6 legs, fuzzy ears, and a long tail?
     I don't know, but there's one on your neck.

     SD:g.12.75

274. What's red, purple, green, yellow, gray, purple, sky-blue,
     and green?
     I don't know, that's why I'm asking you.

     SD:g.10.75

275. What is round and green, it's covered with blue hair, has big
     scaly clothes, weighs 5000 pounds, and goes peckity peck
     peck?
     Nothing.

     SD:b.10.75

276. What is green and has wings and it does not fly?
     A football pitch.

     (pitch = football field)
     Ld:b.10.73

277. What's green and swims in the ocean?
      Moby Pickle.

      NJ:g.11.61

278. What's green and flies through the air?
      Jonathan Livingston Pickle.

      SD:b.9.75

279. What's green and flies through the air?
      Super Pickle.

      SD:g.10.75

280. What's green and has warts?
      Super pickle.

      SD:b.10.75

281. What's yellow and points north?
      Magnetic banana.

      SD:b.10.75

282. What rides a banana and wears a red hat?
      The Long Pickle.

      SD:g.10.75

283. What's green, flies in the air, and is highly dangerous?
      A flying cucumber with a machine-gun.

      L:g.11.75

284. What's red, white, blue, and flies?
      Evil Knieval.

      (Evil Knieval = stunt motorcyclist)
      SF:g.10.74

285. What is green inside and white outside?
      A frog sandwich.

      L:b.9.74 (Eng:b.10.74)

286. What's green and jumps about?
      Spring cabbage.

      L:b.9.74

287. What's green and waits under water?
      A ballpoint gucein.

      (child's spelling) L:b.7.74

288. What's purple and burns cakes?
      Alfred the Grape.

      Ld:b.8.73

289. What is purple and is always going into battle?
      Alfred the Grape.

      Ld:b.8.73

290. What weighs 2 tons and is purple?
      2 ton grape.

      CA:g.12.61

291. What's red, then purple, then red, then purple?
      A cherry that works at night as a grape.

      SD:b.10.75

292. What is red and is upside down in the gutter?
      A dead bus.

      Ld:b.8.73

293. What's yellow, has 22 legs, and goes munch, crunch, munch?
      A Chinese football team eating crisps.

      (crisps = potato chips)
      Ld:b.12.73 (Eng:g.10.73, b.11.74)

294. What's yellow and spins round and round?
      A banana in a washing machine.

      Ld:g.8.73

295. What's yellow and goes click-click?
      A ball-point banana.

      (Ball-point pen = biro)
      NJ:g.11.61

296. What is you best colour? Pink. What is your best animal?
      Horse. What is you best number? 7. I have never seen a horse
      pink and 7 legs.

      L:g.8.74

297. What is like us but a different kind?
     A man turning into an ape.

     L:b.9.74

298. If a blue house had made out blue birkeer (bricks) and if and a
     red house and made of red birkcer and what is a green a made
     of?
     Glass.

     L:b.9.74

299. What's the difference between a saloon and an elephant's fart?
     A saloon is a bar room, and an elephant's fart is a barROOM!

     SD:b.14.71

300. What's the difference between a flea and an elephant?
     An elephant can have fleas, but a flea can't have elephants.

     SF:b.9.74

301. What do babies and basketball players have in common?
     They both can dribble.

     SD:b.12.75

302. What's the difference between Prince Charles and a ball?
     One can be thrown in the air, and the other is heir to the
     throne.

     Ld:b.9.73

303. A dad says to his boy: What's the difference between an
     elephant and a postbox? And the boy says, I don't know, and
     his dad says, I'll never send you to post a letter then.

     Ld:b.9.73

304. What's the difference between an egg and an elephant?
     If you don't know, I'll never send you to get eggs from the
     shop.

     Ld:b.9.73

305. What is the difference between a glass bra?
     Smash and grab.

     (reference to display-window stealing)
     L:g.9.74 (Eng:g.9.74)

306.   What time is it?
       Half past the monkey's ass, quarter to his balls.

       SD:b.10.75

307.   What's the definition of agony?
       A woman standing outside a toilet with a bent penny.

       Ld:g. & 73 (Eng:b.12.73)

308.   What's the definition of agony?
       A fly sliding down a razor using his balls as blades (brakes).

       Ld:b.12.73 (Eng:b.13.73)

309.   How would you picture a guy sliding down on a razor blade,
       and having to use his balls for brakes, and landing in a pool of
       alcohol?

       SD:g.12.75 (US:2-b.12.75)

310.   What is the definition of a cat going down the motorway?
       Meown.

       L:b.10.74

311.   What's the definition of success?
       Two pouffs walking around with a pram.

       (pouff = a homosexual)
       Ld:b.13.73)

312,   What's the definition of noise?
       Two skeletons in a biscuit-tin.

       (sexual reference) Ld:g.11.73

313,   What's the definition of a skeleton laying on a bed?
       Lazybones.

       Ld:b.12.73

314.   What's the definition of a skeleton?
       A striptease gone too far.

       Ld:b.12.73 (Eng:g.10.74)

315.   What's the definition of depressed?
       A ant trying to climb Mr. Everest with a stepladder.

       Ld:b.13.73

316. What's the definition of blockbuster?
Square tits.

Ld:b.13.73

317. What's the definition of a mental child?
Potre.

Ld:g.8.73
(mental = deficient)

318. What's the definition of a belt?
A topless mini-skirt.

SD:g.16.67

319. What is hot when you put it in the refrigerator?
Mustard.

SD:g.10.75 (Eng:2-b.10.73, b.11.74)

320. What's this? (move fingers across front of your body, in mid air, flapping and wiggling the fingers)
I don't know, but there it goes again (movement again)

NJ:g.11.61

321. What would you do if coppers were surrounding you?
'Pick 'em up and spend them.

Ld:b.10.73 (Eng:b.8.73, b.10,73, b.11.73)

322. If a king were cut in half, what would he wear on his head?
Half a crown.

Ld:g.10.73

323. What would the number one be doing at the end of a relay race?
Because you won, one.

SD:b.10.75

324. If you took the middle of a hot dog out what would you have?
A hollow weenie.

SD:g.8.75 (US:g.12.75)

325. There's this boy, and he's in a classroom. And the teacher comes up to him and says, Oh Mark, if you have 6 weeks and I took 3 away, how many would you have?

So he said, I don't know how many I'd have, but you'd have a broken arm.

Ld:g.13.73 (Eng:b.11.73)

326. If you've got forty apples in one hand and thirty in another,
      What have you got?
      Mighty big hands.

      Ld:g.10.73

327. If you threw a white ball into the black sea, what would it become?
      Wet.

      L:b.10.74

328. What will you get if you come across a black cat?
      Bad luck.

      L:b.9.74

329. What has lots of legs and has a furry coat?
      A caterpillar.

      Ld:b.10.73

330. What has 6 legs, 2 heads, and a tail?
      A man on a horse-back.

      SD:g.10.75 (US:g.10.75, Eng:b.12.73)

331. What has a camel always have?
      The ump.

      L:g.9.74

332. What has a hump, is brown, and lives at the North Pole?
      A lost camel.

      SD:b.10.75

333. What maths book do you get splinters from?
      A log book.

      Ld:b.9.73

334. What planet makes children go to the dentist?
      Mars.

      (Mars — chocolate candy bar)
      L:b.11.74

335. What animal falls from the clouds?
     A rain, dear (reindeer)
     Ld:g.11.73

336. What engine has ears?
     An engineer.
     Ld:b.10.73

337. What dog hasn't got a tail?
     Hot dog.
     L:g.8.74

338. What fish scares other fish?
     Jack the Kipper.
     Ld:g.10.73 (Eng:2–b.10.73)

339. What pet is kept in a car?
     Carpet.
     Ld:b.11.73

340. What pet makes the loudest noise?
     A trumpet.
     L:g.8.74

341. What pie can fly?
     A magpie.
     Ld:g.10.73

342. What meat do policemen eat?
     Truncheon meat.
     L:b.11.75 (Eng:b.11.75)

343. What makes a pickle laugh?
     Tell him an elephant joke.
     SF:g.10.74

344. What vegetable can see?
     A potato, it has eyes.
     SD:b.10.75

345.　What part of your finger gets hit with a hammer?
　　　The nail.
　　　SD:b.10.75

346.　What bed is a three-season bed?
　　　One with a spring.
　　　SD:g.9.75 (US:b.10.75)

347.　What time is it when the clock strikes 13?
　　　Time to get a new clock.
　　　SD:g.8.75

348.　What always weighs the same?
　　　A hole.
　　　SD:g.8.75

349.　What weighs 2000 pounds and wears flowers in it's hair?
　　　A hippy-potamus.
　　　SD:b.11.75

350.　What kind of an animal can jump higher than a house?
　　　All kinds, houses can't jump.
　　　Ld:g.12.73 (Eng:b.10.74, US:g.11.61)

351.　What kind of money do people eat?
　　　Dough.
　　　SD:b.10.75

352.　What kind of fly do you wear on your foot?
　　　A shoe fly.
　　　SD:b.10.75 (shoo – fly!)

353.　What kind of animal has a different kind of baby than others
　　　do?
　　　A baby kangaroo.
　　　SD:b.9.75

354.　What kind of lotion do werewolves use?
　　　Moondown lotion.
　　　SD:b.9.75

355. What time did the Chinaman go to the dentist?
At 2.30 – tooth hirty
Ld:g.12.73 (Eng:2-g.10.73, g.10.74)

356. What tree is about that size (3 ft. from floor) and never grows?
A lavatory.
Ld:b.8.73 (= lavat'ry)

357. What goes from London to Norwich without running?
Gas.
Ld:g.8.73

358. What goes round an ashtray at 120 mph?
An E-type Fag.
Ld:b.12.73

359. What goes ha ha ha plop?
A man laughing his head off.
Ld:b.9.73

360. What goes 99 clump?
A centipede with a wooden leg.
Ld:b.11.73 (Eng:b.9.73, B.12.73, B.10.74)

361. What goes 89 mph clunk clunk?
A centipede with 2 wooden legs.
Ld:b.12.73

362. What goes to bed with its shoes on?
A horse.
Ld:b.11.73

363. What goes pick pick bang, pick pick bang, pick pick bang?
Three chickens in a mine-field.
Ld:b.9.73

364. What lies with a hundred feet in the air on the ground?
A centipede on its back.
Ld:b.10.73 (Eng:b.11.73)

365.   What lives under the sea and carries lots of people?
        An octerbus.

        Ld:b.9.73

366.   What kind of transport do witches use?
        Witchcraft.

        Ld:g.12.73

367.   What lives at the bottom of the ocean and has a double-barrel
        shotgun?
        Billy the Squid.

        IN:g.8.62

368.   What makes budgies bounce?
        Rubber boots, bom bom.

        L:g.8.74

369.   What happened when the lady backed into the airplane?
        Disaster — dis-assed her.

        SD:b.16.73

370.   What happened when the cow jumped over the barbed wire
        fence?
        Utter destruction.

        SD:b.16.73

371.   What happens if you phone 666?
        Get 3 policemen walking on their heads.

        L:b.11.75

372.   What happens when you cross a cow with a duck?
        Creamed crackers.

        L:b.11.75

373.   What happen when pigs fly?
        Price of bacon and sausages goes up.

        L:b.10.74

374.   Why did the pig fly up in the air?
        The backers gone up.

        L:b.10.74

375. What can't you ever answer no to?
      Are you sleeping?

      SD:g.8.75

376. A vampire wants to stay warm in a woods. What does he do?
      He builds a vampire fire.

      SD:g.8.75

377. What was Tarzan's last words?
      Who greased the vine?

      SD:b.7.75

378. Which is the latest way to get to work?
      Shut off the alarm clock.

      Ld:b.10.73

379. Which is faster — hot or cold?
      Hot because you can catch cold.

      Ld:g.9.73

380. Where do you find prehistoric cows?
      In a mooseum.

      Ld:b.10.73

381. Where do you weigh whales?
      In a whale weigh station.

      Ld:b.10.73

382. Where does a bird go to if its ill?
      It goes for tweetmint.

      Ld:g.10.73

383. Where do sick ships go?
      To the dock.

      SD:b.12.75

384. There was a man on a building site looking for a job.
      He met a man and said can you tell me where Wheetibix the
      builder is?

      (Wheetibix the builder = breakfast cereal advertised as the builder)
      Ld:b.9.73

385. How do you communicate with a fish?
     Drop it a line.

     Ld:b.10.73

386. How do you start a flea race?
     One, two, flea.

     Ld:g.10.73

387. How do you start a rice pudding race?
     Sago (say go).

     (Sago = tapioca, rice pudding)
     Ld:g.10.73

388. How do you hire a horse?
     Put four boxes under its feet.

     Ld:b.12.73

389. How do you make gold still?
     Add 40 carrots.

     SD:b.8.75

390. How do you make a hippopotamus float?
     With lots of root beer.

     (Ice cream floats = ice cream plus soda, either coke or root beer)
     SD:b.10.75

391. How do you tell when a motorcycle driver is happy?
     When you see bugs on his teeth.

     SF:b.11.74

392. How does a rabbit dig a hole without putting dirt on top of
     the hole?
     Dig it from bottom up.

     SF:b.11.74

393. How do you raise strawberries?
     With a spoon.

     SD:b.9.75

394. How do you get an alligator into a matchbox?
     Go to the African jungle, take a telescope, turn it, turn the

telescope around the other way, so it makes things smaller, look through the telescope so it's small, get a pair of tweezers, open matchbox, and put the alligator into the matchbox.

L:b.11.75

395. How does an elephant put it's trunk in an alligator's mouth?
Very carefully.

SD:b.10.75

396. How do monsters count to 19?
On their fingers.

SD:b.8,75

397. Three men dived into water. Two got their hair wet. How come?
One was bald.

SD:b.9.75

398. My dog has no nose. How does it smell?
Terrible.

L:b.11.75

399. How do Chinese get their children's names?
Well, they get all the knives and forks and throw them in the air and they go fing fong fie.

Ld:g.12.73

400. How do you have a paper baby?
Marry an old bag.

L:b.9.74 (Eng:b.9.74)

401. What do you do when you're surrounded by lions, tigers, and elephants?
Get off the merry-go-round.

SD:g.10.75 (Eng:b.8.73)

402. What should you do if you see 3 Frankensteins, 2 Draculas, and 4 Wolfmen in a room on the same day?
Hope it's a costume party.

SD:b.8.75

403. How many insects does it take to make an officer?
Tenants.

Ld:g.9.73 (Eng:g.12.73

404. Donkey on one side of river, and on other side of river there's
beautiful carrots. Rivers right wide, and he can't jump over it,
and its so long that by the time he walked to the end of it he'd
have to walk all the way back on the other side to get to
carrots. And there's no boat, and he can't fly, and he can't
swim, or anything like that, so how does he get across? How?
Do you give up? So did the donkey.

Ld:g.13.73

405. This old lady, you see, she goes to this inspector,
"How long will the bus be?"
And the inspector goes the same as any other.

Ld:b.12.73

406. There's this boat out in the middle of the sea, and the man said
to the captain how far is it to the nearest land?
6 miles straight down.

Ld:g.8.73

407. How deep does the water have to be for a frog?
Knee-deep, knee-deep (said like a frog, low deep voice)

SD:b.10.75

408. How many sides has a table tennis ball?
Two, an inside and an outside.

Ld:g.8.73

409. How could soap save you from a sinking ship?
By washing you ashore.

Ld:g.12.73.

410. Why is a football ground always cold?
Because there's so many fans.

Ld:g.8.73

411. Why is the emblem of the United States more enduring than
that of France, England, Ireland or Scotland?

The Lily may fade, and the sleeves decay,
The rose on it's stem may wither. The shamrock will just pass
away, but the stars will shine forever.

SD:g.10.75

412. Why is everybody tired on April Fool's Day?
They just had 31 day March.

SD:b.12.75

413. Why is a banana skin like a pullover?
It's easy to slip on.

(pullover = sweater)
SF:g.10.74 (Eng:2–b.8.73)

414. Why is a banana peel like a pot of grease?
Because it is easy to slip on!

SF:g.11.74

415. Why is a banana peel like a pair of shoes?
Because they're easy to slip on.

SF:g.11.74 (Eng:b.8.73)

416. Why is wheat like a donkey?
Because they both have long ears.

L:g.9.74

417. Why is grass so harmful?
Because it has blades.

SD:b.7.75

418. Did you hear Betty Crocker is in the hospital?
She burnt her buns.

(buns = buttocks).
(Betty Crocker = brand name packaged cake mixes)
NJ:b.10.67

419. Why is the Statue of Liberty standing in New York harbor?
Because it can't sit down.

SF:b.11.75

420. Rasmus, why's you got a hole in your upper lip?
So's I can sees where I's agoing when I's a whistling.

Ld:b.13.74

421. Why are dark-haired boys white?
     Cause they're going to be fair.
     Ld:b.8.73

422. Why are fish so smart?
     Because they travel in schools.
     SD:g.9.75

423. Why can't a nose be twelve inches long?
     Because it will be a foot.
     L:b.10.74

424. Why can't you play cards in a jungle?
     Too many cheetahs.
     Ld:b.13.73 (Eng:g.10.73, g.8.74, 2-g.9.74, 3-g.10.74, b.8.74, b.10.74)

425. Let me see, why couldn't they play cards on the ark?
     Because Noah sat on the deck.
     SF:b.9.74

426. Why can't candy be mean?
     Because it's sweet.
     SD:b.10.75

427. Why do birds fly south?
     Because it's too far to walk.
     L:b.8.74 (Eng:2-b.8.74, b.10.74)

428. Why do birds fly to the south in the winter?
     Well they have to have a holiday sometine.
     L:b.9.74

429. Why would a compliment from a chicken be an insult?
     Because it would be fowl language.
     SD:b.12.75

430. Why do white sheep eat more than black sheep?
     Cause there's more white sheep than black.
     L:g.11.75

431. Why do we have coke?
     Because we like jokes.
     SD:g.8.75

432. Why do witches use broomsticks?
Because vacuum cleaners are too heavy.

Ld:g.9.73 (Eng:g.10.73, g.12.73)

433. Why does a duck walk softly?
Because it doesn't know to walk slow.

SF:g.11.74

434. Why does a cherry go in a Shirley Temple?
Cause it wants to go on the ice when it's real cold.

(Shirley Temple = non-alcoholic drink served to children. Contains soda, cherry & orange slice)
SD:g.7.75

435. Why does a traffic warden have a yellow band around her head?
So nobody can park a car on her.

L:b.11.75

436. Why does a monkey have hairs?
Because it was hairy.

L:b.8.74

437. Why does Smoky the Bear wear a forest ranger's hat?
Cause he just ate one, ate a ranger.

SD:b.10.75

438. There's these 3 schoolgirls walking out along the road, 3 fat schoolgirls, and only 1 had an umbrella. How do you think they didn't get wet?
Cause it wasn't raining.

Ld:b.8.73

439. Why did the blind chicken cross the road?
To get to the Bird's Eye factory.

Ld:g.13.73 (Eng:b.12.73, g.9.74)

440. Why did the chicken go across the road for?
To get its pension.
Do you get it? No? Neither did he.

Ld:b.13.73

441.   Why did the chicken cross the road?
       The eggs were smashing.

       (smashing = very good)
       L:b.9.74

442.   Why did the chicken cross the road?
       To get to the other side.

       Ld:g.10.73 (Eng:2-g.9.74, g.11.74)

443.   Why did the man cross the road?
       Cause he wanted to get to the other side.

       Ld:b.12.73

444.   Why did the dinosaur cross the road?
       Because there weren't any chickens.

       Ld:g.10.73

445.   Why did the man with one hand cross the road?
       To get to the second hand shop.

       L:b.8.74 (Eng:g.10.73, g.13.73, 3-g.10.74)

446.   What do you call a chicken that crosses a street, goes in the
       mud, and comes back?
       A dirty double-crosser.

       SD:b.12.75

447.   Why did Silly Billy take a ladder to school?
       Cause he wanted to go to high school.

       SD:g.8.75 (Eng:3-g.8.73)

448.   Why did the man take a drawing-pad and pencil to bed?
       So that he could draw the curtains.

       Ld:b.9.73 (Eng:2-g.8.73, b.10.73, g.8.74, g.9.74, g.10.74, b.11.75)

449.   Why did the man dip the pen in the sugar?
       He wanted to draw flies.

       SD:g.12.75

450.   Why did the man bring a ruler to bed?
       To see how long he slept.

       Ld:b.9.73 (Eng:g.9.73, g.8.74, b.11.75)

451. Why did the banana stop running?
Because it ran out of skin.

    L:g.10.74

452. Why did the rainbow have no rain?
Because it was thirsty.

    L:b.8.74 (Eng:b.8.74)

453. Why did the monster go to college?
Cause his extension cord was too short.

    SD:g.8.75

454. Why did King Kong climb the Empire State Building?
Cause he wanted to catch a plane.

    SD:b.9.75

455. Why did the monkey get his head stuck in the tree?
Because he wanted some bananas.

    L:b.8.74

456. Why did they have to change the water in the Olympic's pool?
Because Mark Spitz.

    SD:g.8.75

457. Why did the lady say she didn't have anything to do with the accident?
Because she didn't have a driver's license.

    SD:g.10.75

458. Why did the cow jump over the moon?
There was a short circuit in the milking machine.

    SD:b.12.75

459. Why didn't the skeleton jump off the cliff?
He had no guts.

    L:g.9.74 (Eng:g.9.74, 2-b.8.74, 2-b.10.74, US:g.8.75, b.10.75)

460. Why didn't the ape go with the parrot?
Because the parrot's a pretty boy and the ape is a ugly.

    L:b.8.74

461. Why was Cinderella dropped from the netball team?
     She ran away from the ball.

     Ld:g.12.73

462. Why do you go to bed?
     Because beds won't come to you.

     Ld:g.12.73

463. Why did the golfer wear two pairs of trousers?
     In case he got a hole in one.

     Ld:b.10.73 (Eng:b.10.73)

464. Why do zebra have stripes on them?
     To go to bed in.

     Ld:b.10.73

465. Why does Prince Charles wear red, white, and blue braces?
     To keep his trousers up.

     Ld:b.8.73 (Eng:g.11.75)

466. Why does a giraffe have such a long neck?
     Because he didn't want to smell his feet.

     Ld:g.8.73

467. Why do cows have bells round their necks?
     Because their horns don't work.

     Ld:b.10.73 (Eng:b.11.73)

468. Why did Eve never fear the measles?
     She already Adam.

     Ld:g.12.73 (Eng:g.9.73)

469. Why was the tomato embarrassed?
     He saw the salad dressing.

     OR:g.8.58

470. What did the mayonnaise say to the refrigerator?
     Shut the door, I'm dressing.

     SF:b.10.74

471. Why did the boy put a loaf of bread in his comic?
     Because he liked crummy jokes.

     Ld:b.10.73

472. Why did the boy throw the clock out of the window?
     See time fly.

     L:g.9.74 (Eng:g.10.73, g.10.74, g.11.75, US:g.8.58)

473. Why did Silly Billy tiptoe past the medicine cabinet?
     Cause he didn't want to wake the sleeping pills.

     SD:g.8.75 (US:g.8.58, Eng:b.7.73, g.11.75)

474. Why did Silly Billy take a hammer to bed?
     He wanted to hit the hay.

     SD:g.8.75

475. Why did the moron jump off the tall building?
     He wanted to make a smash on Broadway.

     OR:g.8.58

476. Why did the vicar go into the church with a machine-gun?
     To make all the people holy.

     Ld:b.12.73

477. Why did the vicar walk about on his hands?
     Because it was Palm Sunday.

     Ld:g.11.73

478. Why did Batman climb up a tree?
     Cause he wanted to get Robin out of his nest.

     Ld:b.8.73

479. Why did the 2 potatoes fight?
     They couldn't see eye to eye.

     Ld:g.12.73

480. Why did the owl 'owl?
     Because the woodpecker would peck her.

     Ld:g.12.73

481. Why did the sailor know there was a man in the moon?
     Because he went to sea.

     Ld:g.8.73

482.   There's a man in this house and he didn't have any hair and he
        went out and he looked out a window. Why do you think he
        went and looked out a window?
        To get some fresh air.

        Ld:b.9.73

483.   You know why a monkey stepped down a hole?
        Cause it lost its baby monkey.

        Ld:g.6.73

484.   Why did Cliff Richard die?
        He fell over his first name.

        (Cliff Richard = pop singer)
        Ld:g.11.73

485.   Why can't a cross-eyed teacher teach properly?
        He can't control his pupils.

        Ld:g.12.73

486.   Why can't a one-legged woman change a pound note?
        She's only got half a knicker.

        (knickers = panties)
        Ld:b.8.73

487.   Who wins the fight between a dog and a hedgehog?
        The hedgehog wins on points

        Ld:g.12.73

488.   A man coming down the road, and he saw these trees moving
        and he said, Who are you?
        And they said "Special Branch."

        Ld:b.8.73 (Eng:b.7.74)

489.   Who's the toughest pickle in Dodge City?
        Marshall Dill.

        (Marshal Dillon = from "Gunsmoke" TV western)
        SF:g.10.74

490.   If the king sits on gold, who sits on silver?
        The Lone Ranger.

        SD:g.10.75

491. Who wrote the cliff tragedy?
Eileen Dover.

(See 1074–1092)
Ld:g.11.73 (Eng.b.10.74)

492. Which is the fastest person at running?
Adam because he was the first in the human race.

Ld:g.9.73

493. If one snail was on the grass, and one snail was in a jar, which one would be singing "boy you're good"?
Neither one, snails can't sing.

SD:b.10.75

494. When do horses have 4 legs?
When its a cloth horse.

Ld:g.12.73

495. What horse can't you ride?
Clothes horse.

SF:g.10.74

496. If I was you and you was me, who would you be?
You.

L.b.8.74

497. When's a bus not a bus?
When it's a street.

SF:g.10.74 (Eng:g.8.73, b.11.75)

498. When is the best time to eat a door?
When it is jammed.

L:b.9.74

499. What's the only kind of jam you can't eat?
A traffic jam.

SD:b.11.75

500. When is a door not a door?
When it's a jar.

L:b.11.75

501.   When can 8 be more than 10?
        When you spell it.
        SD:b.10.75

502.   When does a frog jump the higher?
        In spring.
        L:b.10.74

503.   Shall I tell you about the rubbish bin?—
        Oh, I better not tell you because it is rubbish.
        Ld:g.10.73 (Eng:g.8.73, 2-b.9.74, b.10.74)

504.   Did you hear the joke abouh the dirty windows?
        No, you wouldn't see through them.
        L:g.10.74 (Eng:b.9.74)

505.   Do you know the joke about the butter?
        I better not tell you, you might spread it.
        Ld:g.9.73 (Eng:g.11.75)

506.   Shall I tell you the joke about the pencil?
        No, there no point.
        Ld:g.9.73 (Eng:g.8.73)

507.   Shall I tell you the joke about the oil?
        No, its too crude.
        Ld:g.9.73

508.   Shall I tell you the joke about the high wall?
        No, you will never get over it.
        Ld:g.9.73 (Eng:g.10.74)

509.   Have you heard the joke about the jump rope?
        Skip it.
        SD:g.11.75

510.   Did you hear the joke about the bed?
        It hasn't been made up yet.
        SD:g.11.75

511.   Do you want to hear a clean joke?
        I've just had a bath, bom bom.
        L:g.8.74

512. Do you want to know a dirty joke?
      Two boys fell in the mud, bom bom.

      L:g.9.74

513. Do you want to know a dirty rude joke?
      Two boys fell in the mud with no clothes on, bom bom.

      L:g.9.74

514. I'm going to tell you a dirty joke.
      The boy fell in the mud.

      L:b.11.75

515. Sure ya want to hear a dirty joke. You're sure ya wanna do?
      You're sure, you're really sure, you're positive. Okay, what's
      really dirty?
      Mud.

      SF:g.10.74

516. Want to hear a dirty joke?
      A pig took a bath.

      SF:b.10.74

517. Who killed the Osmond's?
      Crazy Horses.

      (famous single by Osmond's)
      Ld:b.12.73

518. What did Donny Osmond say when he fell of a cliff?
      Help me, help me, help me please.

      L:g.10.74 (Eng:b.13.73, 3-g.9.74, g.10.74)

519. What do you get if you mix Donny Osmond, Gary Glitter,
      and Chuck Berry?
      Do you want to touch my dingaling. Why, cause I love you.

      (Do you want to touch me = Gary Glitter, My dingaling = Chuck Berry,
      Why, cause I love you = Donny Osmond)
      Ld:b.13.73

520. How did Larry Grayson die?
      He went into a gas chamber and said, "Shut that door."

      (Larry Grayson = English TV comedian, catch phrase "Shut that door")
      Ld:g.10.73 (Eng:g.10.73, g.13.73)

521. How did Tommy Cooper die?
      "Just like that."

      Ld:g.13.73 (Eng.b.10.74)

522. What would you do if you saw Jesus in the street?
      Go up to him, give him a Bible, and say, this is your life.

      (This is your life = TV show – life of celebrity)
      Ld:b.12.73 (Eng:g.13.73)

523. What do you call a doctor and you don't know his name?
      Dr. Who.

      (Dr. Who = English science fiction TV show)
      L:b.8.74

524. Who is a robin and is he on telly?
      Robin Day.

      L:b.9.74

VI. KNOCK KNOCK JOKES

525. Knock, knock, who's there? Agnus. Agnus who?
      Agnus me coat up please.

      Ld:b.8.73

526. Knock, knock, who's there? Aim. Aim who?
      Aim at me if you dare.

      Ld:g.12.73

527. Knock, knock, who's there? Alisin. Alisin who?
      Alisten to the radio.

      Ld:g.10.73

528. Knock, knock, who's there? Amos. Amos who?
      A mosquito.
      Knock, knock, who's there? Anna. Anna who?
      Another mosquito.
      Knock, knock, who's there? Helen. Helen who?
      Hell, another mosquito.

      Ld:b.13.73 (Eng:b.13.74)

529. Knock, knock, who's there? Amos. Amos who?
A mosquito bit me.
Knock, knock, who's there? Andy. Andy who?
And he bit me again.

    SD:b.12.75 (US:g.7.75, 3-b.8.75, b.10.75, b.6.75)

530. Knock, knock, who's there? Amos. Amos who?
Amos why don't you stop knocking on my door.

    SD:g.8.75

531. Knock, knock, who's there? Arthur. Arthur who?
Arthur Apple.

    Ld:b.8.73

532. Knock, knock, who's there? Arthur. Arthur who?
Arthur Teacake.

    Ld:b.12.73

533. Knock, knock, who's there? Arthur. Arthur who?
Our thermometer is broken.

    SD:b.7.75

534. Knock, knock, who's there? Artichokes. Artichokes who?
Artichokes when he eats too fast.

    SD:g.10.75

535. Knock, knock, who's there? Avon. Avon who?
Avon calling, your bell's broken.

    (Avon = brand name of cosmetics, sold door to door)
    Ld:b.13.73 (Eng:b.8.73, b.9.73, b.13.73, g.11.75, US:g.11.61)

536. Knock, knock, who's there? Banana. Banana who?
Knock, knock, who's there? Banana. Banana who?
Knock, knock, who's there? Banana. Banana who?
Knock, knock, who's there? Orange. Orange who?
Orange ya glad I didn't say banana.

    SF:g.10.74 (US:g.9.75, b.8.73, g.6.75)

537. Knock, knock, who's there? Banana. Banana who?
Banana split.

    SD:g.12.75

538. Knock, knock, who's there? Betty. Betty who?
Betty Crocker, your cake's burned.
NJ:g.11.61

539. Knock, knock, who's there? Boo. Boo who?
Boo, don't laugh.
Ld:b.9.73

540. Knock, knock, who's there? Boo. Boo who?
Don't have to cry about it.
SD:g.10.75 (US:g.10.75, b.12.75)

541. Knock, knock, who's there? Cargo. Cargo who?
Car go beep beep.
SD:g.10.75

542. Knock, knock, who's there? Check. Check who?
Check book.
Ld:g.10.73

543. Knock, knock, who's there? Chine. Chine who?
Chinese.
Ld:g.10.73

544. Knock, knock, who's there? Cooh. Cooh who?
You said it.
L:g.9.74

545. Knock, knock, who's there? Cow's go. Cow's go who?
Cow's go moo.
L:g.11.75

546. Knock, knock, who's there? Despair. Despair who?
De spare tire is in the trunk.
SD:g.10.75

547. Knock, knock, who's there? Doctor. Doctor Who?
You peeped.
Ld:b.12.73 (Eng:3-g.8.73, g.10.73, g.13.73, 2-b.8.73, b.9.73, b.12.73, g.9.74, g.10.74, 2-b.10.74)

548. Knock, knock, who's there? Donald. Donald who?
Donald Duck.

    SD:b.9.75

549. Knock, knock, who's there? Dwain. Dwain who?
Dwain the bathtub, I'm drowning.

    SD:g.11.75 (US:g.10.75, g.11.75)

550. Knock, knock, who's there? Eggburt. Eggburt who?
Egg but no bacon.

    Ld:g.7.73 (Eng:g.10.73, 2-b.9.74)

551. Knock, knock, who's there? Either. Either who?
Either come in or come out.

    L:g.9.74

552. Knock, knock, who's there? Ether. Ether who?
Ether bunny.

    SD:g.6.75 (US:g.10.75)

553. Knock, knock, who's there? Father. Father who?
Father, dear Father.

    Ld:g.10.73

554. Knock, knock, who's there? Felix. Felix who?
Felix me lolly, I'll bash him.

    Ld:g.10.73

555. Knock, knock, who's there? Frankenstein Junior.
Frankenstein Junior who?
Will you please open the door, my foot's stuck in the door.

    SD:g.6.75

556. Knock, knock, who's there? Garnelie.

    L:b.10.74

557. Knock, knock, who's there: Go. Go who?
Go to bed.

    L:b.9.74

558. Knock, knock, who's there? Grendre little pussy cat, what you want a pint of milk, where you money, in my pocket, where I forgot it I you silly little pussy cat.

    L:b.10.74

559. Knock, knock, who's there? Himidge. Himidge who?
    Are you? (I'm a Jew)

    Ld:b.12.73 (Eng:b.12.73)

560. Jane: Knock, knock. Julie: who's there? Jane: I live in London's. Julie: I live in London's zoo. Ha, ha.

    Ld:g.10.73

561. Knock, knock, who's there? I-it. I-it who?
    I 'ate you.

    SD:b.8.75

562. Knock, knock, who's there? Ipoo. Ipoo who?
    Do you? (I poc)

    Ld:b.12.73

563. Knock, knock, who's there? Ipe, Ipe who? Do you really?

    Ld:g.9.73

564. Knock, knock, who's there? Ivan. Ivan who?
    I've an eye on you.

    SD:b.10.75

565. Knock, knock, who's there? Ivor. Ivor who?
    Ivor lot of money.

    Ld:g.9.73

566. Knock, knock, who's there? Kit. Kit who?
    You suck.

    Ld:b.9.73

567. Knock, knock, who's there? A lass. A lass who?
    A lass knocking.

    L:b.9.74

568. Knock, knock, who's there? Lass. Lass who?
    That's who.

    L:g.11.75

569. Knock, knock, who's there? Lean. Lean who?
Lean over and tie my shoes.

SD:b.10.75

570. Knock, knock, who's there? Lettuce. Lettuce who?
Let us in and you'll find out.

SD:g.10.75

571. Knock, knock, who's there? Lettuce. Lettuce who?
Let us sing.

SD:b.7.75

572. Knock, knock, who's there: Lidia. Lidia who.
Lidia your spins blow off.

Ld:g.13.73

573. Knock, knock, who's there? Like. Like who?
Like you.

L:b.10.74 (Eng:b.9.74, b.10.74)

574. Knock, knock, who's there? A little boy who can't
reach the doorbell.

Ld:g.9.73 (Eng:b.13.73)

575. Knock, knock, who's there? Little old lady. Little old lady
who?
I didn't know you could yodel.

SD:b.10.75 (US:b.7.75, g.9.75, g.9.75)

576. Knock, knock, who's there? Mark. Mark who?
Mark, Mark, a dog with teeth in.

Ld:b.8.73

577. Knock, knock, who's there? Marmite. Marmite who?
Marmite smack you if you tell lies.

(Marmite = yeast extract spread on toast)
Ld:g.10.73 (Eng:g.10.73)

578. Knock, knock, who's there? Medame. Medame who?
Me damn foot's caught in the door.

SF:g.10.74 (US:g.12.75, g.11.75)

579. Knock, knock, who's there? Michael. Michael who?
Michael othes are dry. (My clothes are dry)
Ld:b.13.73

580. Knock, knock, who's there? Micky. Micky who?
Micky Mouse.
SD:b.9.75

581. Knock, knock, who's there? Micky. Micky who?
Micky Mouse's underwear.
SF:g.10.74

582. Knock, knock, who's there? Molasses. Molasses who?
Me glasses is dirty.
SD:g.10.75

583. Knock, knock, who's there? Nickolas. Nickolas who?
Nickolas girls must not climb trees.
Ld:b.13.73 (Eng:g.8.73)

584. Knock, knock, who's there? Nickolas. Nickolas who?
Nickolas girls shouldn't ride bicycles.
Ld:g.8.73

585. Knock, knock who's there? Official. Official who?
Official will do if you haven't any chips.
Ld:b.12.73

586. Knock, knock, who's there? Olive. Olive who?
I love you.
SD:b.9.75 (US:b.10.75, g.6.75)

587. Knock, knock, who's there? Oliver. Oliver who?
I'll leave you alone if you leave me alone.
SD:b.6.75

588. Knock, knock, who's there? Oorer. Oorer who?
Our you cassers.
L:g.9.74

589. Knock, knock, who's there? Orson. Orson who?
'orse and wagon.
SD:g.10.75

590. Knock, knock, who's there? Perry. Perry who?
Periscope.

SD:g.10.75

591. Knock, knock, who's there? Ronald. Ronald who?
Ronald McDonald.

(Ronald McDonald = clown advertising for McDonald's hamburger)
SD:b.9.75

592. Knock, knock, who's there? Santa. Santa who?
Don't ya know him?

SF:b.11.74

593. Knock, knock, who's there? Senior. Senior who?
Seeing you're so nosy, I won't tell you.

Ld:b.12.73

594. Knock, knock, who's there? Sherlock. Sherlock who?
Sherlock Shoelicker.

SD:b.6.75

595. Knock, knock, who's there? Sofa. Sofa who?
Sofa you're glad I'm here.

SD:g.11.75

596. Knock, knock, who's there? Stop. Stop who?
Stop that man.

L:b.9.74

597. Knock, knock, who's there? Terrain. Terrain who?
Trains coming, close the window.

SD:g.10.75

598. Knock, knock, who's there? Tic. Tic who?
Tic 'em up, I'm a tongue tied robber.

Ld:b.9.73

599. Knock, knock, who's there? Titan. Titan who?
Tit in your bell.

SD:g.10.75

600. Knock, knock, who's there? Tomato. Tomato who?
Tomato shoe.

SD:b.7.75

601.   Knock, knock, who's there? Uncle. Uncle who?
        Knock, knock, who's there? Aunty. Aunty who?
        Aren't you glad I didn't say Uncle.

        Ld:b.13.74

602.   Knock, knock, who's there? Winnie the. Winnie the Who?
        Winnie the Pooh, not who.

        SD:g.10.75

603.   Knock, knock, who's there? Who. Who who?
        You do.

        Ld:b.8.73

604.   Knock, knock, who's thereou who. You who who?

        L:b.11.75

605.   Knock, knock, who's there. Youdland. Youdland who?
        Stop youdlaying and I'll tell you.

        Ld:b.8.73

VII. WELLERISMS

606.   What did the big candle say to the little candle?
        I'm going out tonight.

        Ld:b.10.73 (Eng:b.8.73, b.10.73, b.11.73, 3-g.10.73)

607.   What did the big chimney say to the little chimney?
        You're too young to smoke.

        Ld:b.11.73 (Eng: 2-b.8.73, 3-b.10.73, 2-b.11.73, 3-g.8.73, 8-g.10.73,
        b.7.74, 2-b.9.74, b.10.74, 3-g.8.74, 4-g.9.74, 7-g.10.74, g.11.74)

608.   What did the big train say to the little train?
        You're too young to smoke.

        L:g.7.74

609.   What did the big telephone say to the little telephone?
        You're too young to be engaged.

        Ld:g.10.73 (Eng:2-b.8.73, 2-g.8.73, g.9.73, 4-g.10.73, b.9.74, b.10.74, 2-
        g.7.74, g.8.74, 4-g.9.74, 7-g.10.74, 2-g.11.74)

610. What did the ten-p say to the half-p?
You're too young to be in the shops.

(p = pence – British currency)
Ld:b.8.73

611. What did the big pencil say to the little pencil?
You're too young to draw.

L:b.8.74

612. What did the big saw say to the little saw?
Have you cleaned your teeth today?

L:g.8.74

613. What did the big shoe say to the little shoe?
You're too young to walk.

L:g.8.74

614. What did one slice of toast say to the other slice of toast?
I'm browned off.

L:g.10.74

615. What did one pot say to the other pot?
How is stew doing?

SF:b.11.74

616. What did the big firecracker say to the little firecracker?
My boom is bigger than yours.

SD:g.11.75

617. What did one earthquake say to the other?
It was all your fault.

SD:b.12.75

618. Two biscuits walking across the road. One got run over.
What did the other one say?
O crumbs.

Ld:b.10.73,(Eng:b.8.73,g.8.73, 5-g.10.73, b.10.74, g.7.74, g.9.74, 2-g.10.74)

619. Two oranges were walking down the road. One stopped.
The other one said, "what's up", and the other one said, "I've
run out of juice".

Ld:g.10.73 (Eng:b.8.73, 2-b.10.73, 2-b.12.73, g.6.73, 3-g.8.73, 2-g.10.73, g.13.73, b.8.74, b.10.74, g.8.74, 2-g.9.74, 2-g.10.74)

620. There was 2 tomatoes in a desert and they're going to play cowboys and Indians. Who were the cowboys?
None of them, they were both redskins.

Ld:b.13.73 (Eng:b.10.73, b.11.73)

621. One day, two eggs was walking on the pavement and one got run over by a scooter and a boy came along and he laugh. And the other one said, "shut up, it's no yoke."

L:b.10.74 (Eng:b.10.74)

VIII. DOCTOR DOCTOR JOKES

622. A man went to the doctor and said, I feel like a bell.
And the doctor said take these pills and if you don't get any better give me a ring.

L:g.9.74 (Eng:b.10.73, g.10.73, g.13.73, b.11.75)

623. Patient: Doctor, I feel like a telephone.
Doctor: Well sit down and don't be alarmed.

Ld:g.9.73

624. There was this man, and he went to the doctors and he said Doctor, I think I am a packet of biscuits. So the doctor says 'them square ones' and he says yeah, he say, 'and they've got little letters', and he says yeah, and he says, 'you must be crackers.'

Ld:g.13.73

625. Patient: Doctor, my brother thinks he's a chicken.
Doctor: Why didn't you tell me sooner?
Patient: We needed the eggs.

SD:b.12.75

626. This man went to the doctor and says, doctor, doctor, I think I'm a pair of curtains. And he says, ah, come off it man, pull yourself together.

Ld:g.13.73 (Eng:b.7.73, b.9.73, b.12.73, 2-g.10.73, g.12.73, g.10.74)

627. This coloured man goes to doctor's cause he's got diarrhea, and he says doctor doctor, I'm melting.
Ld:b.12.73

628. Doctor, doctor, I think I'm a dog.
Get down, get down.
Ld:b.12.73

629. Doctor, doctor, I feel like a dog. When did you start having this?
When I was a puppy.
Ld:b.9.73

630. Doctor, doctor, I only have 59 seconds to live.
Wait a minute.
Ld:b.12.73 (Eng:2-b.9.73, g.9.73, b.11.75)

631. There[1]s this man, he went to doctors, and doctor said, have you flu? and he said no, I walked in.
Ld:b.7.73 (Eng:b.9.73)

632. Doctor, doctor, I keep thinking I'm a bird. He says right, come back next day. So he comes back next day.
He says, how did you get here? I've just flown in.
Ld:b.12.73

633. Doctor, doctor, can you help me out?
Sure, what way did you come in?
Ld:b.12.73

634. This man goes into doctors and says, doctor, doctor, people ignore me, so he said, next please.
Ld:b.12.73 (Eng:b.10.74, 2-b.11.75)

635. Doctor, doctor, everybody says I'm invisible.
Who said that?
Ld:b.9.73 (Eng:b.9.73, b.12.73, b.13.73, b.11.74, g.11.75)

636. This fellow goes to the doctor and says, doctor, doctor, everybody thinks I'm a liar, so he says, next, no, I don't believe you.
Ld:b.13.73

637. There's this fellow comes rushing at his doctor's and he says, doctor, doctor, I dreamt I've eaten a giant marshmallow last night. And he says, so what? And he says, when I woke up my pillow had gone.

    Ld:b.12.73 (US:g.11.75)

638. A man went to the doctor and said, Doctor, doctor, I think I'm a spoon, and the doctor said, sit down and don't stir.

    Ld:g.10.73 (Eng:g.8.73, b.12.73)

639. Doctor, doctor, I feel very weak.
    Well, just take these pills and you'll feel better.
    So he comes back the next week and he says, Doctor, doctor, I still feel weak, I can't get the cork out.

    L:b.11.75 (Eng:g.10.73)

640. A man went to the doctor, he was knocking his head on the wall. The doctor said, why are you knocking your head on the wall? Because when I leave off it is a lovely feeling.

    L:g.10.74

641. Patient: Doctor, doctor, I keep thinking there's two of me.
    Doctor: One at a time please

    L:b.11.74

642. There's this man, and he had a thing over his head, and he said, Doctor ah doctor, I feel like a bridge.
    And he said, what's come over you man?
    He said, 2 cars, a lorry, and a bus.

    L:b.11.75 (Eng:b.11.75)

643. Doctor, doctor, I feel like a race horse.
    Doctor: Take one of these pills, then breath furlong.

    L:b.11.75

644. Doctor, doctor, I feel like a toilet.
    You were looking a bit flush.

    L:b.11.75

IX. TRICKS, CATCHES

645. There's this king and a castle. Here's the castle, that, and then
      he's got this path, and he's got this pool. Alright, and he goes
      along, and goes into the pool and has a swim, and all of a
      sudden, he says, ah, no, I've lost my key. Where's the key?

      Ld:b.12.73

646. This is an idiot test. What is it? Well, it's 2 Mexicans on bikes,
      doing no handing, and one's going to the butchers.

      Ld:b.12.73

647. What's that? A Spanishman cooking an egg (also a Mexican,
      with his hat, 2 arms, cooking the egg)

      Ld:b.12.73

648. What's that? A giraffe going by a window.

      Ld:b.12.73 (US:g.11.61)

649. What's this? A bear going up the tree, on the other side.

      NJ:g.11.61

650. What's this? A snake who has swallowed an elephant.

      NJ:g.11.61

651. Idiot test: There's a diesal going that way, and a diesal going
      that way.   Now, which way would the
      smoke blow, That way (left), that way (right), or that way
      (up)? No, diesals don't have smoke.

      Ld:b.12.73

652. Idiot test: There's a pond, in the middle of it there's a dead
      frog. How can the frog get across, without getting itself wet?
      It's dead, doesn't need to.

      Ld:b.12.73

653. How can you draw 2 separate lines without lifting up the
      pencil? (from the paper)

Fold the corner of the paper over, draw across the fold touching the paper on both sides of the folded piece, then unfold it, and you have 2 separate lines.

Ld:g.12.73

654. Trick: Clap hands, cross arms, if right arm on bottom, hold nose, while left holds ear. Then clap again, arms cross opposite way, left hand holds nose, and right hand holds ear.

Ld:b.13.73

655. I know what you're going to say next? What? You said it.

Ld:b.13.73 (US:g.11.61)

656. I can turn you into an Indian? How?

Ld:g.12.73 (US:b.10.75)

657. There were 6 kings, whose names were George. Name the rest.

Ld:g.12.73

658. A boy said to another boy, I know a man with a wooden leg called Smith. And the other boy said what's the other one called?

Ld:g.8.73

659. There were two donkeys walking across the road. One called 'Say it again' and one called 'Bob.' Bob got lost, who weren't lost? Say it again. There were these two, etc.

Ld:b.10.73

660. There were three horses in the field. One called Parden, one called Parden Parden, and one called Parden Parden Parden. Parden Parden Parden died, Parden Parden ran away. Who was left? Parden.

Ld:b.8.73 (teller repeats)

661. If Pete and Repeat went out in a boat, and Pete fell over, who'd be left? Repeat.
If Pete and Repeat went out in a boat . . .

SD:g.6.75

662. Hit me (hit). What did I say? Hit me. (hit back)

Ld:g.12.73

663. Hit me, I won't hit you back. (hit). But, I'll hit your front.

Ld:b.13.73

664. There was this sweet all crushed up on the road, so the person I am telling the joke to, they say 'I one it, I two it, I three it, I four it, I five it, I six it, I seven it, I ate it!' And I say do you get it and they say yes, I do. You eat it.

(sweet = candy)
Ld:g.9.73

665. Do you lie? No. You do, you lie in a bed.

Ld:g.8.73

666. Piece of paper, who has a small hand, place it on the paper. Two X's one on each side of hand, near wrist, on paper. That's the school, that's the house. So the boy goes to school, goes all the way round there (drawing around fingers) and there he forgot his homework, so he goes back, and then back, and he keeps forgetting things (still draw around fingers) and then he goes, oh, I got an idea, I can just do that (take pen and draw across top of hand from X to X), take a shortcut.

Ld:b.12.73

667. On top of hand draw two X's, one as far apart from other as possible. One's his school, one's his home. So he says right, anyway, he starts from home and goes to there (school, with pen, draw from one X to other). I forgot me bag (draw back to home X), so he goes back, and back again. and he keeps going like this until he's got pen all over.

Ld:b.12.73

668. Take 1 pence, press it on other's forehead, even lick it to stick, release pressure, and remove coin, but pretend it's still there and tell person to knock back of his head to knock it off — tell them to keep knocking harder, until they realize it isn't there.

Ld:b.12.73

669. Take a coin, say you're going to do a trick. Take coin, and draw around it with a pencil on a piece of paper, about 5 circles. Tell person to take coin, place it on edge of his forehead, and lst it roll down his nose and try to make it fall in one of the circles. Keeps doing it. Actually the coin is leaving a black mark on his face from the pencil residue. If he can't do it after several tries, start again with new circles, until he catches on, or the laughter from the audience makes him suspect something.

NJ:g.11.61 (see joke No. 672)

670. I can make a match burn twice. How?
Light it, that's once, blow it out, and immediately touch the other person with it. Ouch. See, I told you I could make a match burn twice.

NJ:g.11.61

671. Which would you rather be: a faucet, a tree, or an acorn?
Faucet — you drip!
Tree — You sap!
Acorn — You nut!

OR:g.8.58

672. Trick of drawing around a 10 pence coin with a pencil, and person then must roll the coin down his forehead and nose, on it's edge, trying to drop it in the circle. Where ever it drops, you draw another circle, so he has a better chance of dropping the coin into a circle. Each time, the coin gets more pencil residue on it, and it leaves a black line on the person's face. Quit when he succeeds, or he gives up or people are laughing too much.

Ld:g.12.73 (see joke No. 669)

673. Niners: everytime, when reading out loud, a book or anything, any word beginning with 'w' that is said, you hit the person 9 times, unless he says safties.

Ld:b.12.73

674. Constantinople is a big word. Can you spell it?
     I – T.

     NJ:g.11.61

675. While Washington's wife went to Washington, Washington's washwoman washed Washington's woolies. How many "W's" in all?
     None, in A-L-L, all.

     SD:b.12.75

676. What words are on all US bills?
     The United States of America

     (bills = paper money)
     NJ:g.11.61

677. When a plane crashed on the border between Canada and the United States, which side were the survivors buried?
     Neither, survivors aren't buried.

     NJ:g.11.61

678. If you were in a pitch black cold room with a gas lamp, a fire place, and a gas stove, which would you light first?
     A match.

     NJ:g.11.61

679. Which weighs more, a ton of lead, or a ton of feathers?

     NJ:g.11.61

680. There was 10 copycats sitting on a wall. One jump off. How many were left? None, because they were all copycats.

     L:g.8.74 (Eng:b.9.73, g.10.73)

681. If there's 6 birds sitting on a fence, and a man comes up and shoots one, how many are left?
     Zero, none, cause once you shoot one the rest fly away.

     SD:g.7.75

682. Margie lives on the 12th floor of a super high-rise apartment. Whenever she's alone she presses the button for the 6th floor,

and then she gets out at the 6th floor and walks up the next 6 flights of stairs. She would much rather ride the elevator all the way up but she doesn't, why? Cause she's too small to reach the 12th floor button.

SD:b.12.75 (US:g.11.61)

683. There's this little boy, he got caught inside an elephant. How do you think he got out?
He ran around until he got pooped out.

SD:g.11.75

684. If you were put in jail, and all you had was a mattress with springs in it, and a calendar with dates on it, how would you survive?
You'd eat the dates off the calendar and drink the water out of the springs.

SD:b.12.75

685. If you're out and then came back to your house and there was no way in, how'd you get in?
Run around the house until you're all in.

SD:b.12.75

686. There's this man, he's in a room, there's no windows, no chimney, no door, nothing but a table and so, he got his hand and chopped the table in half. Two halves make a whole, he crept through the hole, and he shouted down the hole, made a horse (hoarse) got on horse, and galloped off.

L:b.11.75

687. There was this man in one room, without any windows, anything inside except one door, and a piano. So he thought how am I going to get out. And then he thought well I know. So he took all the keys out of the piano, and tried them in the lock and he opened it.

L:g.11.75

X. ELEPHANT JOKES

688. How can you tell when an elephant has been in the fridge?
By the foot prints in the butter.

Ld:b.10.73 (Eng:g.12.73; US:g.12.62)

689. How do you know when there's two elephants in your fridge?
You can't shut the door.

Ld:g.13.73.

690. How do you know when an elephant's in your bed?
Cause he's got an E on his pyjamas

Ld:b.8.73

691. How do you tell an elephant's in bed with you?
You can smell the peanuts on his breath

NJ:g.12.62

692. How do you know when an elephant's sitting on your shoulder?
When his ears are flapping

Ld:g.13.73

693. How do you put 4 elephants in a Volkswagen?
Two in the front and two in the back.

NJ:g.12.62

694. How do you put 4 giraffes in a Volkswagen?
Take the elephants out first.

NJ:g.12.62

695. Why does the elephant paint his toenails red?
So he can hide in the cherry trees.

CO:g.13.62

696. Why do elephants have flat feet?
From jumping out of palm trees.

IN:g.8.62

697. Why do ducks have flat feet?
From stamping out forest fires.

Why do elephants have flat feet?
From stamping out burning ducks.

IN:g.8.62

698. What did Tarzan say when he saw a herd of elephants coming over the hill?
Here come the elephants.

What did Jane say when she saw the elephants coming over the hill?
Here come the grapes, she was color blind.

NJ:g.12.62

699. What do you do if you have a herd of elephants charging at you?
Make a trunk call and reverse the charge.

Ld:b.12.73

700. What do you do when an elephant's charging?
Take away his credit card.

SD:b.11.75

701. What do you call an elephant with big ears?
Jumbo the elephant.

L:b.8.74

702. Why does the elephant wear green sneakers?
To hide on the billiard table.

(sneakers = tennis shoes = gym shoes)
NJ:g.12.62

703. Why does the elephant wear green sneakers?
To hide in the grass.

NJ:g.12.62

704. Why does the elephant wear pink sneakers?
Because his blue ones are in the wash.

NJ:g.12.62

705. Why did the elephant take a key with him?
To open his trunk.

L:b.10.74

706. What's grey, has four legs, and a trunk?
An elephant going on vacation.

NJ:g.12.62

707. What's brown, has four legs, and a trunk?
An elephant returning from vacation.

NJ:g.12.62

708. What's grey, has four legs, and a trunk?
A mouse going on vacation.

NJ:g.12.62 (US:2-g.10.75, g.12.75)

709. How do you shoot a blue elephant?
With a blue elephant shooter.

NJ:g.12.62

710. How do you shoot a pink elephant?
With a pink elephant shooter?
No, you hold his nose until he turns blue, and then you shoot
him with a blue elephant shooter.

NJ:g.12.62

711. Why does the elephant lay on his back with his feet in the air?
To trip birds.

CO:g.13.62

712. Why does the elephant have a curly tail?
So he can wrap it around daisies and hang over cliffs.

CO:g.13.62

713. When do elephant's have 16 feet?
When there are four of them

SF:g.10.74

714. What's the time when an elephant sits on a fence?
Time to buy a new one.

L:g.11.75 (US:g.8.75)

715. What's a cross between a prostitute and an elephant?
A 2-ton hooker, that will do it for peanuts and never forget you.

SD:g.12.75

716. What's the difference between an elephant and a biscuit?
You can't put an elephant in a cup of tea.

L:g.10.74 (Eng:b.8.73)

717. Two elephants fell off a cliff: boom boom.

L:g.10.74 (Eng:b.10.74, b.11.74, g.8.74, g.10.74, g.11.75)

XI. ETHNIC RIDDLES

718. How do you kill a Jew?
Roll a penny under the bus

Ld:g.12.73 (Eng:b.13.73)

719. How do you get a Jew mad?
You put him in a round room and tell him there's a penny in the corner.

Ld:g.12.73 (Eng:b.12.73) (See Polish joke No. 771, Irish joke No. 732)

720. How can you tell a Jew's house?
Bog rolls up on the washing line.

(Bog rolls = toilet paper; bog = toilet)
Ld:b.12.73 (Eng:b.13.73)

721. How can you tell a Jew's garden from another?
There's a padlock on the dustbin.

Ld:b.13.73 (Eng:b.13.73)

722. How can you tell a Jew's house from another?
There's a parking meter on the chimney on Christmas.

Ld:b.12.73

723. How do you get a Jew in a telephone?
Throw a ha'penny in.
How do you get him out?
Shout gas.

Ld:b.12.73

724. Why are Jewish synagogues round?
So the Jews can't hide in the corner when the collection
coming round.

Ld:b.12.73 (Eng:b.13.74)

725. How can you tell a Jew's house?
Fork in the sugarbowl

Ld:b.12.73

726. The biggest book in the world is the Jewish book of savings.

Ld:b.12.73

727. What did the Jewish Father Christmas say to the little boy?
Do you want to buy a toy?

L:b.10.74 (Eng:b.10.74)

728. It's about what do you call a half-Irishman who has big hob-
nailed shoes on, a studded jacket, and a machine gun? What?
Sir.

Ld:b.13.73

729. What does it say on the bottom of a Guinness bottle?
Open other end.

Ld:b.13.73

730. Why did Irishman drive a 2-ton truck over edge of cliff?
To test his air brakes.

Ld:b.12.73 (US:g.9.55-moron) See Polish joke No. 772

731. How do you aggravate an Irishman?
Put him in a barrel and see if he can find the four corners.

Ld:b.12.73

732. How do you confuse an Irishman?
Put him in a round room and ask him to stand in the corner.

L:b.11.75 See Joke No. 719, and No. 771

733. How do you confuse an Irishman?
First, put out three shovels, and ask him to take his pick.

L:g.11.75 (Eng:g.11.75, b.13.74)

734. How do you brainwash an Irishman?
Put water in his Wellingtons.

(Wellingtons = black shiny rubber boots, waterproof, usually worn by the Irish)
Ld:b.13.73 (Eng:b.11.74)

735. How many Irishmen do you need to paint?
One to hold the ladder, one to hold the paint, and a hundred to move the wall up and down.

Ld:b.10.73

736. How many Irishmen does it take to clean a top floor skyscrapper?
One to hold the ladder, one to wash the window.
How many Irishmen does it take to clean bottom floor window of a skyscrapper?
One to hold the ladder, one to wash the window, and one to dig the hole.

L:b.11.74

737. It takes a 100 Irishmen to screw into a wall. One to hold the screw, one to hold the screw driver, and 98 to turn the wall.

Ld:b.13.74

738. What do you do when a pin hits you?
Look for an Irishman holding a grenade.

Ld:b.10.73

739. Have you heard of the Irishman that wanted to be buried at sea?
Six men drowned trying to dig his grave.

L:b.11.74

740. How do you get an Irishman on the roof?
Tell him the beer is on the house.

L:b.10.74 (Eng:b.10.74)

741. Where do Chinese people bury Irishmen who die in China?
In the paddy fields.

L:b.11.75

742. What are the 3 shortest books in the world?
Well the first one is the Italian book of heroes, the second one
the Biafran cook book, and the third one is the Irish book of
knowledge.

Ld:b.13.73

743. What do you call some Irishmen sliding down a hill on tin
tray?
Anavylanche (an avalanche)

Ld:g.10.73

744. There's a boy in a classroom and a teacher comes up and says,
Mark, how far is Africa?
He says, well, it can't be far away cause he goes home to his
dinner.

Ld:g.13.73

745. Who's the founder of Poland?
The Rotor Rooter Man

(Rotor Rooter = company that cleans blocked drains and sewers)
SF:b.11.75

746. Why is a Polish dog afraid to walk in the woods?
He's afraid the trees will pee on him.

SF:b.11.74

747. Why did the Polacks lose the war?
The French walked in Backwards in their fort and they
thought they were leaving.

SF:b.11.74

748. If there's a bunch of motorcycles going down the road, which
one can you tell the polack is?
The one with training wheels.

SF:b.11.74

749. How does a Polack clean the water out from the bottom of his boat?
Puts a hole in the bottom of the boat.

SF:b.11.74

750. Why does a Polack carry a piece of shit in his pocket?
Identification

SD:b.14.71

751. Why does a Polack carry a piece of shit in his pocket?
Spare parts.

SD:b.14.71

752. Why does a Polack carry a piece of shit in his pocket?
Two heads are better than one.

(head = toilet)
SD:b.14.71

753. How does a Polack take a shower?
Spits in the fan.

SD:b.10.75

754. How does a Polack take a shower?
He pees in the wind.

SD:b.9.75

755. Well, there's 3 houses, each one of them has a sewer in front. How can you tell which one the Polack lives in?
Cause there's a diving board in front of the sewer.

SD:b.12.75

756. How come the Polack stapled his balls together?
Because if ya can't lick them, join them

SD:g.9.75

757. How do you tell when a Polack lady is having her period?
When she only has one sock on.

SD:g.11.75

758. What kind of airplane has hair under it's wings?
Polack Airplane

SD:b.9.75

759. How do you sink a Polack's boat?
    Put it in the water.
    SD:b.11.75

760. What's the Polack's national bird?
    They don't have one, it crashed.
    SD:b.11.75

761. How does a Polack scratch his elbow?
    First he scratches the wall, then he puts his elbow to the wall.
    SD:g.11.75

762. The Polack Test: (I need somebody else to help me.) Repeat
    after me. Red — red. Blue — blue. Blue — blue. Blue — blue.
    Red — red. Red — red. Blue — blue. What color is the sky?
    Blue. You're a Polack, you didn't repeat after me.
    SD:b.11.75

763. Did you hear about the Polish national fish?
    It drowned.
    SD:b.11.75

764. How do you break up a Polish party?
    Flush the punch bowl.
    SD:b.10.75

765. What happened when the Polack shot an arrow in the sky?
    He missed.
    SD:b.10.75

766. When Polacks put their shoes on, they have these initials on
    the front of them, TIF. What do they stand for?
    Toes in First.
    SD:b.9.75

767. Why do Polack's have green hair?
    Cause this: (answer is a gesture. Bring flat hand, palm toward
    face, from nose upward to hair.)
    SD:b.9.75

768. How did the Polack get 43 holes in his head?
    Learning how to eat with a fork.
    SD:b.10.75

769. Why did the Polack stick a knife up his butt?
He wanted to cut a fart.

SD:b.9.75

770. Why did the Jew Polacks bust all the windows?
Cause they wanted to go window shopping.

SD:b.11.75

771. How do you drive a Polack crazy?
Put him in a round room and tell him to pee in the corner.

SD:b.12.75 (US:b.10.75) See Joke No. 719 & No. 732

772. Why did the Polack run his car off the cliff?
Because he wanted to try out his new air brakes.

SD:g.8.75 (See joke No. 730)

XII. ETHNIC JOKES – IRISH

773. There these 2 Irishmen, and they are both drunk, just come
out of a pub, and they see this, you know, they see this bag of
apples on this tray, and they go oh, we'll get them, and they
pinch them and take them down to the cemetary and between
2 gravestones and they're going, one for me, one for you, one
for me, one for you, and anyway this fellow comes along and
he hears this one for me, one for you and he thinks its God and
the Devil sharing out the dead. Anyway, he's in hysterics, and
he's going afff (shout, scream) you know, and he runs down
to this policeman, a cop, anyway, when he tells him about
them, when they're coming up, they're both scared, you
know, shivering, anyway, when they're coming up, they're
still going one for you, one for me, one for you, one for me,
anyway, they go right, we're finished, but then he goes, ah,
but don't forget the two outside. They're in hysterics.

Ld:b.12.73 (Eng:b.8.73)

774. There's this Irish fellow driving down the motorway
100mph, and the motorway police were standing behind a
poster, a big poster, for advertisments. And he sees this Irish

fellow going 100mph down the motorway so he comes out, with his siren on, and he stops him and he gets out, and it's going on for 12.00 midnight, and he says, uh, will you get out and take a breathe analyser please. And he says no. And so he's shocked with this and he says will you get and take a breathe analyser please. So he says no. So he puts down his dummy address and enters the car. And he's in car and he said do you plead guilty and so he says no. He says will you stand down from the car please and walk along the white line. And he says no. So he says why not? Cause I'm drunk.

Ld:b.13.73

775. This Irishman, and he's drunk, and he's driving down this road, about 120mph, reving his car (make noise of rev) anyway, this copper pulls him off and he says, will you blow into this bag sir, and the drunken Irishman goes why, are your chips cold?

(Chips = french fries)
Ld:b.12.73

776. There's this Irish woman and her husband and they're wanting a drink, so she says, Samos, go get a point of bitter and we'll share it out. So she gives him a jug, and he puts on his hat that got a hole there and hole on the inside, trilby, and he's walking down and he drops the jug, and it smashes. Bother, I can't be bothered to walk up there for another jug. I'll go get it in me hat. So he walks in the pub — a pint of bitter please. So, he says where are you going to put it? Oh, in me hat, and so, he turns it that way (upside down, fill inside) filling it up inside it from the tap, and there's a bit left and he says where do you want this bit put and then he turns it over and says put it in there (in dent in the top) and he says oops, I've blown it, oops, look what I've done.

Ld:b.12.73

777. There was this Irish, there was this man and his wife was watching him all night, and she saw everytime she went to bed he was drinking out of a bottle of whiskey you see so uh, so the next night, cause he always went past the graveyard on a bike, on his bike, you see, so so his wife dressed up as the

devil, you see, and when came back, uh, pass the graveyard, his wife jumped out at him and he said, I haven't got it in me, I haven't got it in me, me wife.

Ld:g.6.73

778. An Irishman came back to London, after being in Ireland for four years. He went into a shoemenders, where he remembered giving in his Wellington boot for repair. He asked for them back. The shoemender said, 'come back next week, they will be ready then!'

L:b.11.74 (Eng:b.12.73)

779. There's this Irishman and he comes in doctors and he's got that many bandages on his feet, he's about 8 feet. And he says doctor, can you help me, so he says, yeah, if you tell me what's wrong. So he says well, yesterday, I went to supermarket and I bought a tin of treacle pudding and it said, pierce hole in tin and stand in boiling water for 20 minutes.

Ld:b.12.73

780. There were two Irishmen down a pit. One said to the other, it's dark down here. The other said, I don't know, I can't see.

Ld'g.11.73

781. There's a joke about an Irish lumberjack. There's this Irish lumberjack he went over to Canada to do some lumberjacking. And he went up to the boss, and he says, uh, can I, can I get a job please? And he says, and the boss says, yeah, sure. And he says, I'll have the trial tomorrow. So next day comes, and he says, all right, start there, show me later, when you finish. He says, my top men do about 50, 60, 60 trees a day. And he goes, and afterwards he does some trees, and he says, how many did you do Paddy? And Paddy goes two. And he says two, oh, we'll have to try it once more, and if you can't do it again, you'll, you're going to be in bother, cause ya bought all this gear and that, and so the next day comes and he goes and the Paddy goes up to the boss and he says, can I have another go, and the boss goes okay. So he goes into the forest, and cuts down some more trees. He says, how

many did you do today Paddy? And he goes three. He says
three. He says, you got the sack, you can't do it. And he says,
how about all my equipment? He says, can I sell it back to the
shop? He says probably. So he goes back to the shop and he
says I only used it for two days, so its probably clean. He says
okay, says the shopman. So he gave it to the shopman, and
then suddenly he heard, broomm (machine noise). He says,
what's that? And it was the electric saw, he'd only been using
it by hand.

L:b.11.75

782. My joke is about an Irishman as well. He goes to the show and
there's a ventriloquist on, you know, and then he starts to
telling jokes about all different people, all religions and
everything. He says, well, someone said now lets tell a joke
about the Irish people so a big man stands up in the audience, a
big Irishman, says, I'll not having you tell jokes about the
Irish, we're not as 'tic as you 'tink you know, and so he says be
calm sir, be calm, please, and sit down. And he says I'm not
talking to you, I'm talking to the wee fellow on your knee.

Ld:b.13.73

783. There's this Englishman and Irishman, you see, and
Englishman he brought a present to the Irishman, and
Irishman opened it you know, and there was a big card on it,
it says, How to keep an Irishman amused, please turn over.
Turn over, how to keep an Irishman amused, please turn
over.

Ld:b.13.73

784. Here's a quick newsflash, a pregnant Irish woman was
stopped in the Headrow in Leeds today. Child she was
carrying was a dope.

(Headrow = main street in downtown Leeds)
Ld:b.13.73 (Eng:b.10.74)

785. An Irish road sweeper sweeping up leaves fell out of a tree and
broke his neck.

L:b.11.74

786. Did ya hear about the Irishman who drowned himself when a policeman told him to dip his headlights?

L:b.11.75

787. How does an Irishman throw a hand grenad? He reads the label – must throw before 15 seconds. So he gets the hand grenade in his hand, so he reads 15 seconds and pulls out the pin, and he forgets he can't count so (standing up, hold Grenade in one hand, starts counting on his fingers of the other hand) he says 1,2,3,4,5, (must switch hands, so he puts grenade under his arm and counts the fingers on the other hand) 6,7,8,9,10 (switch back to other hand) 11,12,13,14,15 (grenade still under his arm when it goes off)

Ld:b.12.73

788. There was Paddy and Murphy, 2 Irishmen in Belfast, and Paddy had a sack over his shoulder and Murphy says to him, what you got in the sack Paddy? So he says I've got some chickens. So Paddy says, if I can guess how many there is in there, can I have one of them? So he says if you can guess how many there is in there you can have both of them.

Ld:b.12.73

789. Two Irish fellows, Paddy and Murphy on the scaffolding. And there's a man looking for new acts for the varieties and he's walking past the scaffolding and all of a sudden he sees Paddy doing a triple somersault off the top of the scaffolding, a backflip, another double somersault, and lands on his feet. And the fellow, who was looking for these acts, thinks that's tremendous and he goes to Paddy and says Paddy, would you like to come to my varieties and do an act for me and so he said yes, how much do you want? So he said 100 pounds, and he says 100 pounds and he says yes, well there's 50 for me and there's 50 for Murphy who hit me on the foot with a hammer.

Ld:b.13.73

790. There's this little Irishman and everytime he walks into this pub, these 2 big Englishmen bash him in, keep on bashing and kicking him and kicking him in guts, and he goes in and I

can't get a pint of bitter when I want, and and he goes home, and everytime he come in he keeps on getting bashed in, bang bashed in. So he goes right, I'm going to learn judo, the art of Kung Fu. Anyway, he starts off with lollypop stick, and goes hiya hiya ho, crack, and he breaks it in half. Anyway, he starts off with a little piece of, you know, plywood, and he goes, ahiya, etc. and it takes 10 minutes to say it all, and he breaks it. Then he gets a right big plank, about that big, hiya, etc., takes 20 minutes to say it all, breaks it in half again. Anyway, he takes 5 bricks, standing in a row, hiya hiya hiya, etc etc., anyway, he hits them and they all crumbles to bits. Right, let them try it on me now. Anyway, he goes, he goes, he's going to the pub, and these 2 big tall Englishmen looking down on him, and he goes ha, hiya, boom boom boom (got beat up) he was taking so long to say ha hiya.

Ld:b.12.73

791. There's an Irishman, who made his own 10 pence pieces. He just filed the corners off the fifties.

Ld:b.13.74

792. There's this Irishman, and he's only about 3 foot high, and his name's Anemic.

Ld:b.13.74

793. One day an Irish soldier was caught by the Germans. They said he could have one request before he was shot. He asked if he could sing a song. So they said he could. So he started to sing "1,000,000 green bottles standing on the wall, and if one green bottle would accidently fall, there would be 999,999 green bottles standing on the wall," etc.

Ld:b.10.73

XIII. ETHNIC JOKES – JEWISH

794. There's this Jew fellow and he's going to get shot before the
      firing squad, and before he gets shot the commodant says,
      your last request, what do you want? So, the prisoner who's
      getting shot says, can I sing a song please, and have a right big
      party? So he says yes, you can sing your song, so he says right,
      9000 green bottles standing on the wall (sung)

      Ld:b.12.73 (see Joke No. 793)

795. There's another one about Olympic Games in prisoner-of-
      war camps. And they're having a race, and its Germans
      against Jews, and who ever loses will win, commodant gives
      last words, ready Jews – yes, ready Germans – yes, rev rev
      (like motor reving)

      Ld:b.12.73

796. There's these Englishman, Irishman, and there's this Jew in a
      prisoner-of-war camp, and as you know, Germans don't like
      Jews. And he says, today we will have a sort of Olympic
      Games. The English will climb the water-tower, the Irish will
      climb the barracks wall, and the Jews will climb the electric
      fence.

      Ld:b.12.73 (Eng:b.11.74)

797. About this prisoner-of-war camp, and every year they have
      this contest to see who were the brainest people in the prison,
      so they wanted to see the brainest people, and 3 people
      entered, there's an Englishman, Scotsman, and a Jewish man.
      And the winning prize was, if they all passed the test they
      could get free the next day, and they would be set out. So the
      Englishman is questioned, he says in what year did the Titanic
      sink? (I'm not certain of the certain year but supposed he said)
      1903, so he said exactly right, yeah, right, you can go
      tomorrow. So the Scotsman come along How many people
      were on board? Ah, it was about 12,559 people, and he says

exactly right, you can go tomorrow. So the Jewish man comes along, he says what were their names?

Ld:b.13.73

798. These 2 Jews in 1944, night before they fall up against the German firing squad, and you know, the officer says do you have any last request before you die? And this Jew steps forward and he goes "you lousy German rotbags, I hate you and I always will, and I'll come after you when I'm dead", anyway the other Jew quickly pulls him back and says hey man, stop causing trouble.

Ld:b.12.73

799. There's this Jewish fellow standing around the bus stop, and the Pakistani man is not sure of the bus times because he's new in the area, and he asked the Jewish man what time is the next bus due and he thought he was making fun of him by saying Jew so he said, Half Paki seven.

Ld:b.13.73

800. There was a man and he walked into a Chinese restaurant and said to a waiter "have you any Chinese Jews?" I do not know sir, I'll go see, said the waiter. He came back five minutes later and said, no sir, but we have orange juice, blackcurrant juice, and lemon juice.

Ld:g..73

801. See there was there, there was a Jewish you know, a Christian man and a Methodist, and a Jew you know, and they're all in different, in a, you know, so in, they're in this hut together, in the middle of lake you see, and they're all discussing how to get all their religions together. So you know, but, nothing, you know, but they couldn't work out anything, so you know, the Jew says one of you had better go get some food you see. So the Englishman, the Christian man goes, I'll go get it, so he just went tut tut tut tut (hand motion of hopping over water) running along the water and he went to some shops and the Jew thought, God, how did he do that? He must have some faith. So he came back you know, tut tut tut along

the river. So you know he goes, he wants to know what happened. So next day he goes, somebody else had better go get the food, because they were hungry. So the Methodist man goes I'll go so he goes tut tut tut right along and back in again. So the Jew really flattened, to know what had hit him. So the next day he goes, I think I'll better try it, try it out you see. So he goes tut tut and he drowned you see. So he came back up went to them and goes how come well how come I tried it and couldn't get across? So the Methodist man goes, ah, how stupid of you. We walked on the stepping stones.

Ld:b.12.73

802. There's this Jew and he goes to Eiffel Tower, and he thinks he sees a 10 pence piece you know, down at the bottom. He's got good eyesight, so he jumps from top to get everything, and in newspaper it says Jew jumps from Eiffel Tower and dies in a dustbin.

Ld.b.12.73

803. There's 3 fellows, a Moslem, a Christian man, and a Jew you see. So the Moslem so this fellow goes, what do you do with all your spare money? So he goes, well the money I get I keep all to myself but all the rest I give it to the charity. So you know, the Englishman, he do the same thing, he give his spare money to the charity. But the Jew says, I get all my money and I throw it up to God. What he wants he gets, but what comes down I have.

Ld:b.12.73

804. There's these 2 Jews, and they're going to Heaven and they meet St. Paul at the Golden Gates, he says ah, you have been not spectacular all your life, have you, and he says no. And he says I'll have to go inside and consult the other saints, so he goes in and when he gets back the gates are gone.

Ld:b.12.73

805. It's about, in Northern Ireland, the Catholic and Protestant priests, you know, and this Catholic priest is running this Sunday school, there's a mixture. There's a Jew, a Jewish

person, a Protestant, and a Catholic. And they said, they asked a question to all three of them, they said, who's the most famous man in the whole world? So the little Catholic boy stands up and says, Jesus. So, he says, you're nearly right, but that's not quite right. So then he goes in to the little Protestant boy, he says, who's the most famous person in the world? And so he says, Harold Wilson, you know, the Prime Minister. So he says, oh no, you're miles away, you're miles away. So then he asked the little Jewish boy, who the most famous person in the whole world? And he stands up and says St. Patrick. So the Catholic person says, well done boy, how did you guess? He says, well really in my heart it's, it is Moses, but business is business.

Ld:b.13.74

XIV. ETHNIC JOKES — OTHERS

806. There was an Englishman, an Irishman, and a Scottishman, and Englishman says, there's a table in there, and it's got a pound note on it, but that cave's haunted. So Irishman goes in, he looks at pound note, and he's just about to pick it up and this voice says, I'm the ghost of your Aunt Mabel, and this pound note stays on the table. And so he runs out. And Scottishman goes in and he's just about to pick pound not up, I'm the ghost of your Aunt Mabel, and this pound note stays on the table. So he runs out so Englishman goes in. He picks it up and he says, and voice says I'm the ghost of your Aunt Mabel, that pound note stays on the table. So he says, I'm the ghost of Davy Crocket, and this pound note goes in my pocket.

Ld;b.10.73 (Eng:b.7.73, b.8.73, b.9.73, b.12.73, b.9.74, b.10.74, g.11.74, b.11.75)

807. There's these fellows, an Englishman, an Irishman, and Scottishman. And they go to this house where it's supposed to be haunted and they go to this part where there's supposed to be a haunted room. Anyway, and the Irish man goes in and he

hears these voices going YoHo to Chocolate Island (sung) anyway he goes oh, giba giba, and anyway he goes out, has hysterics you see. Anyway, he runs out and this Scottishman comes in and he hears these voices going, YoHo to Chocolate Island, and he goes ahh, and runs in hysterics again, and he runs out. And this Englishman who thinks he's right big and hard and he goes in and he hears the same voices and he runs out, you know, petrified, and they go what good does it to shiver, it seems to be coming from bed stead — YoHo to Chocolate Island, anyway they come to the bed and there's these flies, in the middle, in a little matchstick box, rowing, rowing to this pisspot you know, rowing with matchsticks for oars to Chocolate Island.

Ld:b.12.73 (Eng:b.12.73)

808. There's an Englishman, Irishman and Scottishman walking down the lane. And this lady came out of her house and said, if you sleep in the bedroom, I'll give you a thousand pounds. So Scottishman went in, at 12.00 midnight he heard this voice coming from somewhere saying 'sailing round the river in a chocolate boat'. So he ran out, and then Irishman went in, at 12.00 he heard this voice coming from somewhere saying 'sailing round the river in a chocolate boat'. So he ran out, then Englishman said, went in and at 12.00 he heard this voice coming from somewhere saying 'sailing round the river in a chocolate boat.' So he looked all over the place and he couldn't find where the voice was coming from and so he looked in toilet and saw 2 mice sailing round, going round toilet in, on some plop.

Ld:b.7.73

809. There's this Irishman, Englishman, and Scotsman, and they're all gone to stay in this little hut, little house, and they sent Irishman upstairs for a blanket and he goes upstairs, and he hears this noise, 'if I catch ya, I'm going to eat ya.' So he runs downstairs, and he shouts, he says, I'm not going up there, there's a ghost up there. So Scotsman goes up and he hears this

noise, 'if I catch ya, I'm going to eat ya.' So Scotsman runs downstairs, and tells Englishman, and he goes alright, we'll all go up together, and they all go upstairs, and they all hear this noise, 'if I catch ya, I'm going to eat ya.' So they hear where its coming from and they open this cupboard door and there's this boy, and he's picking his nose and he's going, 'if I get ya, I'm going to eat ya.'

Ld:g.13.73 (Eng:b.12.73, g.9.73, g.12.73, b.11.74)

810. There were these 3 sailors and they went into this house cause they haven't got no place to go. So the first one goes go upstairs and see if there's a blanket up in the attic, so the 2nd one goes up, and and he's just about to open the door when he hears this voice go, when I get ya, I'm ging to tear every part of your body apart. So, he runs down, he says oooh, I'm getting out of here (shaky scared voice), so he goes down and says you go up and get a blanket to the 3rd one. So the 3rd one says alright, so he goes up and he's just about to open the door when, all of a sudden, he hears this noise, when I get you, I'm going to tear every part of your body apart. (almost scream this) So its getting louder, and so, he goes down and he says to the first one, you go up and get one, and he goes ah no, let's all go up together. So they all go up together and they open the door, and to their suprise, there's a cat, and he's got a mouse, and he's saying, when I get you, I'm going to tear every part of your body apart.

Ld:b.12.73

811. This ones ancient, There's this Irishman, this Englishman, and a Scottishman and this cow in this field and the Irishman he says that's an Irish cow, and Englishman goes no it ain't, it's an English cow, and the Scottishman says nay, you're both wrong. It's a Scottish cow, it's got bagpipes.

Ld:b.12.73 (Eng:b.7.73)

812. Three men on a little island, an English, Irish and Scottish. A giant came along and said I am going to eat you up. The Irish man said if you can do the things we say, you can eat us. The

English man said reach over the sea, the Scottish man said to touch the moon. The giant could do both so they got eaten up. The Irishman spat on the floor and said swim in that.

Ld:b.9.73 (Eng:g.12.73-Englishman spits and survives)

813. There was these Irishman, Scotsman, and Englishman and none of them could get across this bridge unless they were brown. So they all put in, Englishman painted himself all brown, and he got across, Scotsman painted himself all brown and he got across, Irishman only had a half a pot of paint left, so he painted his face, his arms, but not his legs and feet, and man noticed that his feet were white, and his face and arms were brown, so he said take your trousers off, and man said no, and then he took his trousers off, and man goes, you aren't fuckin' brown, so get bloody lost, you aren't bloody brown, you've only bloody painted yourself, you're bloody white.

Ld:g.12.73

814. There was this Englishman, Irishman, Scottishman, and was a lady on a cliff, they all liked her you see, and so she said if you can go down the cliff, well I'll marry ya. So this Englishman came up and he said I'll go first. So he goes down and he goes ahh, so he's dead. Then there's this Scottishman and he goes down and he goes ahhh, and he's dead. And then there's this Irishman, and he goes, ladies before gentlemen, so she goes down and she's dead.

Ld:g.10.73 (Eng:b.8.74-Englishman survives)

815. One day there was these 3 people, an Englishman, a Frenchman, and a Poland. First they put a dead pig in a barn. First of all, the Englishman in. He went in there 2 days, he came back out, phew phew. The next one, the Frenchman went in. He stayed in there 2 months. He came out, phey phew. Then the Poland man went in there. He stayed in there 2 years, and the pig came out, phew phew.

SF:b.11.74 (Eng:b.7.73-Irishman, Scotsman, Englishman is dirty; b.10.74-American, Australian, Pakistani is dirty)

816. There's this Scotsman, Irishman and Englishman, and they couldn't go across this bridge unless they give this man some gold. So Scotsman give him a gold watch, Englishman give him a gold ring, and Irishman give him a golden wonder crisp.

Ld:g.12.73

817. There's this Jew, Englishman, and an American, no, I'll change it, an American, and a Canadian, and an Irishman. Anyway, the American is going to the gas chamber for committing crimes and all that, and he goes, ave you a last request before you get gassed to death, and the American goes, can I have a cigar, a right big cigar, and he gets a right big cigar and he smoking it in the gas chamber. And he goes to the Irishman, what would you like and he goes cause I want a bell, to ring it as I'm dying, just turn around, you know, while I'm dying, and he goes to the Canadian, what would you like? And he goes a piano. Yeah, a piano? And he brings a big piano in, a big Concerto, and he plays Beethovens 6th Symphony, and ding dong, you know. Anyway after 3 hours, the American and Irishman are dead, and the Canadian is still playing away, 7th symphony, after finishing the 6th symphony. Anyway, they put him in for 7 hours ding dong. 7 hours comes, he's still going this, uh (deep breathing) How do you do it? Tunes help you breath more easily.

(Tunes = methalade candy for stuffed noses, ad is 'Tunes help you breathe more easily')
Ld:b.12.73 (Eng:b.11.73, 2-b.10.74, g.11.74-Englishman, Irishman Scotsman)

818. There was a man who was starting work. The boss said this is Nick, he comes from Cockney, this is Mac he comes from Mull, this is Paddy, he comes from Ireland, this is Wack he comes from Scotland. While the boss was out they started fighting. When the boss came in he said, Nick Mac Paddy Wack, leave the man alone.

L:g.8.74

819. There was an Englishman, a Scottish and a Paky and the Paky what would you do if you saw a ghost, they said run for my life. One night a ghost came, the Scottishman and the Paky man ran away, but the Englishman did not. The ghost said I shall give you a wish, what is it? A piece of toilet paper please.

    L:b.10.74

820. There was these English, Chinese and Welsh man, they were in an aeroplane and it was going to crash and there was only one parachute so they let the driver have it. He land safe in a field then the Englishman jumped out the aeroplane and said 'God save me' so he landed safe in the field and then the Welsh man jumped out and said the same and landed safely. Then the Chinese man jumped and said 'God shave me' and he landed up in the barbers, having a shave.

    L:g.11.74 (Eng:b.12.73)

821. There was 3 men in a plane, there was an Englishman, a Chinaman, and a Irishman. The Englishman threw 'is cup down and said there goes my bonnie England. The Irishman threw his cup down and said there goes my bonnie wee Ireland. They went a bit further on and the Chinaman's cup fell down and he said there goes my bonnie wee China.

    Ld:g.9.73 (Eng:b.8.73, g.13.73, b.10.74, g.10.74, b.11.75)

822. There once was a Irishman, a Chinaman and a Scottishman. They all went up on a high mountain, one of the men said I bet you can't throw your watch down and catch it. Then the man said I can you know. He done it but he couldn't then the next but he could not do it and last of all they said the last man you try it and he did but he done it then the men said how did you do that? The man said my watch is half an hour slow.

    L:g.10.74

823. There's 360 people in a plane, and all sudden 3 engines stopped, and there's only one going round, and he says I need four people to jump out of this plane without a parachute to save the rest, 356. Anyway, all sudden, an Englishman stands up and says, before I jump, God save England, anyway, he

jumps down. And then 5 minutes later a Scottishman stands up and goes, God save Scotland and he jumps out and then an Irishman stands up and goes God save Ireland and he jumps out and then an American stands up and goes God save America and he chucks a Mexican out.

Ld:b.12.73 (Eng:g.11.73-English, Scottish, German pushes pilot out, b.9.73-French, English pushes Irish out)

824. There was an Englishman, a Scottishman, and a Frenchman. One day the Scottishman went to the shop and asked for a blue lolly and the shopkeeper gave him a green lolly and the Scottishman said he wanted a blue lolly so the shopkeeper said its the same shape, same size, but only a different colour, 6 pence please. Then the Frenchman came in and said can I have a yellow lolly and the shopkeeper gave him a green lolly. I wanted a yellow lolly. Well it is the same shape, same size, but only a different colour, 6 pence please. Then the Englishman came in and said can I have a pink lolly please and the shopkeeper gave him a green lolly, and the man said I wanted a pink lolly. Well it is the same shape, same size, but only a different colour, 6 pence please. So the Englishman gave him a half a crown. Shopkeeper said I wanted a 6 pence. Well it is the same shape, the same size but only a different colour.

Ld:g.8.73

825. There's this French lady and this Englishman. And the Englishman had a new car, and he say, would you like to come to a cafe with me? And she say oui oui, and he said not in my new car.

(oui = French for yes) Ld:g.8.73

826. There's this Frenchman and this Englishman, and they go to this hotel, and the Frenchman goes first and he says (french accent) excuse me, have you got a spare room please? He says yes, No. 13, but it's haunted. He says, oh, I am not scared of ghosts, give me the key please. So he gives him the key, and he goes upstairs, unlocks the door, puts his case on the floor, gets undressed, into his pyjamas, and goes into bed. And

anyway, it strikes 12, and then he hears this noise, it's a coming, it's a coming, it's a coming. What's that? Oooh, it's a ghost (shaky voice) I'm getting out of here. So he goes away and he isn't seen again. Anyway he goes down the lift (whistle sound) out the door (swish sound) and out again and you never see him again. Anyway, the Englishman says, do you have a spare room please? He says yes, No. 13 but it's haunted. He says ah, I'm not scared o' ghosts, so he goes upstairs, unlocks the door, put his case on the floor, gets undressed, puts his pyjamas on and gets into bed. And all of a sudden it strikes 12, dong dong, so he says, what's that? (shaky voice) Oooh, it's a ghost, I'm getting out of here. So he goes out, but he's got some sense you see, so he goes, he goes to Scotland Yard and he goes, up all the stairs (pant, pant, heavy breathing) go to the top, opens door (pant) there's a ghost in a hotel, and he drops down on the floor and they pick him up. So they go to the hotel, he says, uh, right, which is the room, No. 13, but it's haunted. He says right, we'll go up and search the whole place. Anyway, they search the whole place, but they forgot to search a toilet. So anyway, a little boy comes in, you know, cause it's getting demolished, he comes in, and he opens the door, and then there's a skeleton on the toilet with a pirates hat on saying, it's a coming it's a coming.

Ld:b.12.73 (see next joke)

827. There's these 3 guys, one with a rifle, one with a lantern, one with a knife. And they all 3 of them, first there's the guy with the rifle, he wanted, he went into a hotel and asked for a room. And he said, well the only room we have, everybody thinks it's haunted. So he went, so he's in that room that night and he kept on hearing, it's coming it's coming it's coming. And so, so he was quiet for a while and then he said, and then he heard it again, and it said, it's coming it's coming it's coming. And so he shot himself and he fell out the window. And so the next guy came the next night, and he had a knife and so he came in the night, and he asked for a room. And he said well the only one we have everybody thinks it's haunted. And so that night he heard, it's coming, it's coming it's

coming. So he shut his eyes for a while, and then he heard it
again and it goes, it's coming it's coming it's coming. And so
he stabbed himself and he fell out the window. And then the
next guy with the lantern came in and asked for the room and
he said, he said, I want a room, give me a room. Come on,
give me a room. So he said, well the only room we have,
everybody thinks it's haunted and all you have is a lantern. He
said, oh I don't care, I'm not afraid of ghosts. And so he goes
in, he goes in the room and he hears, it's coming it's coming
it's coming. So he shut up and went back to sleep. And then
he heard it's coming it's coming it's coming. And he didn't
jump out the window, but he hid under the bed, you know,
cause then he thougt he wouldn't hear it. And so he heard it
again, and it goes it's coming it's coming it's coming it's
coming (louder voice, stronger). And so he went in the other
room and he saw, he saw a piece of poo and a whole bunch of
ants around it in the toilet.

SD:g.12.75 (see Jokes Nos. 807, 808, 831)

828. There's this lady, and she married a foreigner, you see, from
Italy you see. It was the first day of the marriage you see and
she goes on go on darling, go and learn yourself some English.
So he went to the airport and learned the word takeoff, then
he went to the zoo and he learned the word zebra, then he
went to the hospital and he learned the word baby. So he
came back and home and she goes what did you learn luv, so
he goes 'take off ze—bra baby' (said with foreign or Italian
accent, accent on baby)

Ld:b.12.73 (Eng:2-g.8.73)

829. There's this Englishman and he wants to go abroad, but the
only ship available in his town is for a, you know, black man,
anyway, he was going in there, sneaking in and all of a
sudden, out sir, only black men can come in here. Well he
gets a bright idea — big bulb on the top goes bulm bulm
(flashing) Anyway he goes home and paints himself black,
with shoe polish, anyway oh, alright, so he leaves and oh
alright, you can go in, and he was walking up the aisle and all

of a sudden his trousers dropped down and they see this blackman go in and the last blackman I saw, but I've never seen a nigger with a white ass though.

Ld:b.12.73

830. There's this fellow and he's going to be shot before firing squad, and the Germans are going to shoot him and the Germans says, your last request, what do you want? So this English officer says, can I have just one cigarette, to smoke, so he says Nein, that's German for no, and so he says, no I only want one.

Ld:b.12.73

831. There was these 3 men, 2 were Muslems, and an Englishman. And one day, they were supposed to be camping, and the 2 Muslem men said, if you want to do a fart, just say he's coming, and so we'll lift a bit of the cover and then you can do it. And then, one of them wanted to do it, and he goes, it's coming, and so they put the cover up and he farted. And after that, the Englishman, he wanted to do a number 2, so he goes, his dad's coming. But they didn't know what he meant so, just left the cover, and he goes, his dad's coming, and he goes, they didn't do it, so he goes his dad's coming he's coming; he's coming faster and faster, and he's here. And so he shitted all over bed.

Ld:g.12.73

832. There was this Englishman, and this Pakastani man and they thought right, we'll go for a hike on the mountains. So they went along, and the Pakistani man says oh, I'm the greatest, I'll go up in front and show how good I am. So he goes up in front, and he falls down in this great big hole, it's about, oh, 250 feet deep. And the Englishman says, are you alright? He says no, I broke me arms. He says well then climb up with your legs. He says no I broke them too. So he says climb up with your teeth. So he climbs with his teeth and it took about oh, a long time. And then he gets him up to the top and the Englishman says you alright? He goes yesssss (fainter and fainter as he falls down again)

Ld:b.12.73

833. This is a story about an Italian and an Englishman. They live
      next door to each other and they each had a horse. And they
      were friends so they wanted to cut down the fence between it.
      Then they couldn't tell them apart. So they clipped off part of
      their ear, then they grew back so they couldn't tell them
      apart. They clipped off part of their tail then it grew back and
      they said, it's no use, it's a no use, we can't tell the white from
      the black. (last line with a slight Italian accent)

      SF:b.11.74

834. There's this Scotsman and he's carrying this case and he goes
      into this boat you know, an he goes I want to go to the
      Avenue of Parliment and I'll go to that, and I got this thing
      that says, and he goes that will be 5 pence for you and 2½pence
      for your kids. And he goes God, and he goes that will be 5
      pence for you and 2½ pence for the kid and he goes I'm not
      paying it. And he goes, if you don't pay it, I'll have to chuck
      your case in if you don't pay it. Anything, this goes on for
      about 10 minutes, and he goes downstairs and chucks the case
      in Thames, and the Scottishman comes down and goes, you're
      not satisfied trying to rob me, you're trying to drown my wee
      boy as well.

      Ld:b.12.73

835. There was these 3 fellows, up at sitting in the gates, up in
      heaven, there was a white fellow, there was 2 English fellows
      and a Black man, and St. Paul says, before you get in you got
      to spell a word. So he goes to the first English fellow, and
      goes, spell dog, and he goes d-o-g, you know ga, and he goes
      right, you're in, and he gets in and he goes to the other
      Englishman and says spell cat, and he goes c-a-t, and he goes
      right, you're in, and he goes to the Black man and he goes
      spell Constantinople.

      Ld:b.12.73

836. This is a joke that Michael made up, and he said, there's all
      these Black men wanting to be smuggled into England and
      they're on this ship and there's all these coffins on it and when
      they come to the fellows you know to see what they've got to

get past them, the customs, they tell them all get in the coffins, you know, so some get in the coffins, and some carry the coffins, and they're coming along, and just as they're going past the customs man he notices that the coffin carriers are black and he thinks there something fishy here so he goes what's in that coffin and he opens it up and there's this fellow in it, and he gives him the answer. He goes what's in that second coffin, and he opens it up and there's a nigger in it, and suffocating, and he opens a third coffin up and there's nothing in it and it's all laid out for a burial and he says what's this for and the fellow said the first nigger that dies of suffocation.

Ld:b.12.73

837. On the news yesterday it said there were 30 colored people swimming in the English Channel, and they were mistaken for an oil slick.

Ld:b.12.73

838. This American comes over and he's touring London and he sees Big Ben and he says we've got bigger Grandfather clocks and sees Tower Bridge and he says golly we've got a bigger bridge over a stream in our back garden so his tourist (tourman) gets tired of him bragging and he sees Queen Elizabeth sailing and he says Queen Elizabeth sail coming in to port, when they go to see, and so he up one of those megaphones and shouts come on in number 2, your time is up.

Ld:b.12.73

839. There's this American comes over to tour England, and this touring company is showing him around London, and the fellow goes that's Big ben and the American goes oh, I've got grandfather clocks as big as that. And he's going around, and everything he shows him he's showing off, you know, tellin him about America, and he's getting fed up with him and so this fire engine goes wizzing past them and the American hears this bell and he turns around just sees the ladder whizz past and so he goes Godd Golly, what was that? And the Englishman goes, just a window cleaner late for work.

Ld:b.12.73

840. There's this American and an Irishman, and this American thinks he knows every riddle that there is, you see, and he got this Irishman, and I'll give you 3 pounds if I can't answer one of your riddles, and if you can't answer one of my riddles, you only have to give me one pound. And he goes ah that's okay. And the American goes right, you go first. Right, what's yellow, has 500 arms, 10 legs, 300 eyes, 2 lips, 10 teeth, one that goes sticking down there, 2 feet long (down throat) and what is it? and he goes, and the American was thinking, for about half an hour, going what is it, ah, I, I don't know, here's your 3 pounds. And he goes, what is it, you know, What is it? And he goes, I don't know, here's your one pound.

Ld:b.12.73

841. There was 3, you know, fellows in a change room, a Jew, you know, a waiting room, so you know, there were a Jew, an Arab man, and an Englishman, you see, and they were all bored, you see, nothing to do. So a fly came buzzing around you know, buzz, and it landed on the Englishman and the Englishman went oo oo go away (gesture of turn head and brushing fly off shoulder) So it landed on the Jew, and the Jew went oo oo go away. So it landed then on the Arab man and the Arab picked it up and et it. Anyway then another half hour went past, and another fly came buzzing round and then it landed on the Englishman and the Englishman went oo oo go away. Then it landed on the Jew, and so the Jew picked it up and said to the Arab, do you want to buy a fly?

Ld:b.12.73 (Eng:b.7.73, b.12.73, g.13.73)

842. There was this Pakistani you see and he was singing the Paki's took all of the houses. And this vicar came along and he said do you know anything better than that? Then he said yes, Jesus was born in a stable. Then, then, then he said, why was Jesus born in a stable? Because the Paki's took all the houses.

Ld:g.7.73

843. There's This Indian teacher, you know, he's a faker, pins and stuff like that and he's got a load of Indian faker bottle little boys, and they're all sitting on pins and the teacher walks into

the classroom and sits in his chair and then he goes, who stole my pin? (no pins there, the pins are on the floor, you know Indian faker)

Ld:b.12.73

844. There was a man at a train station and he saw a West Indian train driver. So he said to him are you a member of Aslef? Yep he said. Then why aren't you taking out your train? Then the West Indian driver said aslef my train at the junction.

L:b.10.74

845. Once there was this German and this Russian guy. And the German called up the Russian and goes, 'come on over' and the Russian goes, 'I'm rushing, I'm rushing.'

SF:g.11.74 (US:g.11.74)

846. There's this man in hospital and somebody came to see him. And he's talking to him and the Chineseman, that's the man in the hospital, started talking in Chinese, and the Englishman couldn't understand what he says. So he wrote it down on a piece of paper Chineseman, and he couldn't understand what it says, so the Englishman went around to the Chinese restaurant and asked what it says, the the Chinese person in the restaurant said, 'please will you get off my airpipe.'

L:b.11.75

847. Okay, one night this Polish guy walks in this drugstore and he asks for 12 pairs of underwear, and the drugstore man says, 12 pairs of underwear, what for? He says, one for each month.

SD:g.11.75

848. There's this Polack, and he's hitchhiking, and there's this guy coming by in a car, and he has all these antennas all over his car. And Polack says, oh I guess it's all right to ride with him. So he gets in the car, and they're riding for about 3 miles. The Polack says, hey, I want to know why you have all these antennas all over your car? And the guy says, oh I can talk to anybody in the whole wide world. And he goes anybody? He goes anybody. And so Polack goes, can you talk to somebody

in Poland? Ah sure, that's easy. Hey, could you talk to my mother in Poland? He goes sure. Golly, I'd do *anything* to talk to my mother in Poland. And the guy says *anything?* Polack says anything. So he stops car, gets out on side of the road, the guy pulls down his pants, he pulls his "uk-hum" out, the Polack grabs ahold of it, and says, hello mom?

(uk-hum = penis)
SD:g.12.75

849. There's these 3 Polacks sitting on a fence, and this one little monkey. First, they had this one sick cat, that had to shit all the time. So they didn't know how to stop him. So they told the little monkey to put a cork in the guy's ass. So he did it. And days days went by, and he keep getting fatter. And one day he blew it, and he kept shitting all over. And all the reporters and everything were there, and the reporter goes to the Polack what do you see? Tons and tons of shit. The other reporter asked the second Polack, tons and tons of shit. And then the reporter asked the third guy, the poor little monkey's trying to put the cork back in.

SD:b.10.75

850. There's this group of astronauts talking about where they are going, and the Americans go, we're going to Mars. And the Russians say, we're going to Venus. And then they ask the Polacks where they're going. And the Polacks go, we're going to the Sun. And the others say, you're crazy, you'll burn up. And the Polacks say yeah, that's why we're going at night.

SD:g.12.75

851. There were these two Polacks walking down the street, and this sea gull. And the sea gull shit in one of the Polack's eyes. So the other Polack said, let's go get some toilet paper, and the other one said, it's no use, the bird will be 20 miles away by the time we get back.

SD:b.11.75

XV. DOCTOR JOKES

852. There's a woman, and she's having a baby and she goes to the doctor's 'cause she keeps getting terrible pains. So he says, it must be because it can't get out. So he says right, swallow a rocking chair. So she eats a rocking chair. And then she goes back next day and says I'm still getting me pains, so he says right, eat a straw hat. So she eats a straw hat, and she comes back next day and says I'm still getting me pains. So he says right, eat a banjo. So she eats a banjo, and she has one of the babies. So he says oh, I'll have to cut you open for the other one. And they cut her open, and inside is this baby sat in a rocking chair, with straw hat on playing the banjo singing 'you got my brother but ya didn't get me, doda doda day.'

    Ld:g.13.73 (Eng:2-b.12.73, g.8.73)

853. *The Pregnant Lady:* Once there was this lady and she had to go to the doctors. So she went to the doctors and the doctor said she was going to have 2 twins. So she went to the fortuneteller, and the fortuneteller said one's going to be a scientist, and one's going to be just a plain old hippy. So she was so happy, she went to tell her husband. And when she told him, he got so mad, he shot her in the left kidney. And the hippy in, said, 'boom boom, ya got my mother but didn't get me, boom boom boom boom, I was hiding in the left kidney.' (sung as rock star)

    SF:g.10.74 (US:b.11.74, b.10.75)

854. This this lady, this woman, and she's got a problem. She knows she's going to have a baby, but it won't come out. So she goes to doctors and she says, doctor my baby won't come out. So he says right, take 5 gallons of water and 100 pills. So she does. Next day, it still hasn't come so he goes right, take 10 gallons of water and 200 pills. So she does, but nothing happens. Third day she takes 20 gallons of water and 300 pills.

Nothing happens. She comes back next day and he says sorry, I'll have to operate and then he says we're going to operate. And he open her tummy and there's two of them and one's dead, and the other one says ah, you didn't know I could swim did ya?

Ld:b.13.73

855. See there's this woman and she's having a baby. She goes to the doctors and the doctor's not in. She comes home and goes ah fuck, so little lad goes, what does that mean mum so she goes that's the name of me doctor. She goes there next day, doctor still not in. She comes home and goes ah bollucks. Boy goes what does that mean so she goes oh that's the name of me doctor's coat. She goes next day, doctors still not in. She comes home and goes ah Harry, Fanny and Tits. Little lad goes, what does that mean? So that's what I'm going to call me baby. She goes next day, doctors still not in, so secretary goes I'll send doctor round when he comes in. So, when he goes round to this lady's house the little lad answers door and he goes come in Doctor Fuck, hang your bollucks on the wall and come and see me mums harry fanny and tits.

(bollucks = balls = testicles, fanny = female genitals)
Ld:g.13.73

856. There's this, I got this off Paul, well there's this lady, and she hasn't had the baby yet, and her little boy went up to her and said, what's that in your tummy? And she said a baby. And then the little boy said where'd you get it from? And she said you Dad. So he went to his Dad and said, I don't feel you'd better give Mummy anymore babies. And his Daddy said why? Because she's just eaten it.

Ld:b.8.73 (Eng:b.8.73)

857. There's this little lad and he goes Daddy, I want you to tell me about life. So he goes alright, I'll tell you about the birds and the bees. But he goes. I don't want to know about the bees. I want to know about the birds.

(bird = chick = girl) Ld:b.12.73

858. This little boy went into his father and said, daddy how does me mum make a baby, and so he says, well you're a bit young to know, but seeing it's your 12th birthday tomorrow I'll tell ya. So when the father, first of all, goes down warehouse shop and buys a big pole so he says, after that he goes to his mother, goes to your mum, and inside your mum's stomach there's a bench with 5 babies on it, and your father gets the pole and knocks a baby off the bench. And his son is a bit confused and he says, well how come Mr. Green down the road has got 5 babies? So his father said, he was that bloody eager, but he knocked the bench over.

Ld:b.13.73 (Eng:b.13.74)

859. There was this little boy, and he was 2 years old and you see and it was his birthday tomorrow, so his dad goes right son, what do you want for you birthday, a trainset? So the boy goes naw, I don't want a train set. I want a little baby brother. So his father goes don't be silly, in one day. Tuh, so he goes here here, have a football. He goes no, I want a baby brother. You know, tah, don't be silly. So, well you know, his little boy goes, well you work on the builders site now, there's lots of men there. Well why don't they get some more men on the job?

Ld:b.13.73 (Eng:b.13.74)

860. There was these ladies, and one went to the doctor, and the doctor gave her, and she wanted a baby, so the doctor gave her some red pills, and she went off, and there was another lady, and the doctor gave her blue pills, and then the third lady come in and the doctor gave her som iron pills. Then the first lady had a red baby, the second a blue baby, and the third an iron robot.

Ld:g.8.73

861. There's this woman, and she wants a lot of children, and she wants them all to be right polite, so anyway, she has some children, and the doctors are wondering why they're not coming out, so they open her stomach up and they see all these babies saying, after you, no after you.

Ld:g.13.73

862. There was this woman, and she was pregnant, and she could talk to her children inside. So she said to the girl, what do you want, so she said a doll and a pram. And she said to boy what do you want and he said I want a real gun. And then after that she said well, how did you like your pram and your doll? She goes it was beautiful. Then she asked the boy, she said how did you like your gun? And he said it was great. And she said anyway what did you want a gun for. He said, to shoot that big hairy monster that comes in my window everyday.

Ld:g.12.73

863. There's this fellow and he goes to the doctor and says doctor, I've got worms, what can I do? So he says, bring a sandwich and a cream bun. And so he brings a sandwich and a cream bun. And he says take your trousers down, and sticks the sandwich up his bum, and then he sticks cream bun up. And he do same next day. And this treatment goes on about a week. And then he says, Doctor, I'm getting fed up with this, when's the treatment going to cure me. And he says, well, tomorrow your last day, tomorrow just bring a sandwich and don't bring a cream bun, bring a golf club instead. And so he brings a sandwich and a golf stick and the doctor says pull your trousers down and he sticks sandwich up his bum. All of a sudden a worm sticks his head out and says – here, where's cream bun? Doctor picks up the golf stick and goes bam.

Ld:b.12.73

864. A man and lady came into the doctors, the man wanted some cream for more hairs on his head, and the lady wanted some cream to make her busters bigger, so he gave them some. At home the man put the lady's cream on her and the lady put the man's cream on for him. The next day the lady had hair on her busters, and the man had busters on his head.

(busters = breasts)
Ld:g.10.73

865. There was this fellow and he went to doctor's and he said doctor doctor, my willy's too short. So he gave him some pills, and his, well you know, it grew too long. And then next day he wanted to go to a football match, so he wrapped it

around his neck and painted it as a scarf. And so, and when his team won, he went around with it, and then he goes wackoo (twirling it around his head, use arm motion) and then, and then somebody shouted, would the person who's squirting ice cream please stop it.

(willy = penis)
Ld:g.12.73

866.   There's this guy he had a really high voice (said in high voice) so he went to the doctor and the doctor said, the doctor said, well, uh, I'll have to cut off your "beep". And he goes no no, not me, no. And he goes okay. So the doctor and the patient got to be really good friends, and one day when they went to the beach and the guy was out, and the guy with the high voice went out swimming and he was going shark shark (high voice) shark shark (low voice)

("beep" = penis)
SD:g.12.75

867.   One day a man goes into the doctors and tells him that his finger wouldn't grow. So the doctor put some ointment on it that whenever somebody said pardon, his finger would grow one inch. One day he met a Jew and he bumped into him and said a thousand pardons.

Ld:b.10.73 (Eng:b.12.73, b.9.74)

XVI. SEXUAL JOKES

868.   There's this woman, and the milkman takes her milk every morning. And one morning the milkman goes to this woman, I'll give you 10 pints of milk if you'll let me come in house. So she says alright. He goes, I'll give you 50 pints of milk if you'll take me upstairs. She says alright. He goes I'll give you 100 pints of milk if you'll get undressed. So she goes alright. He says I'll give you 200 pints of milk if you'll get into bed with me. She goes alright. You see, this girl's names called Shagarada, and her mother comes home and she shouts

Shagarada, so milkman shouts down, bloody hell, I'm shagging her as fast as I can.

Ld:g.13.73 (Eng:3–b.12.73, b.13.73, b.13.74)
(also Fuckarada and Kissarada)

869. Johnnie Fuckerfaster, named that by his mom, was under the house with girl, and his mom didn't know he was there with a girl. And she called Johnnie come here. And Johnnie goes I guess I'll have to go, even though they were in the middle of it, and she yells again, Johnnie Fuckerfaster, and so he yells back, I fucking her as fast as I can.

SD:g.12.75

870. There were these three guys, and they went to this farm. They asked the farmer if they could stay overnight at the farm, and the farmer said they could each sleep with one of his daughters, as long as they didn't make his three daughters pregnant. Well, in the morning, the three girls were pregnant, so the farmer told the 3 boys to go out in the fields and pick whatever fruit they wanted. The first boy went out and picked grapes, and when he came back, the farmer said, stick them up your ass, or I'll blow your head off. So he did. The second boy went out and picked raspberries, and when he came back the farmer told him to stick them up his ass or have his head blown off, so he did. Then the third boy went out, and the other two boys started laughing, and the farmer said why are you laughing? and they said, he's picking watermellons.

SD:g.12.75 (US:g.12.75)

871. This is another story about the milkman. And this little boy, when he was a small baby, he was gifted with an advantage of seeing into the future, and predicting things you know. So, what happened was, when he was five, this little boy, people got to hear about him. So every night the boy used to go up to his bedroom, kneel down beside his bed, and say his prayers. He said, God bless mummy, God bless daddy, God bless grandma, and goodbye grandad. And his grandad's listening to this. Next day his grandad dies. So, in next night, his

grandma takes him to bed. He says God bless mummy, God bless daddy, and goodbye grandma. And his grandma is listening. And the next morning she dies. So anyway, his father takes him up to bed next time. And he said, God bless mummy, and goodbye daddy. So his dad's listening to this and he's scared stiff, and he's watching every step, and he's going to work, when he's going to work he's watching all the cars, so he doesn't die. And he going all around, all around the town making sure he didn't put a foot wrong. And when he gets home his father says, to his wife, well, I didn't die today, I guess his prediction was wrong. And she goes yeah, cause the milkman died.

Ld:b.13.74

872. There's a woman in the bathtub, and the postman comes and he has to ring the bell, it's one of these big parcels, and she comes down, and he says parcel for you, so she signs it. So he says, tell you what, I'll give you your money back for the parcel if you'll take the middle towel off. So she says alright, and she does. So he says I'll give ya 5 pounds if you take top towel off. So she says alright. And he says I'll give you 10 pounds if you take the bottom towel off. So she says alright. So he says if I put a penny in the slot will the bells ring?

Ld:g.13.73

873. There was this lady and she went for a bath, and that day the milkman comes, so she wraps 3 towels around her. And Milkman says, and she lets him in and he says I'll knock 10p off if you take your top towel off. So she took it off. So he says I'll knock another 10p off if you take other one one off, so she took it off. And he said, I'll knock 20p off if you'll take the bottom pair off, so she took it off, and he gives it what's the bloody hells is that? And she gives it me tits, me privates, or me backside.

Ld:g.12.73

874. There's this lady you see, you know, she lives in a right big house, a mansion house you see, and this tramp came along you see, and he had nowhere to stay, so he says, please lady,

can I stay in your house? She goes, you can't stay in my house, but you can stay in the garden, so, but as long as you don't drink me milk, the milk on the doorstep. So you know, he couldn't resist the milk cause he was so hungry, so in the morning she goes I told you not to drink me milk you know, I'll give you a last chance, so you know, so, another day goes, this time, as long as you don't pull me cats hairs out and so she goes this is your last chance. So she goes, you know, you can stay, as long as you don't pull me knickers down from me washing line. So he goes okay, so you know, he saw the knickers you know, he goes, oo I can't resist it, pulled them down you see. And the lady goes right, I'm going to call the police now. So you know, she rang up and goes police police, there's a tramp you know, he's drunk me milk, pulled me hair out and pulled me knickers down.

Ld:b.12.73 (Eng:g.13.73)

875.   There's these 2 boys playing marbles and one won, and the other one lost, and he said, he said bastard. So he went home and asked his mom what bastard meant and his mom said people, people who visit you. And then he had another game next day and he said fuck, and so he went home and asked him mum what fuck meant and she said, mother and father upstairs getting washed. And so he has another game and boy says shit, so he went home and asked his mum what shit meant and his mum said food on table. And so that day a visitor come, and he said hello bastard, fuck upstairs and shit on table.

Ld:g.12.73 (see next joke)

876.   This ones the other one, so there was this kid, he went out and this girl cussed at him and he goes, mommy, what does shit mean? And she goes food. And then he goes out, and he goes upstairs, and then he goes, then this girl goes fuck, and then he goes back in and he goes, mommy, what does fuck mean? She goes dressing. And then this girl goes out and he goes out again. He goes what does bastard mean? and he comes back in, what does bastard mean? And she goes priest. And then,

that night, priest came over, and his mom told him to tell the priest that the foods on the table, and mommy and daddy are upstairs dressing. So, priest comes in, and the kid goes, hello there bastard, shits on the table, mom and dad are upstairs fucking.

SD:b.11.75

877.　There's this fellow and he can't speak very good, can't even say a word, or some words, you know, and he goes in to a bun shop, you know, cake shop, and he goes can I have a bum please, he goes a bun, and he goes no a bum, a bum, and he goes you mean a bun, and he goes yeah, a bum. Anyway, he gets his bun, and he's carrying it in his hand, and he goes into this clock shop and he goes can I have a cock please and he goes a clock, and he goes yeah, a cock. Anyway he gets his clock, and he goes into this blanket shop and he goes can I have a wanket please and he goes you mean a blanket, and he goes yeah, a wanket. And he goes, right, and he's carrying them all, and he's walking up, and he drops his bum, and this lady's walking past and he goes, will you hold my cock and my wanket while I pick up my bum.

(wanket = masturbate)
Ld:b.12.73

878.　There's this little girl and this little boy says to her can I come to your house with you so she says, you're not allowed to, but I'll let you, seeing you're my friend. And so they go to house, and he says, can I come to your bedroom with you, so she says, well you're not supposed to, but seeing you're my friend, I'll let you. So he says can I get in bed with you, and she say, seeing you're my friend, I'll let you, but you're not supposed to. So little lad says, can I put my finger on your bellybutton, so she says yeah, but you're not supposed to, but seeing you're my friend, I'll let you. So he does, and she says that's not my bellybutton, and he says that's not my finger.

Ld:b.12.73 (see next joke)

879.　There's a little boy and a little girl. And the boy said to the girl, can I stick my finger in your bellybutton? Girl said, uhnuh. And he said pretty please? Oh all right. So, he sticks his finger in. And she says, that's not my bellybutton. Surprise, surprise, surprise, that's not my finger either.

SD:g.12.75

880. There was this woman, and she lived in a house, and she had a table she called it strip me and she had a chair called uh tits, and she had a uh, dog called, no, her house was called strip me, and her table was called Bust, and her chair was called bum. And one day, when she came back, she lost, she went out, you know, and she lost her way home, so she goes, she went to the police station, and she goes, I've lost, and she stops, then she says strip me. So they stripped her and she goes, how dare you. And she went out and she found it. And after that she lost one of her chairs, so she goes so she went to the police station and says I've lost my bust. And so, you know, they start looking for it all over for it, and they go it's there. No not that, my chair, how dare you and she walked out again. And then the, then she lost her chair, so she goes, she went to the police station, and says, I've lost my bum, and so they took her knickers off and then said, it's there. And she says no, not that bum, my chair I call it bum.

Ld:g.12.73

881. There's a man with a horse and car, and he walking along, no, in car and he sees a fairy on the road fallen down. So he gets out of his car and picks it up and she says, oh thank you. Now I'll grant you 3 wishes. So he says right. First of all I wish I had a face like Rock Hudson, I wish I had a body like Mr. Universe, and I wish I had a dooda like me horse's. So she says right, I grant you your 3 wishes, and he goes home, and he gets this right nice bird. And he's getting undressed and she says, ah, haven't you got a handsome face, and haven't you got a big muscular body, and he takes off his trouser, and she says oh crikey, so he say what's the matter? She says look, so he looks down and says oh crikey, I forget me horse was a mare.

Ld:g.13.73

882. One time there was this man, and there's this fairy lady, and she goes, I'll give you 3 wishes. He goes all right. And she goes, what's your first wish? He goes, well I wish I had a big black limousine. She goes okay, it's yours. And she goes, what's your second wish? He goes, well I wish, I had in the back of my limousine I wish I had bags and bags full of money in the back of my car. She goes, okay, it's yours. She goes, what's your next wish? He goes, I'll have to wait until tomorrow to tell you. And he goes I'll have to think about it. And he goes driving and she goes, whatever you say wish it will come true. He goes okay. And he was driving along one day listening to his radio and the Oscar Meyer weiner song was on, and he was singing along with it, "I wish I were an Oscar Meyer weiner". And then, this guy drove by and he saw this Oscar Meyer weiner sitting and driving in a black limousine with money in the back of it.

SD:g.10.75

883. There's this little lass, and her mothers in bed poorly and she don't want to be disturbed, and so she says to her father, daddy, can I come to bed with you. So he says no, so she says I'll scream, so he says okay then. So they go to bed. And the daughter says daddy, what's that long thing? So he says it's a teddy bear, so she says can I play with your teddy bear Daddy? So he says no, so she says I'll scream, so he says okay then, but let me get to sleep, got to go to work early tomorrow. So in morning he wakes up and there's blood all over the covers, and he says, what you done, so she says your teddy bear spit at me so I bit it's head off.

Ld:b.12.73 (Eng:g.9.74, b.13.74; US:b.10.75)

884. There was this girl, and her mum and dad were going to bed, and so she saw them undressed and she said mom, what's that? So she said, ah, and so she said dad what's that? And her dad goes oh it's just something you can play with. And she goes can I play with it then? And so he says no. And so that night, she sneaks into their bedroom and got under the covers and started playing with it. And next day, he says mother, have

you been playing with my prick last night and so she says no. So he asks his daughter, and his daughter says yes. And he says, well remember it's your moms', it ain't bloody for you.

Ld:g.12.73

885. There's a woman, and she's right old fashioned, you know, she doesn't know much. And she goes to bed with this man, and then you know, all suddenly, she jumps out of bed and says eek Henry, there's a worm in the bed.

Ld:g.13.73

886. There's this boy and he goes to his mother who's getting changed, mom, what's that, what's them? Oh, they're my headlights son. Mom, what's that? That's my grass. So he goes to his dad in the next room. Dad, what's that? That's my snake son. So that night, his mum and dad were in bed, he comes in and says, mom, dad, can I come in bed with you, I'm cold. Alright son, as long as you don't look under covers. So he gets into bed, and about 5 minutes later he looks under covers and says, mum mum, switch your headlights on, me dad's snake's going into your grass.

Ld:g.13.73 (see next joke)

887. *The Little Red Wagon*: Little boy always loses his little red wagon. One day, he is looking for it, and goes to his sister who's in the shower. Have you see my little red wagon? She goes no. He goes what's those? She goes those are my headlights. Again he loses the wagon, and he goes in to his mom who's in the shower. Have you seen my little red wagon? She goes no. He goes, what's that? And she says, that's my cave. He lost it again, and he goes in to his dad who's in the shower. No he hadn't seen it either, but dad, what's that? That's my train. That night, his parents are in bed, and the little boy comes in and says, can I get in with you? Only if you don't look under the sheet. So the little boy looks under the sheet, and yells, hey sister, come and turn on your headlights, dad's train is going into mom's cave.

SD:g.12.75(US:b.10.75 – car and garage) (A continuation of this story has

the mother pregnant, and the little boy goes, I know where the little red
wagon is now. It went in with dad's train)

888. This is called the 3 holes. Okay, there's this guy who went
into this hotel, and he wanted a room, and the guy said, okay,
well the only one we have is the one with 3 holes. And so he
rented the room with the 3 holes. And the guy said whatever
you do, don't stick your "ukhum" in the first hole. And so he
went and got some sheets and when he came back the guy did
what he told him not to do. And so he went and got some
towels, and he said, whatever you do, don't stick you
"ukhum" in the second hole, and so he went and got some
towels and he came back and he was sticking his "ukhum" in
the second hole. So he went and he said, whatever you do,
don't stick your "ukhum" in the third hold, cause if you do,
something will happen. And so he went, he went to get some
sheets and he came back and he was sticking his "ukhum" in
the third hole and he was sitting there ow ow, and so he came
and so he said what were these 3 holes. And he said, well the
first one was a goat's butt, the second was a lady's vagina, and
the third one's a cow's milking machine that won't stop until
it gets 10 gallons.

(ukhum = penis)
SD:g.12.75

889. There's this guy, he just fired his secretary because she got bad
in typing. And so, this lady comes walking in, real sexy, and
he goes, okay, you can have the job. You work every Friday.
Next week, she comes in walking in with her legs spread
apart, walking. And he goes what happened to you? And she
goes, oh I'm having a party tonight, and had to put curlers in
my hair.

SD:g.12.75

890. Two little kids going to the movies to see Cary Grant and this
beautiful girl. And so they're watching the movie and Cary
Grant goes, I want what I want when I want it, and then he
kisses her. So, the 9 year old kid, they're walking home from

the movie, and he says to his girlfriend, I want what I want when I want it, and she says, I'll give what I got when I get it.

SD:b.10.75

891. Well, there were 3 mice, a chief and 2 of his servants. One day they decided to look around the house so the chief went straight, one of the slaves went on the left, and the other went on the right. And, the chief saw something, and he came back, and then one saw something and he came back and the other one saw something and he came back, but the chief, he took quite a long time before he came back. And the first one said I saw something squared and it was white, it had a hole at the bottom. Do you know what that was, anybody? It was a sink. And then the other one said I saw great big pool full of water, do you know what that was? A bath, a bath, ya, bath, and then chief now said, I saw something, it was quite round at the top, had a bit of water in it at the bottom. Do you know what that was? A toilet, yes, a toilet. And he goes, while I was looking I fell in, and then it grew dark, somebody sat on the top and then he said, it started to rain, and I got wet through and then a big log came down and if that log didn't come I would have drowned.

Ld:g.12.73

892. There's these 3 ants on a lady, or a woman, and they say, right, let's go explore. There's a leader and he goes, you go that way, I'll go that way, and you go that way. So, takes an hour, and they all come back and the first one says, when I went there, there were these 2 mountains, and I nearly got drowned cause all this white stuff, all this white lava came out and nearly drown me. So the second one says, oh you were alright, I had to, when I got there, there was this great big hairy jungle and this pool, so I drank it, and the other one says, you're alright. I went around this corner, and there was this great big hole, and when I tried to get in this big brown thing came out and knocked me out.

Ld:b.13.73

893. There was this bus conductor and this lady got on. She dropped her ticket and bent down to pick it up. As she did he said, oooh, she's got black knickers on, she must support Liverpool. Another lady bent down when she dropped her ticket and she had red knickers and the bus conductor said oooh, she must support Manchester United. Another lady got on and she had no knickers on and he said oooh, she must support Arsenal.

(Liverpool, Manchester United, Arsenal = football (soccer) teams)
Ld:g.10.73 (Eng:b.12.73, 2-g.73)

894. There was Blackpool town, and the lift was comimg down right fast, and he said, and this fellow said, have you had a nice ride? She said, yes. Why? Cause me knickers are down to me ankles.

Ld:b.8.73

895. One mate said to his mate, when I get home I have to rip my wife's knickers off. So his mate says why? So he says cause they're killing me.

Ld:b.13.73 (Eng:g.8.73)

896. I know a joke like that, but it's involving an old woman and a parrot. A woman with the parrot on her shoulder and a hat on, and she sits on the bus, and she sits there and the bus conductor comes and he says, that will be 4p for you madame and 3p for your parrot. And she says if that's not, I'm not going to pay if it's as expensive as that. So she gets off the bus, and she's thinking of a way to get the parrot on the bus without the conductor seeing her. So she decides to stick it in her knickers, and she's sitting there, and a little girl sitting opposite her and all of a sudden there's a little noise, um um um um (hum to tune) and she says there's something murmuring. And of a sudden it's getting louder, hum hum hum hum hum hum hum, and then all of a sudden it gets into full blast and it's the parrot saying "Raindrops keep falling on my head" (sung)

Ld:b.13.73 (Eng:b.8.73, g.8.73, g.13.73, b.8.74)

897. There once was a girl named Sally, and one day she was walking down from school, and a boy goes climb up the telephone pole, so she did and then the next day the same thing happened, he goes climb up telephone pole. And she goes no, and he goes, 'if I give ya a dollar?' And she goes yes, so she did. And then the next day she did it and she did it again for $5, and next day she told her mom that she'd been climbing up telephone poles for a boy and her mother goes 'don't do that again cause all they want to do is sees your underwears.' And then she goes okay, I won't do it again. And so then the next day they go, will you climb up that telephone pole? She goes no, all you wants to sees my underwears. And they go, for $15? And she goes, okay. And then, when she got home she told her mom. She goes, I told you they're only trying to see your underwear. She goes, this time I didn't wear underwears.

SF:g.11.74 (Eng:b.12.73)

898. There was a man walking down the street which was next to a railway line and just then a lady who was hanging out her washing said to him, you know everytime a train comes past and I'm in bed I fall out of it. Eh? I don't believe it. Then come with me and see it for yourself. All right said the man. So he walked up the garden path, up the stairs, and got into bed with her. When her husband came home he said, what are you doing in bed with my wife? And the man said, you'll never believe it but we're waiting for a train.

Ld:g.8.73

899. There's these 2 tramps, and one has 25p so he said to the other tramp, I'm going into a hotel tonight. So he went and the manager said, ooops, sir, it's on the right, is your room. So he went, on the left, and got into bed with the manager's wife. And that night, the manager said, I'm going to fuck my wife tonight. So he went upstairs, and got into bed with the tramp and started working the tramp. And the next morning the manager had all the fleas from off the tramp.

Ld:g.12.73

900. There's a lorry going down and a fellow sees this girl
      bumming a lift, and his, a ginger-haired girl, bumming a lift
      up, and it's slow by there so he pulls up and tells her get in,
      give us a kiss, no, get out. He goes along and sees this other
      girl bumming a lift, and he goes, and he pulls up, lets her get
      in, give us a kiss, no, get out. And he keeps going on like this,
      and all a sudden he hears this siren behind him and he looks in
      his mirror and there's this policecar following him. Pull up, so
      he pulls up and the policecar goes, are those your 4 chickens
      walking along there, and he says, and then they ask us give us
      a kiss, no, get out. So then they went out back the lorry and
      they opened this cage and there's this parrot grabbing among
      all these chickens going, give us a kiss, no, get out.

      Ld:b.12.73

XVII. VICARS, PRIESTS, CHURCHES

901. There's this man and he goes to a massive monastary, knocks
      on the door and the chief monk comes and he says, can I stay
      here for the night! So he says yeah, so he goes and gets all his
      clothes out, and puts them in his drawers, and before he goes
      to bed, he says Chief Monk, can I have an apple, an orange,
      and a piece of string? And the father goes yeah, of course you
      can, if you want it really. So he gives him it and he goes to
      bed. Next day, can I stay again? So he stays again, same thing
      happens that night, can I have an apple, an orange and a piece
      of string? So he says yeah, of course you can. And this goes on
      for about 8 weeks, until this chief monk is going to die soon
      he's getting right old, an apple, an orange and a piece of string
      every night. And so he goes up one night and gives him an
      apple, orange, and a piece of string and he says, look, will you
      please tell me why you want this apple, orange, and piece of
      string? So he says no, I can't tell you. So he says no please tell
      me. So he says, I can't tell you unless you keep your word as a

true monk, so he says okay, and he told him. And the monk was a true monk and he never told no one.

Ld:b.12.73 (Eng:b.13.74)

902. It's about this monastary, up in the hills, and you see, and you see all these tramps you see and poor people that haven't got homes, they go to this monastary to see if they can sleep there. So this, the first one walks to the monastary door and knocks on the door and the monk comes to the door and opens the door and says, yes my son, and he says can I sleep here for the night please, and he says, and the monk says yes. So he says well what would you like for your breakfast? And he says I'd like an orange, a banana and a crust of bread. And he thinks it's odd, is that, but anyways, he does as he wishes and gives him his food for the morning, and in the middle of the night there's a big bang, and all the monastary explodes, but he's still alive, this man. And after a couple of years the monastary is rebuilt, and he goes to the monastary again and knocks on the door and the monk comes to the door and says yes my son, he says could I, can I please sleep here for the night? He says yes, what would you like for your breakfast? So he says I would like an orange, a banana, and a crust of bread. So he thinks this is a bit odd, and it's not the same monk, because the other ones were killed. And in the middle of the night a big bang, and the monastary explodes, and there's only him alive. Well after 5 years, they build an even bigger monastary, and the same fellow comes to the door, knocks on the door, and this new monk comes to the door and says, yes my son, and he says could I please sleep here for tonight? He says yes, what would you like for breakfast? And he says a banana, an orange, and a crust of bread. And he thinks ah, alright then, so he gives him his orange, banana, and crust of bread. And in the middle of the night, a big bang, and the monastary explodes, again so anyway after another 10 years they build an even bigger monastary, like the Empire State Building, and it's thousands and thousands of feet up into the air, and he

comes to the door and knocks on the door, and he says could I sleep here for the night please? And he says of course my son. What would you like for your breakfast? And he says a banana, an orange, and a crust of bread. And he says alright then, here's your banana, orange, and crust of bread and he sleeps there. And in the middle of the night there's another big bang, and the whole building falls down and he's still alive. And you know, the people are getting used to this, and they're watching this man. And there's one man, there's one monk, that was asked to watch him all the time, and to not sleep in the monastary, because they know it's going to fall down, they knew it was going to explode. So anyway he goes for the last time and knocks on the door and says could I sleep here for the night? He says yes my son, what would you like for you breakfast? So he says an orange, a crust of bread and a banana. So he says alright, my son. And again, as expected, the monastary fell down. Well this monk, goes right, this is got to be the last time. So he gets this fellow and he takes him to the cliff face and says, now will you tell me why this monastary everytime you sleep in our monastary it always falls down, it always explodes just for no reason? So he says I'm not telling you. Look will you tell me please? He says no. So he gets him by the throat and says, if you won't tell me, I'll push you over the cliff, so he says no, so he pushes him over the cliff.

Ld:b.13.73

903. There's this vicar in an airplane, and he's going over to somewhere, and they're right, and they hear over the microphone we are now flying at a thousand, so many thousand feet, and the vicar goes 'Good God' and he hears the voice say, 'yes my son.'

Ld:b.12.73

904. Then some more news comes over and it says, I am sorry, there will be a slight delay, engine No. 1 has now cut out, there is only 3 engines left. And then about 10 minutes later, there is another slight delay, we will be a bit later, engine No. 2 and 3 have cut out, there is only No. 4 left. And so, the vicar

says to the person next to him, good golly, if other one cuts out, we'll be up here all night.

Ld:b.13.73 (US:g.11.75-Polack, b.12.75 a- 2 people, wife) See next joke

905. See a Polack, he was flying in an airplane and one of his engines burned out, and he called down to his men below, that I'll have to stay up here for a half an hour cause one of my engines burned out. So then, a second one conked out, so he said he'd have to be up there for around 2 hours. Then the 3rd one came out, and he said that he'd be up there for 5 hours. Then he said, oh my god, if the 4th one comes out, I'll be up here all day. But if the 4th one went out, he'd crash.

SD:g.11.75

906. This fellow, and he goes up to this woman and he says is your dog black with a white collar? She says no, he says is it white with a black collar? She says no. And then he says oh god, I must have knocked the vicar over.

Ld:b.12.73

907. There was man standing at church, and the preacher said put money in box and he says okay, I'll put it in. So he put it in and he says blasphemous. And he came in again and says blasphermous and priest says if you say that again God will send a thunderbolt down. So he says it again and God sent a thunderbolt down and it hit the priest instead.

Ld:b.7.73

908. There's this boy, and his red wagon, it's wheels always fall off. And so, a priest walks by and his wheel falls off and he goes God damit. And the priest says, don't say God damit, say God help me. And so, next time his wheels break off, and he says well the priest was walking by, he says God damit, say God help me. Next time, he goes God dang everytime. And then the next time his wheels fall off he goes, God, and then he goes God help me. And then the priest goes, God dang, cause the wheel fell off on him.

SD:g.11.75

909. This boy was walking down the lane, bouncing a bottle of acid, and this priest said to him, 'huh, that bottle of acid can't

do anything, so the boy said huh. The priest said, I dipt my hands in some holy water and placed my hands on a woman's stomach and she passed a baby.' Then the boy said, 'so what, I put a bit on my cat's bottom and it passed a motorcycle.'

Ld:g.10.73

910.   Policeman to Clergyman stopped for speeding:
       Sorry Reverend, I'm afraid your speedometer runneth over.

SD:b.12.75

911.   Once a man in church listened to a very interesting sermon but when he came out the man said, 'it was a nice sermon but I've got every word of that in a book at home.' 'But you can't have' he said, 'I wrote it only last night.' So the next morning the man sent him a copy of the English dictionary.

Ld:g.10.73

912.   There's these 2 nuns walking down a dark alley and this man with a big dark mask on jumps out and rapes them both. As they're walking back home from being raped, one of them says to the other nun, what shall we tell Mother Superior when we tell her we've been raped twice? And so the other one says we've only been raped once haven't we? And she says yes, but we're going back again aren't we?

Ld:b.13.73

913.   There's this fellow and he's interviewing this monk you know, and he says what was it like in the WWII? So he says well when the Americans came, you know, they raped us, everybody except Sister Matilde, and he goes really, and he goes yeah, and he says and when they came back they raped us all except the Sister Matilde. And then when the Germans came they raped us all except the Sister Matilde, and when the English came they raped us all except the Sister Matilde. And when they all came back they raped us all except for the Sister Matilde. And he says, why, why didn't they rape the Sister Matilde? And he goes, Sister Matilde doesn't like that sort of thing.

Ld:b.12.73 (Eng:b.10.73)

XVIII. BODY FUNCTIONS

914. There's a woman and her son in a big large store. And her son
      goes, Mom, I want to wee wee (shout). So she goes, with a
      bright red face, sshh son, everybody will hear ya. She says
      next time say mom, I want to whisper. So he says alright. And
      then he's at home and he wants to go to toilet, so he says to his
      dad, dad I want to whisper. So he says, go on son, whisper in
      my ear.

      Ld:g.13.73

915. This boy says to the teacher, sir, can I go to the toilet? And so
      he says, and the teacher says no, sit down and do your work.
      And he says, but sir, I can't swim.

      Ld:g.12.73

916. This is my joke, and I warn you it's a long one. It's the middle
      of the night, in London, and this old backyard, in some old
      tattered house, and this dog is scrounging around this dustbin,
      something to eat. And suddenly this horrible growling noise,
      from behind this dustbin, and out comes this hairy hand with
      blood on it. And dog scared, for out comes Wolfman. Along
      trudges Wolfman, and until he comes to this pub, he gets
      down to the cellar and drinks 15 pints of beer. He gets out, he
      comes out drunk. A few days later, these circus men have
      heard of him, cause he's been, you know, going around to all
      the houses, doing all these horrible things, killing a few
      people as well and they set out to catch him, and they catch
      him. Well, one day he's travelling along on this old country
      road in one of those cages, on wheels, suddenly he breaks out,
      cause he's sick of being in it, and comes along until he comes
      to a farmhouse. He knocks on the door, and farmer opens it
      and says, I know who you are, you're Wolfman aren't you?
      And he says yes in wolfman language. He says you're just
      escaped the circus haven't you? And he says yes. He says what
      do you want? He says can I go to your toilet?

      Ld:b.8.73

917. Well you see, last Friday night I was washing up all the dishes and this flying saucer came and landed on the grass outside the window. And out came this what looked like a 6 foot raspberry pudding pie and you see, he came in, he knocked on the door, knock knock knock, and he said who's there? and he say me, and he said, who's me? So he said come in and he said I've been travelling all these light years and I've never stopped before, and then I say to him, what do you want here? And he said, like this, I want to go to the toilet.

Ld:b.8.73

918. See there's this monkey sniffing around these dustbins and this man looks out the window and he saw this monkey sniffing around these dustbins, and the other thing, this man went downstairs, and opened the door and he said, can I go to the toilet please? And he escaped from the circus. And there's these other men came along, and said have you ever seen a monkey around here? Yes, he's just gone to the toilet.

Ld:b.9.73

919. You see, you know, there's this other teacher, you know, in a class you see, and this boy goes, Miss, I got to do a piss. So the teacher says, you don't say that, how rude of you. You say, Miss, I want to do my number 1. So the boy says okay Miss, I want to do my number 1. So he goes out. So this other boy goes Miss, I want to do my shit. So she goes how dare you, you don't say that. You say I want to do my number 2. So the boy goes I want to do my number 2 then so he goes out you see. So this boy shouts, Miss, Fred wants to fart, what's his code number?

Ld:b.12.73

920. There was once a boy who was asked by his teacher to say his ABC and the boy said but Miss can't I go to the toilet and his teacher said no, say your ABC first and so he got to the 'o' and missed out 'p' and so his teacher said you missed out the 'p' and so he said Miss the pee is running down my leg.

L:g.11.74

921. A boy said to his teacher can I go to the loo, and she said say the alphabet and he missed the loo out and he done a loo in his pants.

L:b.8.74

922. I was at my friend's birthday party, and the other guy said I'm going to go to the bathroom. So the other guy said, don't fall in.

SD:b.9.75

923. This boy dann a wie (done a wee) in his pustrs (trousers) and a car come along and dann a sarrasmk (?)

L:b.8.74

924. There I sat broken-hearted, paid a penny and only farted.

Ld:g.13.73

925. There's this Indian chief, and he can't fart you see, and he, anyway, he goes to doctor and says I can't, honest doctor. So he says well take this pill. So he takes the pill and comes back and says I still can't fart. And he goes, oh you can't well, take this larger pill, it's about this big you see. Oh okay, and he come back again and he says I haven't farted yet. And he goes, take this massive big pill, as long as this, nope, and then he gets a pill just as big, you know, bigger than this building. Next day, well these Indian braves comes back and say, Big Fart No Chief.

Ld:b.12.73

926. I was walking down the path one day, when I looked up in the sky to see a birdey with a merrgeag blop right in my eye, I'm glad my cows don't fly.

L:b.10.74

927. There was an old lady of seventy and who wanted to go to the lavatory. It must be done it will be done so out of the window she popped her bum. A copper came by and looked up high, dollop right in his eye.

L:g.8.74 (fragment of a song)

928. Once there was this guy who went to Rome and he says, where's the john? And he goes, there is no john, just stick your butt out the window. So this far-sighted guy and near-sighted guy comes along and says, and the near-sighted guy goes, you should have seen the guy who spit on me, and the far-sighted guy goes, you should have seen his lips.

(john = toilet)
SD:b.11.75

XIX. CHILDREN

929. Well, there was the boy, and he was playing very nicely and his mother said, uh, just stay there while I go to the shop. So, when she came back, she saw him crying and she says what's the matter luv? He said, I've lost me green ball (points to her nose, nose snot)

Ld:g.12.73

930. This boy is asked by his mum to go to the butcher's to get a half a pound of bacon and when he got there butcher's was shut, and then on his way home he lost 50p down the gutter, so he cut half of his ass off and cut it up into slices of bacon and wrapped it up in a piece of paper, and took it home to his mom. And his mom fried it and they ate it for supper that night. She said that was nice. Next day she sent him for another half pound, and he lost another 50 p and so he cut the other half of his ass off, and wrapped it up, and his mum ate that. And then next day she said go up and get ready for your bath and I'll come up in a minute to bath you. So he went upstairs and got ready for his bath and his mom started washing him and she said turn around, and she said where's your ass gone? He says you ate it for your supper. And so she took him to the doctors, and the doctor gave him a wooden ass, and that broke, and so he went back and the doctor gave him a glass ass. And he went to school that day, and sat down

and it broke and teacher goes what was that? And they all shouted out glass bum.

Ld:g.12.73 (NJ:b.10.28)

931.   This man goes into a pub and he puts 5 pounds on the bar and he says, give me a glass of beer, and I bet you the rest of that money that I can make you sick. So he says oh, I'll give you 10 pounds if you can and you give me 5 pounds if you can't. So he puts his 10 pounds down next to the other 5 pounds so there's 15 pounds for the winner. And so this man who's going to make the other man sick puts his finger right down his throat, pulls his guts up, and he's all sick. And other man behind bar is sick, all over the table. So the man takes the 15 pounds. So this barman thinks gosh, I've lost 10 pounds there, I'll have to get it back somehow. So he goes into another pub, and he sees this man set down at a table, this old fellow, and he goes over to him and he says, I bet you 10 pounds I can make you sick and he says I'll give you 20 pounds if you can make me sick, so he says okay then and he puts his finger down his throat, pulls his guts up, and he's sick all over the table. And the little old fellow says that ain't make me sick, bet I can make you sick now, and he starts to eat it.

Ld:b.12.73

932.   There's this man, and he goes in a bar, and he's pig sick, he's just about to be sick, and there's a little dog sat down by the side of it, and he's sick all over the dog, and he looks down and there's this dog covered in sick, and he goes funny, I don't remember eating that.

Ld:b.13.74

933.   There were 3 boys who were called Mindyourownbusiness, Manners and Trouble. One day Trouble got lost. A policeman found them trespassing, and took them to the police station. Mindyourownbusiness went inside and Manners stayed outside. The sergeant asked Mindyourownbusiness his name. He said Mindyourownbusiness. Then the sergeant said where are your manners? Outside. Are you

looking for trouble? said the sergeant. Yes, said Mindyourownbusiness.

Ld:b.10.73 (Eng:b.7.73, b.8.73, g.6.73, g.8.73, b.10.74, b.11.74)

934. There's this man in church, and he didn't know what to say so
he walked in dustbin and he didn't find naught, so there was
one called Getaway, and one called Stupid. Getaway said get
away, and stupid said get, uh, stupid get away. And they both
run out of church, and they uh, they didn't know what to say,
so they banged their heads and they were unconscious.

Ld:b.7.73

935. There's this little boy called Nickabar and he's waiting at the
bus stop for the bus with his mum and he says can I have a bit
of chocolate please and she goes alright, here's 5 pence and he
goes to the shop and there's a big long queue, and he's just
going to be served, and his mum sees the bus coming so she
shouts for him, Nickabar, so he nicks a bar and runs.

(nick = to steal)
Ld:b.12.73

936. There's this lad and he's called Jesus and his mom says to him,
on a Sunday, it is, cause it's a funny fish shop, she says go to
fish shop and get me twice fish and a bag of chips, and anyway
he goes alright mom, but, what do I know a fish shop looks
like cause I'm only 3 and I haven't seen one before. Well she
goes, there'll be a long queue outside. And anyway well he
goes to the fish shop wandering about the streets and he comes
across this church and there's a queue of people outside and he
goes ah, fish shop this. Anyway he's going in and picks up a
Bible, ah, this is a big menu. Anyway he goes in and sits in
front row and vicar stands up and goes first we shall serve
Jesus, and then Jesus stands up and goes twice fish and a bag of
chips please.

Ld:b.12.73

937. There's this teacher, and this boy and the boy says, oh Miss, I
don't want to do me homework. So she says, right, go and ask
your brother, sister or your dad what Constantinople mean
(Constamptinopile was how they pronounced it). So he goes

and asks his dad what Constantinople means. So anyway he goes in and his dad's watching telly, and he says dad, dad, what does Constantinople mean? So he says ah shut up. So he goes into his sister's room and she's playing her records you see, and he says sister, what does Constantinople mean? So he says ya ya ya. So he goes into his brother's room and he's got another telly, so he says brother, what does Constantinople mean? So he says dana nana nana Batman. So he goes back to school and teacher says, have you found out what Constantinople means? So he says ah shutup, so she says are you looking for the cane? He goes ya ya ya. She says who do you think you are? Dana nana nana nana Batman.

Ld:b.12.73 (Eng:b.6.73, b.10.73, b.12.73, g.8.73, g.13.73, b.11.75)

938. A little rich boy was attending school for the first time. His mother told him not to tell the class that his family was rich. His first assignment was to write about his family. He wrote: 'my parents are poor. Our maid and butler are poor, and so is the lifeguard at our pool.'

SD:b.12.75

939. Four college students, overcome with spring fever, came to school late one morning. The teacher asked them why they were late and informed them they had missed a test. They claimed their car had a flat tire. To their surprise he smiled understandingly. "Please take seats apart from each other, and take out your notebooks," he said. When they were settled he asked them to answer one question in their notebooks. "Which tire was flat?"

SD:b.12.75

940. You see, there was this teacher in a class and he goes right, I want you all to, you know, make a poem of what you're going to do when you grow up. So you know, you know, Billie starts, he goes, no, Sam stands up and goes 'My name is Sam, and when I am a man, I'm going to Japan if I can, and I know I can.' So Sadie stand up, you know a girl, she goes, 'My name is Sadie, and when I'm a lady, I'm going to have a baby, if I can and I know I can.' So you know Jock stand, he's the bad boy in the class you know, and he goes 'My name is

Jock, and when I'm a man, to hell with Japan, I'm staying at home and helping Sadie with her plan.' (said with different voice, Jock gruff, his own voice for Sam, higher for Sadie)

Ld:b.13.73

941. There was this phone call into head mistresses office and she picked it up and a voice says, Tommy Brown won't be at school today, so Head Mistress says, why not? So the voice says cause he's going to dentist. So Head Mistress says, who's speaking please? So the voice say, uh, it's me dad.

Ld:b.12.73

942. This little boy, he went up to his teacher, and he goes, teacher, if my dad says if somebody doesn't get better grades around here, somebody's due for a spanking. And it doesn't make sense unless you make a man spanking a lady. Yeah, you see, what he's trying to say that is his, that he's trying to get his teacher to give him better grades, because if he doesn't his teacher's in for a spanking.

SD:g.10.75

943. Two children, there's a boy and a girl, and they share a bedroom and they're shouting down to their mum and dad, when they're in bed, and their dad shouts, look if you two don't shut up I'm coming up to sort you out. So a few minutes later they shout, dad when you come up to sort us out will you bring us a drink of water?

Ld:g.13.73

944. There's this boy, and he's always telling lies, and his father says, Winston Churchill's son never used to tell lies. (or George Washington, but it doesn't matter) and he said, cause one day his son chopped down his best tree and he said did you chop down my best tree and he said yeah, and he says, he never did anything to him cause he's been so honest. So he said alright dad, I'll try and be honest. And so his dad has got this brand new tool shed by the river and he can't resist the temptation of pushing it in, so he pushes it in and then his dad comes in and he says come here, I want you. Did you push my

good tool in the river? And he said yeah, and so he give him a good hiding, and then the boy said to him, I thought you said Winston Churchill's son didn't get a hiding cause he told the truth, he said yeah yeah, but Winston Churchill wasn't up the tree when he did it.

Ld:b.12.73

945. There's this woman, and she loved living an ordinary working class town, and the queen comes to visit it, the queen's got to visit it. So she says, she says to her daughter, who's always rude and all that, she says, now you must be on your best behaviour, be very polite, and you must really be courteous to the queen cause she's coming to visit us this afternoon. So, the daughter starts thinking, she says, well instead of me staying in I think I'll go out. So then I won't have to slick up. So then the queen comes to visit the mother, and they're having a cup of tea in the front room and the little daughter runs in and says mum mum our cat's just spewed up a dead cats.

Ld:b.13.74

946. A working mother, living in a tenement in New York City, had twin boys, Ikey and Mikey. And she's going to work, and the baby sitter has already left, so she stands outside on the sidewalk and yells, "Ikey, Ikey, throw me my key." so he picked up his brother and threw him out the window.

NY:g.12.61

947. There's this fellow being burglared, and he gets this gun, and he's holding up the burglar, and a little lad goes and gets a glass of water and goes, you better fill it up dad.

Ld:b.12.73

948. There's this fellow and he's been in a place, and he's coming through customs, and he has a little boy and this customs officer thinks he's got some luggage that he's trying you know, to smuggle in to the country. Anyway, he opens his case, and he's smuggled in this packet full of clothes. And the little boy goes, he's getting close dad isn't he?

Ld:b.12.73

XX. MEN

949. It's about a young boy, who on his first birthday, his father asks him for, what's he want for his birthday so he said he wanted a yellow ping pong ball so his father was a bit confused and he decided to say you don't want a yellow ping pong ball, you want a teddy bear. He said alright, I'll have a teddy bear. So he buys him a teddy bear. So he goes in for his 11+, and his father says, for passing your 11+ what would you like, and so he said I'd like a yellow ping pong ball, so he said you wouldn't like a yellow ping pong ball, you'd like, say, a brand new bike, so he says alright, then I'll have a brand new bike. So he goes, he decides to join the University and his father is very pleased about this and asks him what he'd like for joining the University so he said I'd like a yellow ping pong ball and his father said, look, you don't want a yellow ping pong ball, you, you want say a brand new car. So alright, a brand new car. After 3 years at University he decides to join the Army, and his father is very pleased with this so he asks him what he wants for joining the Army so again he replied a yellow ping pong ball and his father is really getting mad and he says look wouldn't you like a brand new tank, your own tank, oh alright then. So after 3 years in the Army he starts fighting, he's in combat, and he gets wounded, and he's in the battle field and his father got rushed to the scene where he was wounded, and he's there, laying on the floor, and he's dying, and it's the last minutes of his life, and his father says, just before you die my son, will you tell me what you wanted a yellow ping pong ball for? So his son replied, well I wanted a yellow ping pong ball for — ough (sound of dying)

Ld:b.13.73

950. There was once a man and he wanted a house built of 500 blue and white bricks. The truck went for them and came back.

But on the way the truck dropped a blue and white brick. The house was built and then they noticed they had one missing. So the truck had to go all the way back again and come with one brick. They fixed it on, the house was built. (then you say, 'do you get it?'. Then after that you say 'I will tell you another joke then.') There was once a man and a woman who had a dog. They were in the same compartment in a train. The man started to smoke. The dog started to cough, like this, coh coh coh coh. The lady said, 'if you don't stop smoking I'll throw your cigarette out the window.' The man didn't stop smoking so the lady got his cigarette and threw it out of the window. The man started smoking another cigarette. The dog went coh coh coh coh. The lady said 'if you don't stop smoking I'll throw your cigarette out of the window.' The man didn't stop, so the lady got his cigarette and threw it out of the window. The man started smoking another cigarette. The dog went coh coh coh coh. The lady said 'If you don't stop smoking I'll throw your cigarette out of the window.' So the man said, 'if you throw my cigarette out of the window I will throw your dog out of the window.' He carried on smoking. So the lady got his cigarette and threw it out of the window. So the man threw the dog out of the window. When they arrived at the station the dog was there. What do you think he had in his mouth? A blue and white brick.

Ld:g.11.73

951.   This man right, and he asked this other man to help him to get this horse in to through the door. So he pushed and pushed and get it through the door. He says, will you do another favor? He says what? He says, help me get it up the stairs. He says alright. So he gets it up the stairs, uph, upug (noises of great struggle) and he gets it up stairs. (panting, heavy breathing) and when he's put out, he says will you do us another favor? He says what now? He says will you help me put it in the bath? So he says okay, agph (more sounds of effort) lift 1,2,3 ooh, and they get it in the bath. And he says excuse me but why were you asking me to put it in the bath

for? He says well my wife always says that she knows everything, and this time, when she comes in, and goes up the stairs she'll say, I'll say, she'll say Albert, do you know there's a horse in a bath? He says, I know everything.

Ld:b.12.73

952. There's this small man, who was walking along the path at night, and he wanted to get from Manchester to Liverpool. And he saw this car coming along with no driver, and he thought this is strange, no driver. Well, he got in the car, and he went along, no driver, and he stopped, he stopped just outside Liverpool, just where he wanted to go, and he got out of the car and this big fellow came around, and little fellow said to him, shouldn't get in that car, it's got no driver. Big fellow said yeah, I know, I've been pushing it all the way from Manchester.

L:b.11.75

953. As he paid his hotel bill, the departing guest turned and yelled to the bellboy, "quick boy, run up to room 999 and see if I left my briefcase and overcoat. Hurry up, because I've got six minutes to catch my train." Four minutes later the bellboy was back all out of breath. "Yes, sir" he reported, "they're up there."

SD:b.12.75

954. This fellow, and he goes up and he's going to buy a brand new car and he goes up, and he goes up, and he's going to buy a big Jaguar, and a fellow says well this is too big for you, you want a smaller car, like a Mini. And so he goes to buy a Mini and then he says can you drive? And he says no and he says, you can't buy a car. Go to a bicycle shop and they'll fit you up. So, he goes over to the bike shop and is just going to buy it and the fellow says can you ride and he says no, well, go to Fine Feather, they'll fit you up and so he goes in, but just in the doorway there's these wheels with hoops on them, hoop and stick, and he says I'll have them and he pays his 2 schillings and goes out. And he's going down, along the road with his

own hoop and stick. And you know those over night things where you can sleep in them, hotels, and he stops there, and he puts it outside and ties it up and goes in and sleeps the night, and he comes downstairs next morning and it's gone, someone nicked it, and he goes to the manager and says here someones nicked my hoop and stick and the manager says well so what, and he says well how am I going to get home?

Ld:b.12.73

955. There was this fellow who was carrying this big wardrobe you see, full of clothes. So this silly little boy came across the street, he goes, isn't anyone helping you? so he goes ah ya, me mate is inside the cubboard, he's carrying the clothes.

Ld:b.13.73

956. You see, there's this man, going along the desert, in a car, and the car suddenly stops. And so he starts walking, and there's no water and no petrol left. And so he starts walking and it's in the middle of the afternoon and he's crawling along. He sees this Arab on a camel, and he's crawling along shouting for water. But the Arab goes no, I only sell ties. And he keeps going, and later on in the afternoon he sees another Arab on a camel, and the Arab says no, I only sell ties. And he comes up to the hotel, in a middle of a desert, a hotel nowhere, he's just going to crawl in the door, and a doorman says, I'm afraid you can't come in dressed like that, you haven't got a tie.

L:b.11.75 (Eng:b.11.75)

957. There's this man, and he was hungry, and he didn't have no money, and he was skinny like, and so he saw a newspaper ad where, and it said on the newspaper, 'the detectives are finding out criminals nowdays by the fingerprints.' So he thought, oh well, I'll be able to open the safe with out them. So he went into the bank, and took his shoes and socks off, and started to open the safe with his feet. And when he got the money out, he said to himself, oh well, that ought to keep the fingerprint men amused.

L:b.11.75

958. A man went into the woods and he bought a horse from a man who lived in the woods. He was sort of like a hermit. He bought the horse. He had 4 horses, he bought one, and he said I'm not sure my wife will want me to have this. So the little man rode back on his horse, and the man rode back on the horse he was going to buy to his home. And the little man said, and his wife was glad, and the little man said amen, and the horse stopped. And then the next night he had a party, and everybody wanted to see his new horse ride so he got on it and said giddup ya, and nothing he wouldn't go at all. And then the next day he went back to the man and said, my horse won't go. And he just won't go. And then the little man said, to make it go say 'thank the lord', to make it stop say 'amen.' And so he got on when he got home he got on the horse and said, 'thank the lord', and the horse went really fast, he was amazed at the speed it went. And then it was going straight for a cliff, and he forgot the word to make it stop. And right at the minute he said 'amen'. And then he goes (gesture: wipe sweat off forehead), thank the lord, he goes swish (gesture) thank the lord.

SD:b.10.75

959. Once there was a man, his name was Jose, and he went to a baseball game, and he got a ticket, and there was no seats left for the baseball game, so they said that he could sit on top of a flagpole, and so he did. And at the end of the game they asked him how did he like it up there and he said, oh sure, everybody was nice to me today, they said, Jose can you see.

SF:g.10.74

960. There was this man, he was amusing people in the doctor's ward, in the ward kind of thing, and he was trying to make them all happy, and he was telling jokes and things, and this man came in, an old man. He said, coming into a doctor's ward isn't funny as you think. I come here to have my eyes checked, and he said, isn't that funny, I thought that your eyes were brown. And then the doctor came in, checked his back, and said I think you ought to go home and have a glass of

orange and then a hot bath. And he said, I don't mind having the glass of orange, but I think the hot bath might be a bit too much.

L:g.11.75

961. There's this fellow and he wants to be a chef, a cook and he goes to a plush hotel and he sees manager and says I want to be a chef, I got four 0-levels in cooking, or whatever it is, and so can you test me out in kitchen, so he says okay, come in kitchen. And he gets 2 eggs in his hands, throws them up in the air, they hit his head, slide down back of his neck, down his trousers into his shoe, kicks his shoe up in the air, they go up in air, land on the light, fall into a pan, crack, the eggs jump into a bin. So he says hay, that's good, so he says do you want me to do it again, so he says no, I've seen enough. So he says well have I got the job, so he says, you would have, but you take too long.

Ld:b.12.73

962. Well, there was this man, and he was going to have his walls painted yellow, and there was going to be a Chinese painter. And they covered all the furniture with yellow sheets, and the painter came along, and he painted it, and then the man went into the room and he said, where are you?

Ld:g.8.73

963. This man goes into the hairdressers to get his hair cut and you know done, and he gets hair cut and a lot of it dropped out, and he's only got a bit of hair, at the top sticking up, Well, how do you want this bit hair sticking up? Well part one bit this way, and a one bit that way. Well, he gets the comb and he puts it in the middle and one bit that way and one bit that way and a bit drops out of each side, and he says oh I'm sorry sir, but some hair has dropped out of each side and he's only got 3 hairs left. So what do you want me to do with these? Well, I'll tell you what, one that way, one that way, and one sticking up. And so he says alright sir. So he combs one hair and it comes out, and he combs another hair and it comes out.

So he says, oh I'm sorry sir but two of your hairs have come
out and you only have 1 hair left. What do you want me to do
with it? So he says, that's alright, just leave it for the food.

Ld:b.13.73

964.   There are two barbers in this one city, and this man needs a
        haircut. And so he goes over to a policeman, he says, where is
        the nearest barbershop? And he goes, well there's one on the
        South Street, and there's one on North Street. And then he
        goes, first I'll look at them and then I'll decide which one I
        wanna go. He goes to the one on North Street and it's really
        messy, but the guy has a really good haircut but the place is
        really slopped up, and there's hair all over the ground stuff. So
        he goes the one on South Street and it was really clean, but the
        guy had a really ugly haircut. So he decided to go to the one
        on South Street. Why? Because the guy on North Street had
        to cut that guys hair.

        SD:g.11.75

965.   This man's house, crawling with rats his house, and then he
        called the health society and this, and some of these people
        came, and he said, there's loads of rats in this house. So he got
        a loaf of bread, cut it in half, and put half on the floor. And
        then a big rat came out of the join, uh, skirtingboard, took
        half a loaf and went back. Then this fish came out and took
        other half, went back, and the man, he said never mind the
        damp, gets rid of the rats.

        Ld:b.11.73

966.   These two people, the Spaniard women, come to get into a
        hotel, and he says, here's your 2 keys. And they each pay the
        money. Then they go up, night, and then there's 3 men, it's
        $30 for them to get in. They each pay $10. And they give the
        man $5 for a tip. And so they go up to their rooms. And the
        man goes up to give him the money back because $5 is a little
        bit too much for a tip, and he doesn't need them anyways,
        cause he's a millionaire. So he gives them the money. He's
        supposed to give the whole. $5. He gives them $4, how many
        are left over? The one's left over for the candy bars in the
        bathroom.

        SD:g.10.75

967. There's this fellow and he's waiting for the train, and he says to this porter, what time is the next train for London, and he says, well by the timetable half-past six, but it generally comes in at 7. He says what's the next time for the train going to Brighton? And he says, well, by the timetable its quarter past six, but it always comes in at half-past six. And he says well what's the time for the trains to go to Liverpool? And he says well by the timetable it should be five past six, but it generally comes in about 10 past six. So he says what's the use of having a timetable it they always come in late? So he says, well you wouldn't be able to tell if they were late if we didn't.

Ld:b.12.73

968. One day a plane went up into the sky and in the plane went 50,000,000 feet and the pilot said good morning, and he said you look to the right you will see new lands, and if you look to left you will see the left wings on fire, and if you look down you will see a runway. I am sick to you from it.

L:b.9.74

969. There were two women who got on a bus. Busdriver – where do you want to go? One woman – can I have a ticket for Flora? Busdriver – that's a long way. One woman – oh no it, it's not. She's right next to me.

Ld:g.8.73

970. There's this man and he goes to, and there's a right long bus queue and they all got on and there's no room downstairs so he pulls his eye out, throws it up in the air, catches it, throws it up in the air, catches it, throws it up in the air, and puts it back in, so a fellow says what you do that for? So he says only to see if there's any room upstairs.

Ld:b.12.73

971. There was this man stood at bus stop, and he was bouncing, and he had a glass and he was bouncing it up and down to see if there was any room upstairs, and it bust.

Ld:g.8.73 (see preceding joke)

972. A man goes on a bus with a lemon behind his ear. The bus conductor said, what is that behind your ear, a hearingaid? No, a lemon, it's a lemonade.

   L:b.10.74

973. There was this man, and he had a banana in his ear. And this man asked him, why do you have a banana in your ear? And he said I can't hear you. And he says excuse me, you've got banana in your ear. He said, can't hear you, and he said cause I got banana in my ear.

   L:b.11.75

974. There was a man going along the road Then a man come in his car and said, Get in then he said get out and see if my light is working and he said yes no yes and yes no.

   L:b.9.74

975. There's this man, in his car, driving down the road, and this bee flies in the window. So he shuts the window up, so then the bee wants to get out, so he lets the bee out. He driving along, and suddenly he runs out of gasoline. So this swarm of bees come, and they take the tank and take it to the garage. And when they come back the man says, what did you fill it up with? B.P. (bee pee)

   (B.P. = British Petrol, brand of gasoline)
   L:g.11.75

976. There's this man standing at bus stop and he had no arms and no legs, and the bus pulls up and the driver knew him so he says, how you getting on Fred?

   Ld:b.8.73

977. There's this man with 3 eyes, no arms and 1 leg hitchhiking and wanting a lift, and a car came up and the man said eye eye eye, you look harmless, hop in.

   Ld:b.8.73

978. Daddy, daddy, everybody else is calling me a 3-headed monster. What should I do? Oh don't worry about it son, that's all right. (gesture of patting head, 3 heads)

   SD:g.12.75 (Eng:b.11.73)

979. Well there was this boy walking on this road, and he saw a
birds eye, and so he picked it up, and then he walked on a bit
and saw a fish, and so he picked it up, and he was walking
along and saw a finger, and so he picked it up and then the
policeman came along and says what do you got in your
pocket? And he says Bird's Eye Fish Fingers.

    Ld:b.8.73 (Eng:b.8.73, b.8.74, g.9.74)

980. See Dracula comes up to this cart, and inside this cart is this
man, see this man is selling oranges and apples, and Dracula
says to man, can I have ½ pound of blood oranges please?

    Ld:b.8.73

XXI. MEN AND THEIR OCCUPATIONS

981. Two workmen had been working all day and one said to the
other, is there a pub round here anywhere? And the other
man said there's one down the road called the Queen's Legs.
They went there and it was closed so they waited outside and
a policeman came along and he said, what's going on here so
they said, we're waiting for the Queen's legs to open so we
can get a drink.

    Ld:g.10.73 (Eng:b.8.73, g.10.74)

982. This man went into this bar and said can I have a gin and
tonic? The man said, get out, you drunk. So he went out
round the corner, round back into the same bar and said can I
have a gin and tonic? And he said get out you drunk, so he
went out round the corner round back and went into the same
bar and said can I have a gin and tonic? And the man said get
out you drunk and the drunk man said, do you own all the
pubs in town?

    Ld:b.9.73 (Eng:b.9.73)

983. There was a ghost, he went into the pub and the ghost said can
I have a drink and the barman said sorry, we do not sell spirits.

    L:b.9.74

984. There was this man, and it was his anniversary, and he
thought right, I'll go have a boozer, you know, have a party.
So he was there, he started at 6 o'clock and then he came back
at 12. And he opened the door, and he went upstairs, and he
had a bottle of whiskey in his back pocket. Anyway, by his
mistake he fell down the stairs, and the bottle of whiskey
smashed all on his ass. And so he went upstairs and went ooh
ah, you know going ooh agh (sounds of pain and grimaces)
So he went upstairs, and he got this mirror, but he couldn't see
it properly, and he got these plasters, and so he going, that one
goes there, that one goes there and that one goes there
(Motions: turns around head, looking over shoulder, to put
on the plasters) So, he says ah that feels better, and so he goes
into bed. Next morning, his wife comes in and says, you've
been drinking again, haven't you? No I haven't, he says. Well
why the bloody hell are all them plasters on the mirrors?

(plasters = band-aids)
Ld:b.12.73

985. There's this drunk man, outside this pub. And this other man
comes along, carrying a box of bananas. He says, excuse me
sir, can you keep guard of this box of bananas while I go in
and have some Guiness. So he says okay, and he says, now, if
anyone comes along, and asks you how much they are, say
they are 10p a quarter, and 5p for 2ozs. of them. Well he goes
in and drunk man is left outside with the box of bananas. And
this man comes along and he asks, and he says to drunk man,
excuse me sir, do you know what time it is? and he says 10p
for a quarter sir. And the other man said, what do you mean
10p for a quarter, I asked you what time it was. Well forget
about that then, do you know whereabout is Waterloo
Street? And he says 5p a quarter.

Ld:b.8.73

986. There's this fellow, and he's driving home about 12.00 at
night. And he goes, I might as well have a drink, and he goes
to this pub, and he goes in, and the carpark is full and he has to
go ½mile down the road, just to park and he's walking back

and he gets into the pub, and he goes, and there's nobody in there, the carpark is full, but nobody is in there, not a desolate soul, only the, you know, landlord. Anyways, he going, he goes why is your carpark so full but there's nobody in there, you know, you know. And he goes, well its oot oot (like owl sound) night, anyway, he goes, what is this oot oot night, and he goes, well the landlord says you've got to drink 2 rums and a pint of bitter. And he goes, I might as well have a go at this, and then you've got to go down to these old caves, and you've got to go oot oot, and then if you hear someone going oot oot back, well you go in with them. Anyway, ah, I'll have a go at this. So he drinks 2 rums and a pint of bitter and he's going down and he goes to the first cave and he goes oot oot and he goes, nobody there and he tries again, and goes to the second one, oot oot, nobody there. Anyway, things that he drank are going around, and the effects of the drink are beginning to wear off and he goes oot oot (really loud) and all of a sudden he hears oot oot and anyway he runs in, and he's got the lot, and he goes in and gets run over by a train.

Ld:b.12.73

987. There these two tramps, you see, and the first one says, do you want to know how to get some grub? He says yes please. So he says first, go and get some horse muck, manure, horse muck, so he says right. So he goes and gets some, and he gives it to the other tramp. He says right, he goes and knocks on a door, he says please, can I have some salt to put on this? So the old lady says, oh no, you're not going to eat that, come inside and have a big feed. So he says alright. So the other tramp gets a morsel, and he said, and he goes, he says, and he goes to a bigger house, so he says bigger house, bigger feed. So he knocks on the door and he says, please, could you put some salt on that. So the lady at the house says no. I won't let you, no you're not going to eat that. Go around to the stables and get a bigger hunk.

Ld:b.12.73 (Eng:b.12.73, g.13.73)

988. This man, he was reading his book one night so, and uh and he heard this noise, so he looked out his window, and he saw an old drunk in his backyard so he went, so he went to door, and drunk said, drunk said, so mister said what are you looking for? So he said I'm looking for something to eat cause he's so weak cause he hadn't for 50 years. So he said you wait there. And he went in stable, and he said what's that? And he said that's cow's do-ee-do-ee-do.

Ld:b.7.73

989. There's this tramp and he's hungry and so he pinches this duck and he's plucking out feathers off it, and there's this pile of feathers by him and a farmer comes along and so he puts the duck back in the pond and it's swimming about with no feathers on, and then farmer says, what happened to that duck's feathers? And the tramp says, ah it decided to go for a swim and I'm minding its clothes for it.

Ld:b.12.73

990. A policeman came up to an old tramp and said have you taken a bath this morning? And the tramp said why, is there one missing?

Ld:g.10.73

991. *The three tramps.* There was this govement who had some hot rice and he said the one who has the best dream can have my hot rice. So in the morning the first tramp said I dreamed but I was the king, the second said I dreamed that I was the govement, and the third tramp said I dreamed about that hot rice getting cold so I went down and ate it.

Ld:g.9.73

992. There these 2 tramps walking down this lane, one said to the other, I'm so hungry I could eat a dead dog. And so they're walking along and his mate sees a dead dog and he says, there, there's your dead dog you said you could eat. And so he picks it up and starts eating it, and he offers the other one a piece of the leg. And he says, I couldn't eat any stuff like that. So he ate it all, and they're walking on, on their way, and then he was

sick, and it all came back up, and the other tramp gobbled it all up, and he says, I thought you said you couldn't eat anything like that? And he says ah, I can't stand cold food.

Ld:b.12.73

993. 12 skinheads, bubbleboys, walk into a pub, all with levi jackets on and all their equipment, and they walk up to the landlord and says 13 pints of bitter please. But they're only 12 of you, look look I want 13 pints of bitter. So he says alright, and he gives him 13 pints of bitter. And they all get settled, and there's a little Irish fellow sitting inside in a corner, he's only a little navvy fellow, and the head skinhead walks over to him and says here you are dad, here's a pint of bitter for you. And he says thank you sir, thank you, you are so generous son. So he says, it's alright, we don't mind helping the cripples. So he says but I'm not a cripple. He says, you will be if you don't buy the next round.

(skinheads = bubbleboys = Hell's Angels; navvy=navigator, a worker on the road, usually Irish)
Ld:b.13.73

994. There's these 8 bubbleboys with long hair coming to this cafe, coming to this roadside cafe, and they see this fellow sat at a table, and he's got a cup of coffee, and bacon and egg on a plate, and fried bread and stuff like that. And they go over to him, 8 of them, well the first one he gets hold of the cup of coffee and pours it over his head, second one, he gets a knife, jams it through sausage, through plate and shoots it in his eye, forked sausage in his eye. Third one, he gets hold of plate, crashes it over his head, fourth one, get his bacon and shoves it in his ears, fifth one, he says oh, we better leave him now and go get something to eat and drink. So they go over to the fellow that's serving them and he says, and all 8 of them say, boy, he isn't much of a man to stick up for himself is he? So he says, so the fellow goes no, and he's not a very good driver, he just ran over 8 motorbikes.

Ld:b.12.73

995.   Mines about a queer. He walking down the street with his
        dog, Pinkie he's called, Pinkie. So it's a big Julip's dog, with
        hair all over it and he has a flowered handbag, and all these
        flowered things. And he walks into the pub with his hat on,
        and he walks into the pub, and he says to the landlord he says,
        could I have a gin and tonic please sweetie? So he says I'm
        sorry but we're not allowed to serve people like you. So the
        queer says look surgar lips, will you give me a gin and tonic
        please? He says no, I'm sorry, we can't serve people like you.
        Look, will you give me a gin and tonic please sweetie? He
        says no, I'm sorry, we can't serve people like you. So he says,
        now look sugar lips, if you don't let me have a gin and tonic.
        I'll set my big dog on to you. And he says, I'm sorry we can't
        serve people like you, and he goes right, Pinkie, so Pinkie
        jumps upon the counter, catches the landlord up against the
        glass pane at the back and says bowsie wowsie.

        (queer = homosexual)
        Ld:b.13.73

996.   This queer walked into a pub, it's the same queer, still trying
        to get served, and he walks into this other pub and says, can I
        have a gin an tonic please sweetie? So he says, I'm sorry, we
        are not allowed to serve people like you. Oh no, look sugar
        lips, can I have a gin and tonic please? And he says I'm sorry,
        we can't serve people like you. And this time he hasn't
        brought his dog, so he decides to just sit down. And after him
        a big Hells Angel walks in, he was 7'5 with a lots of muscles
        and a big strip of belt with him, and he goes to the landlord,
        buy me your best bitter please, and throws him back. Yes sir,
        and he gets it, gets it, walks down and sits in the corner. He
        was right hard looking and the queers watching this and he
        thinks he'll try this and so he goes to him, a gin and tonic
        please, or he says, or else, or else a packet of crisps please.

        Ld:b.13.73

997.   There's this queer cleaning his eyes. (takes one out, breathes
        on it, rubs on his shirt, puts back in, takes other, same thing,
        then takes both out, breathes on them rubs them, tosses them

up in air, crossing in air, catch them, and puts them back in, when he opens his eyes, he's cross-eyed.)

Ld:b.12.73

998. There was these 3 mental fellows you see and they went to see the doctor, so the doctor said right, first man please. So, first man, so doctor goes, where's your mouth (points to mouth) He goes here. Where's your nose? He goes here (points to nose) Where's your eyes? He goes here (points to ears) So he goes pft, you're stupid, so go out. So the second fellow comes in, so he goes well, where's your mouth? He goes here (points to mouth) Where's your nose? He goes here (points to nose) Where's your eyes? He goes here (points to ears). So he goes pft, you're a bit mental, go away. So the third one comes in, He goes where's your mouth? He goes here (points to mouth) Where's your nose? He goes here (points to nose) Where's your eyes? He goes here (points to eyes) so he goes out, and the other two goes, how do you do it, how do you do it? So the third one goes I use my kidneys, I use my kidneys. (points to brain, head)

(mental = crazy)
Ld:b.13.73

999. There was a man in the nuthouse and the man who owned the nuthouse that the man was all right to go. I will give you a test he said. Oranges tits, pears tits, mellons tits, nipples window screen wipers, pu pu pu

(pu pu pu = kissing sound)
L:b.8.74

1000. There's these 3, there's this warden and a lunatic asylum and he's looking at all sorts to see what they are occupying their minds with, and he goes into the first room and they're all looking fell and stupid. And the second one, it wasn't too bad in this cell, they're all standing on the table, and he goes into the third one, and he sees this fellow reading a book and he says ah, that's very good and then he looking around a bit, round the rest of the room and he sees this fellow swinging on the light bulb, so he walks in and says to the man reading the book what does he think he is? He thinks he's a light bulb. So he says, well I'm glad to see you're occupying your mind with a book, something decent. So he says, will you tell him to get down? Stop being daft, I won't be able to read.

Ld:b.13.73

1001. There's this, you know, you know, looney fellow, you see, and he went to this farm you see, and he saw the farmer put manure over the rubbard you see. He goes, oo ugh. So he went over to the farmer and he goes what are you doing that for? So he goes well to make it grow. So he goes, well over at our place, we put custard over ours.

Ld:b.13.73 (Eng:b.9.74)

1002. There were these 3 nuts in this looney asylum, and the fellow says to them, if you can pass this test, you can go. And there is all these lists of birds and they have to pick which one can't fly. And the first fellow goes in, looks down the list, uh, crane, everyone knows that is a thing to lift, and no, you're wrong, you have to stay in for the rest of your life. The second one goes in and looks down and stork, everyone knows that's a packet margarine. And he goes on, the stork is a bird that can fly, you have to stay in for the rest of your life, and the third man comes in and he goes, looks down, penguin, and he goes yes, you're right, and just as he's going out the front door he says how did you know anyway? And he goes, everybody knows penguin is a chocolate biscuit.

Ld:b.12.73 (Eng:b.12.73)

1003. A man got out of prison, and was given civilian clothes, and he was outside, touching trees, and grass, and yelling, "I'm free, I'm free!" And a little girl tugged on his coat and said, "so what mister, I'm four."

NY:g.13.61

1004. Prisoner being led off through rainy woods to be executed by a firing squad: What brutes you are, to march me through the woods like this. One guard: You're complaining, think of us, we've got to walk back.

SD:b.12.75

1005.   You could say this to your teacher. I had a dream about you
        last night. I goes like this. I dreamt that we were going to
        heaven and we were walking up the ladder and we got to the
        Golden Gates and St. Paul was there and he gave me a piece of
        chalk and he said for every sin you've committed, call in a
        rung on the ladder, and so I started going down, calling in the
        rungs, and I met you on your way back up and I says, where
        you off, and you says I'm off for some more chalk.

        Ld:b.12.73

1006.   There's this fellow, and he's been bad all his life, and he's
        going to hell, and he goes down, and the devil's there and he
        says, I'm going to take you into these 2 rooms and you've got
        to tell me which one you'd like to go in, in the cold, and I've
        numbered them A and B, so go in to Room A and there's all
        these fellows sat around a table drinking cups of tea, and horse
        manure. And he goes in Room B and there's all these fellows
        standing on their heads eating horse manure and he thinks I
        don't fancy that so he says I prefer Room A so he says alright,
        and he goes in and he's on about his fourth cup of tea and devil
        comes in and says alright lads, tea breaks over.

        Ld:b.12.73

1007.   There was a builder, alying down abug (abed) came his
        Governor and said wake up Bill it's time for tea break.

        L:b.10.74

1008.   A man went for a job as a builder, the man in the office said
        we only have one job, laying the tar in the road. When the
        man layed the tar for the first time, he ran over a man and
        when he came back he said I've come for my cards by the man
        in the office said, here's your money and 40 pounds on top.
        Why? asked the man. Any man who can tar the road and put
        the cats eyes in too ought to get 40 pounds.

        L:g.10.74

XXII. COUPLES, MARRIED LIFE

1009.   These 2 people were always complaining, you know, and they're always complaining about, muttering, telling other people about other people, talking to their faces and they're getting a bit sick of these buses coming along the road, they decide, the husband he goes out and says Helda, and she says yes Stanley, he said I've dug that hole, that's a good job, it will stop these buses from coming along now.

'Helda and Stanley = one couple on English TV show, called Coronation Street)
Ld:b.13.73

1010.   There's these 2 men in one's garden and this man has one of these small yachts. And the other side of the fence there's this ship, the Queen Elizabeth the First. And one man says to other man, the man with the boat, he says, it was the same last time, because last time I got a car, my neighbor got a bigger one.

Ld:b.8.73

1011.   There's this fellow and he's going down M1, about 70mph, and his wife sat in the back and she's nagging away, oo, don't go so fast, mind that car, watch that lamppost, go into that ridge, and do this and that and then this police car, he looks in his mirror and behind him there's this police car and it slows him down and he says, did you know sir, that you'd lost your wife out about 2 miles back? And he goes, oh good God, I thought I had gone deaf.

Ld:b.12.73

1012.   A farmer and his wife went to a fair. The farmer was fascinated by the airplanes and finally asked a pilot how much did a ride cost. Ten dollars for three minutes, the pilot said. But I'll make a deal. If you and your wife can go without making a sound, it will cost you nothing, but if you say one word you have to pay ten dollars. They went for a ride and after the ride the pilot said, I want to congratulate you for not making a sound. You are a brave man. Maybe so, said the farmer, but I almost yelled when my wife fell out.

SD:b.12.75

1013. This man and this lady, they got married and lady didn't like this man because he wouldn't give her any money. So she brought a blacky home and she put him in bed, and his feet were sticking out of bed. And then white man got into bed and he says. I'll go wash me feet because blacky's feet were black and then lady said to blacky go down into the pantry. And then white man said I'll go make a cheese sandwich. And when he opened pantry, blacky says hello, I just fell off the marmalade.

(Robertson's marmalade has a golliwog as a trademark-black dolly, with black hair, striped pants and a red shirt waist)
Ld:b.7.73

1014. There's this man, and he's dying, and his wife at the side of his bed, and she goes, and he goes, I want a confession to make dear, uh husband dear, then uh he goes, and he goes do you know those meetings that I went to Manchester, those meetings, so he goes, I didn't, I didn't really go there. So he goes, I went and met with another woman. So she goes, that's why I poisoned you.

Ld:b.11.73

1015. There's these two Eskimo's and one's got this burner, you know, and he's outside his igloo, burning the wall away. And the chap standing out says to the chap with lighter, are you locked out again Fred?

Ld:b.8.73

1016. One day a boy took his girlfriend to a baseball game. The first batter smacked the ball over the fence for a home run. The second batter smashed a line drive for a home run. The third batter did the same thing. Seeing all this the girl said, 'isn't the pitcher wonderful? No matter how the other team holds the bat, he hits it!'

SD:b.12.75

1017. Well you see, there's this lady talking to the policeman outside the house, and her garden looks more like, the thickest jungle you've ever seen. And lady says to the man, to the policeman, yes, you see, my husband went out the other day, into the garden, and he hasn't been seen since.

Ld:b.8.73

1018. There once was an old man and his wife. They lived near a forest, and in the forest was an gnome, and the little old man usually went to feed the gnome. One day the old man fell sick and he had to ask his wife and his wife said she would go, but said the man you must not touch him. She touched him and he caught and he shouted TIG.

Ld:g.8.73 (see jokes Nos. 1019, 1020)

1019. There was once a zoo keeper and an inden (Indian?) came along and said I dare you to go in that cage and hit that gorilla so the zoo keeper said alright, and he went in the cage and hit the gorilla and the gorilla got a bit wild and the zoo keeper ran out of the cage, ran down the street, opened the door, ran up the stairs to his bedroom and got in the cubboard. The gorilla bent the bars and ran down the street, and knocked down the door, ran up the stairs to the bedroom and knocked down the cuboard and said add you.

L:g.10.74

1020. One day after work this guy went into this bar to have a drink before he went home, and he was looking at the list of the drinks. And then he goes, and he saw down on the very bottom, in little letters, a Purple Gorilla. So he orders one, and drinks it. Goes hey, that's pretty good, and when he was done he looked in the bottom of his glass and there was a little purple gorilla trying, running around in circles trying to climb out, and he goes, hey bartender, there's a purple gorilla in my drink and he goes are you sure? And he looks in, there's nothing in there. And he goes, you're crazy mister. And he goes, hey, isn't there a purple gorilla in there? And he goes no. I see, I see purple gorilla in there. And he goes oh, thanks

anyway, and he goes home. And he comes back the next day
and he comes back and orders purple gorilla and the guy goes
okay, here. And then he sees this purple gorilla and he asks
everybody and everybody thinks he's crazy. So he goes home
and tells his wife. Come with me, to this bar, I want to show
you something. And she goes with him. And then they come
and they ask for a purple gorilla and they get it, and they both
see it down there, and they go, and they says to the bartender,
I want to know the secret to this purple gorilla. And he goes
okay. Okay I guess. Meet here around 7 o'clock when I'm off
work and he was there. So he took him to, in his car, down to
this big forest, and they walked down this path, long long
path an there was this big mansion and they go inside and then
they go down to the basement and then they, he pulls off this
big huge rug, and there's this big door, huge door, takes them
about half an hour to open it, they go down, these big curly
stairs, and it takes them around two days. And then they get
way down there and he's really tired and then they go, they
go, see that little bitty door down there, we have to go all the
way down there and then they take them about 5 days, and
they're walking down there and then finally, they go okay,
grab some guns, there's a gun rack there. Then he goes okay,
and grabs some guns. And they go through the door, and
there's all these orange giraffes, and they shoot all the orange
giraffes, and it takes them around 7 days, and then they come
to another door, and they throw down their guns and grab
some more, and they go through the door, and there's all
these pink elephants, and it takes them 10 days, and they shoot
all the pink elephants, and then finally they come to all these
steps, and they go way down, and then they finally come to
this huge cage, and there's this huge purple gorilla, looking
mad and ugly. And then they go back up the stairs, and
through all the pink elephants, and then through the door,
and through all the orange giraffes, and then they go walking
to the door and the guy goes, well that's the secret of the
purple gorilla. And he goes okay, thanks. And he starts
walking back, and he gets really mad, and he goes, and he

goes back, takes a gun out of his shirt, and rings the doorbell, the guy comes, and shoots him and he runs down, pulls the cover off, opens the door, runs down the stairs, runs through the thing, so far it's been 5 days, and then he opens the door, grabs all the guns, and opens the door and runs through, and shoots all the orange giraffes, throws the guns down after he goes through the door and grabs some more guns, goes through the door and shoots all the pink elephants, and it takes 10 days, to get down to the purple gorilla. And he looks at it for there for a couple of minutes, and then he goes down and touches it, and the, gorilla went mad and he's roarrr, and getting all riled up, and he runs, up the stairs, and runs, covers it all up, well he didn't cover it up, but he can hear, hear the monster stamping behind him, trog trog, and he running, and he tripped over this slide, and he goes oh no, and he can feel the purple gorilla breathing down his neck, and he, the gorilla comes down to him, and he turns up and looks up at him and it touches him and it goes, TAG, you're it.

SF:b.9.74

1021. I know one about, and you can tell it at a party, and you need a candle really, but I'll pretend I've got one. There's this candle, and it's in the olden days, and these two, Mr and Mrs Smith, are staying at this hotel, and Mr Smith goes to Mrs Smith, blow out the candle luv. And Mrs Smith, whose always keeps her mouth to one side (twist lips to left side) goes phoo phoo phoo (blow out of twisted lips) I can't blow out the candle luv, (said with mouth twisted), so Mr Smith goes, well I'll have a go. And Mr Smith always keeps his mouth to this side like this (opposite side of mouth) phoo phoo phoo, I can't blow out the candle luv. And then they call down for the landlady and she comes up, and she always keeps her mouth like that (top lip way over bottom lip) and she goes phoo phoo phoo, well I can't blow out the candle. So they call down for the landlady's husband and he comes up, and he always keeps his mouth like this (bottom lip way over top lip) and he's going phoo phoo phoo, I can't blow out the candle luv. So Mrs goes I can't, and Mr goes I can't and landlady goes I can't and Mr goes I can't. And they're all in a mess, and so they're wondering what to do. And then Mr Smith just has an idea – Send across for the schoolteacher across the road and so they send across, and she comes along and she goes, she just goes (takes two fingers and snuffs it out) and then Mr Smith goes, isn't education a wonderful thing.

Ld:b.12.73

1022. These two, Mr and Mrs Hill, and they're going along and it's right steep, and all of a sudden their engine conks out of repair, and they go, oh no, what can we do, you know. So he goes, well there's a house over there, let's go over there. Anyway, they go in there and they knock on door, and anyway the door opens, big hideous fellow, (pause, bend over like a hunchback) anyway and they say can we have a room for the night and he goes, you know, yeah yeah, okay, follow me ugh ugh (all kinds of noises) you know walking about, anyway going up one pair of stairs, you know, then another pair of stairs, then go into this room, anyway, they go into this room and then he goes out. There are the eyes of a portrait, looking all over these eyes in the forehead, and this woman sees this and goes agh (scream) you know, and the fellow looks and sees nothing, obviously just your imagination, you're just spooky. Anyway, they go to sleep and it was late night, and the fellow comes up with a big dagger, and you know he goes creek creek (sound of stabbing) and he stabs them both about 7 times, anyway he carrying downstairs like this (on his back, he's very bent over, like hunchback) you know, anyway he chucks them in, he goes down to this crypt and he chucks them in the coffins, and he's playing the organ (sounds of slow heavy organ music) and all of a sudden, you know, these 2, man and woman, arise, and he looks around he goes 'The Hills are alive with the sound of music.'

Ld:b.12.73 (Eng:b.13.74)

XXIII. QUICK PUNS

1023. A man order a meal in a restaurant, it's supposed to be a right good one, and after he's finished it, waitress comes up and she says, now sir, how did you find your steak? So he says oh, just under the peas.

Ld:g.13.73

1024. There's this man in a cafe, and he orders some soup, and waiter brought it in. Waiter, this plate is wet for my soup, so he says, that not wet sir, it's your soup.

Ld:g.13.73

1025. Waiter waiter, what's this soup doing on my plate? Help to wash the dinner down.

L:b.11.75

1026. This man and he goes into cafe, and he's eating some soup and he shouts, waiter, there's a fly in my soup, what's this fly doing in my soup? So the waiter says, ah, breaststroke I think.

Ld:g.13.73

1027. Waiter waiter, there's a fly in my soup. Don't worry sir, cause you've got a spider on your bread.

L:b.11.75

1028. Waiter waiter, there's a dead fly in my soup. Don't worry sir, it's the heat that kills them.

Ld:g.10.73

1029. Waiter, what your thumb doing in my soup? That's all right sir, it isn't hot.

L:b.10.74

1030. Waiter, what's this feather doing in my soup? You did ask for chicken soup sir.

L:b.10.74

1031. Waiter waiter, bring me a crocodile sandwich and make it snappy.

Ld:g.11.73

1032.   If you go to the restaurant and they serve you chicken, and it's
        barbequed and one's legs bigger than the other, you tell the
        waiter and you say, one legs bigger than the other. And the
        waiter says, what do you want to do with it, eat it or dance
        with it?

        SD:b.8.75

1033.   A little boy says, uncle, how can you eat soup with a
        moustache? The uncle says, it's quite a strain son.

        SD:g.10.75

1034.   How'd you like to be eating a hot dog, and find veins in it?

        SD:b.12.75

1035.   You know what's gross, eating a bowl of tomato soup and
        finding hair at the bottom.

        SD:g.12.75

1036.   How would you like to be eating a bowl of rice and have the
        last piece crawl away?

        SD:b.12.75

1037.   Here's a quick football score. Leeds United 1, Manchester
        City, lost.

        Ld:b.13.73 (Eng:b.12.73)

1038.   Newsflash at Christmas time: All chickens get stuffed.

        L:b.11.74

1039.   Here's a newsflash, the police are looking for a 2 foot man and
        a 12 foot man who have just escaped from prison. The police
        are looking high and low for them.

        Ld:b.12.73

1040.   And here is another newsflash, 8 watches have been stolen,
        police are looking for an octopus with the exact timing.

        Ld:b.13.73

1041.   Here is a newsflash. 500 wigs have been stolen. Police are now
        combing the area.

        Ld:b.13.73

1042.   News: Today a box of wigs fell off the back of a lorry. Police
are combing the area.

Ld:g.9.73

1043.   The lady's toilet were broken. The police are now looking in
to it.

Ld:b.10.73

1044.   Mother (to her son): go and pick that parcel up for that old
lady. Son: no need to mum, it's a packet of self-raising flour.

Ld:g.11.73

1045.   The brown sauce was going for the red sauce. Guess what? He
couldn't get him because he couldn't ketch-up.

Ld:g.8.73

1046.   There's a piece of meat and an egg in a frying pan and fried
egg says to him, I'll be your grilled friend anytime.

Ld:g.13.73

1047.   There was 2 eggs boiling in a pan, and they're brothers. And
one brother said to the other brother, good night, ain't it hot
in here. He said, wait till ya get outside, they'll smash your
egg in.

L:b.11.75

1048.   Snail: I going shopping, back in a fortnight.

Ld:b.10.73

1049.   Man: I thought you said the water was an inch high.
Lady: It looked it on the ducks.

Ld:b.10.73

1050.   I was walking home from school and this man walks up to this
other man and he says, it's raining cats and dogs in that yard.
He said how do you know? Because there was a poodle in the
yard.

SD:b.8.75

1051.   Girl: You remind me of the sea.
Boy: Because I'm so wild, reckless and romantic?
Girl: No, because you make me sick.

SD:b.12.75

1052. Dad, I think my teacher loves me. Why son? She keeps putting kisses by my sums.

   L:b.11.74

1053. How did you get those medals? I saved the Regiment. How did you do that? I shot the cook.

   L:b.11.74

1054. Two men were in a wood. One saw a house and went to it. He said can I have a room? Yes, but there is a ghost. He went up and saw a ghost with a black eye. The man said I give you a black eye like the other.

   L:b.9.74

1055. Wife: Oh I got a ladder in my tights.
   Husband: Well, what do you want, a marble staircase?

   (Ladder in my tights = run in my stocking)
   Ld:g.10.73

1056. Toll collector (to driver of an old broken down car approaching the bridge): 50c. Driver: Sold!

1057. Moe says, I went hunting with a club.
   Joe: With only a club?
   Moe: No, yeah, there were 100 members in the club.

   SD:g.10.75

1058. Lady in the window: Good morning, good night, phew, that day went quickly.

   Ld:b.10.73

1059. There's these 2 cigarette packets talking to one another. And one says to the other, I've been made the Embassador, and you've been the Embassy.

   Ld:b.8.73

1060. The king said 'my bed's too short.'
   Son: Then don't sleep too long.
   Ld:b.10.73

1061. Farmer, this farmer says to the city boy, son, I think you should learn to milk a cow. City boy says, why, shouldn't I just start on a calf.

     SD:g.10.75

1062. City Lady: Look at that bunch of cows.
     Cowboy: Not bunch, herd.
     City Lady: Heard of what?
     Cowboy: Herd of cows
     City Lady: Sure I've heard of cows
     Cowboy: No, a cow herd
     City Lady: Why should I care what a cow heard? I've got no secrets from a cow.

     SD:b.12.75

1063. There was this one old lady, who wouldn't hit flies unless they were open.

     SD:b.11.75 (US:b.10.75)

1064. What's the matter Jack? I can't swim, the tides just gone out.

     Ld:g.9.73

1065. You're in an ice cube says John. What's the matter, are you cold? No, I'm freezing.

     Ld:g.9.73

1066. People in hell need icewater. (used as smart answer, when somebody asks for something, like 'I need a wrench.')

     SD:b.10.67

1067. There was an old man and he lived in a tree and it got chopped down. He said timber.

     Ld:b.8.73

1068. There was an old man called quiet and everything he said was quiet.

     Ld:b.8.73

1069. There were two elephants who lived in a toilet. One said I don't want to go to the toilet.

     Ld:b.9.73

1070. Teacher: Order children order.
       Billy: I will have jelly and custard
       Ld:g.8.73 (Eng:g.8.73)

1071. In case of starvation, eat the last joke. It was full of bologna.
       SD:b.11.75

1072. There are two blood cells. They loved in vein (vain)
       L:b.11.75

1073. Did you know that postman always get the sack everyday,
       but are never out of work?
       L:b.11.75

1074. Batty Books — *Tea Leaves*, by T. Bags
       Ld:g.8.73

1075. Batty Books — *Zebra's* by James Striped
       Ld:g.8.73

1076. Batty Books — *Good Films* by Juliar Seasar and Rome any.
       Ld:g.8.73

1077. Batty Books — *A Pop Song* by The Laughing Gnome.
       Ld:g.8.73

1078. *Rusty Bedsprings*, by I.P. Nightly
       NJ:g.11.61

1079. *Brown Spot on the Wall*, by Who Flung Poo
       NJ:g.11.61

1080. *Yellow Stream on the Floor*, by I.P. Daily
       NJ:g.11.61

1081. *Fifty Yards to the Outhouse*, by Willie Makeit, published by
       Betty Won't
       NJ:g.11.61

1082. *How to be a Millionaire*, by I've Got a Lot
       L:b.11.75

1082. *Loaning Money*, by Buck Owen
       SD:b.12.75

1084. *Stealing Money*, by Sticky Fingers
SD:b.12.75

1085. *Home Run*, by Willie Maket and Betty Don't
SD:b.12.75

1086. *The Light*, by Alec Tricity
SD:b.12.75

1087. *Get Money Easy.* by Rob A. Bank
SD:b.12.75

1088. *All About the Mind*, by M.T. Brains
SD:b.12.75

1089. *Skunk on his Tail*, by Howie Rann
SD:b.12.75

1090. *Air Pollution*, by Carmen Monoxide.
SD:b.12.75

1091. *How to Cut Hair*, by Barb Err
SD:b.12.75

1092. *The Perfect Diet*, by Cal. O. Rees
SD:b.12.75

1093. Daffynitions: Waste of Time – Telling a hair-raising story to a bald man.
SD:b.12.75

1094. Daffynitions: Broadcast – What you put on a fat broken leg.
SD:b.12.75

1095. Some people are like blisters, they appear when the work is done.
SD:b.12.75

1096. Hong Kong played ping pong with Superman's ding dong.
SD:b.6.75

1097. Can I try that dress on in the window? You can if you want but I rather if you tried it on in the changing room.
Ld:b.9.73

1098. A man goes into a shop and says I want a coat, assistant goes alright, then gets one. The man goes yes I'll have this one and the assistant goes do you want a belt? Man turns round and says do you want one back?

Ld:g.10.73 (Eng:g.11.73)

1099. There was this little girl who dropped her orange and a man slipped on it, and the little girl started to cry. The man said don't cry, I am not hurt, and the little girl says, but my orange is.

Ld:b.11.73

1100. A little boy was walking down a street and he slipped in a pile of dog dirt and as he was getting up a man came up and slipped in the same place and the boy said, 'hey mister, I did that' and the man got up and walloped him.

Ld:g.10.73

1101. Sam: My dad shaves once a day.
Henry: Well, my dad shaves 105 times a day.
Sam: He must be balmy.
Henry: No he's not, he's a barber.

Ld:g.8.73

1102. Lollipops: A man went to a shop to buy a lollipop but the shopkeeper said they have ran out. Where to? said the man. To peoples tomeck (stomach) That's funny said the man, I'll go to another shop.

Ld:g.8.73

1103. Alaskan (to newcomer): We have very short summers here. Last year it was on a Friday.

SD:b.12.75

1104. Judge: Why did you park your car there?
Man: Because it said fine for parking.

SD:b.12.75

1105. Musician: Can you tell me how to get to Carnegie Hall?
Citizen: Practice man, practice.

SD:b.12.75

1106.   Willy: Why are you feeding the cat birdseed?
        Billy: That's where my bird is.

        SD:b.12.75

1107.   Tim: What made you decide to become a parachute jumper?
        Jim: A four engine aircraft with three dead engines.

        SD:b.12.75

1108.   Mother: I thought I told you to let your brother have the sled
        half of the time.
        Son: I do. I have it going down the hill, and he has it going
        up.

        SD:b.12.75

1109.   Teacher: Billy, where's your homework?
        Billy: I had it, but I made an airplane out of it and someone
        hijacked it to Cuba.

        SD:b.12.75

1110.   Mommy mommy, it's dark down here.
        Shut up, or I'll flush it again.

        OR:g.8.58

1111.   Mama, can Johnny come out and play?
        But Johnny has no arms and no legs.
        That's okay, we want him for second base.

        OR:g.8.58

1112.   Mummy mummy, can I lick the bowl?
        No, flush the chain like everybody else does.

        L:g.11.75 (Eng:g.11.75)

1113.   Mummy mummy, it's hot in here.
        Shut up and get back in the oven.

        L:b.11.75

1114.   There's this girl, and she said to her mother, mummy
        mummy, I hate my dentist's guts.
        She said don't mind darling, leave him on the side of the plate.

        Ld:b.13.74

1115.   Mum mum, I don't like our Susan.
Shut up and eat your chips.

Ld:b.13.74

1116.   Mummy mummy, can I have a spoon. Susan's been sick and John's getting all the big bites.

Ld:b.13.74

1117.   Mummy mummy, dad's gone out.
Shut up and put some more coal on.

Ld:b.13.74

XXIV. PUNNING STORIES – ANIMALS

1118.   Two flys were playing at football in a saucer and one said I'll be in the cup next year.

Ld:g.10.73 (Eng:b.8.73, g.10.73)

1119.   My joke is, there were these mice and insects, all going to have a football match. And they started it, and at half time it was 6 all, and at the end it was 11-10, and the cats had won. So they went to the centipede's cave and said, why haven't you been at the football match? And he said I've been putting me boots on.

Ld:b.8.73

1120.   See there was this man, and he was standing at the bus stop with this great big pot pie. Anyway this little dog comes along and kept going at his trouser leg and he said, get down get down. And then this lady who owned the dog said no, leave my little doggie there. So he went okay, then, and then he had this piece of pot pie, and the dog wanted some of that and the man said, oh, do you mind I throw the dog a bit? And so she said, oh I wouldn't mind. So he threw it 10 miles down the street.

Ld:b.8.73 (Eng:b.12.73)

1121. There's this fellow and he's in this pub with his dog and he says to this, to this fellow, I bet you a tenner you can't make my dog do what you want it to do. Ah, that's simple, so he puts his tenner down, this fellow puts his tenner down, and he goes sit, and this dog stands up, sit down, stands up again, stand up, sits down, stand up again, stand up and he sits down. He goes, you've done me in, here's your 10 pounds, and he picks it up. This fellow says to this fellow, I bet I can make you do what I want, and he goes ah, bet you can't and he goes. I bet you 20 pounds I can. 20 pounds, put it down. Anyway, he picks it up, puts in on the fire and says get off.

Ld:b.12.73

1122. There's this fellow, with this dog, and he's pug, and it's got black boots on. And this other fellow watching him, and he can't think why this dog has got black boots on. And he's right puzzled, and he comes in the next day and he's got black boots on. And so he goes over to him and says, why does your dog have black boots on? And he says well, his brown ones are at cobblers.

Ld:b.12.73

1123. There's this man in a pub and he's sat down playing drafts with his dog, and a man comes up to him and says hay, that a good dog, ain't it? And he says no, he hasn't won yet.

Ld:b.12.73

1124. This fellow sat down at table, and he's drinking and he calls over to the dog, hay, dog, go get me a pork pie. You can keep change and gives him a 10p piece. It runs outside. And the fellow goes into the bar and says hay, where's my dog gone? He's gone to the porkshop for me to get a pork pie. So he says ah no, and he goes outside and he sees his dog kissing this other dog and he says, you've never done that before, so he says, I've never had any money before.

Ld:b.12.73

1125. I have a very silly dog, his name is Sparky Binner. He always likes to play with us but best he likes his dinner, he always likes to play with us when we play at ball. But when we have some work to do he never helps at all.

Ld:b.10.73

1126. There's this man and he lived by himself, he just had a dog and he had this tree, and he said to the dog, 'mamma mia, what happened to the tree? Last week it was green, this week it's yellow.' (Italian accent) Dog goes, I couldn't hold it.

SF:b.9.74

1127. There's this lady one time and she had this dog named Ralph. So anyhow, she was trying to teach her dog not to crap on the floor. So dog crap on floor. So she pick him up and threw him out the window. Then he done it the next day. So she picked him up and threw him out the window. Then finally she got her dog taught. He crapped on the floor and jumped out the window.

SF:b.11.74

1128. There was this boy who had this dog named Isiah. And his next door neighbor asked him why he called it Isiah. And he said cause one eye's higher than other.

L:b.11.75

1129. There was this man who had a garage and he had a car and a cat. One day the man was filling his car with petrol and just then he gave his cat some milk then just before he had finished he dropped some petrol in the cat's milk, just before the cat had finished. Then it started to run round at sixty miles per hour then it stopped and seemed dead then a customer said is your cat dead? The seller said no, I think it's run out of petrol.

Ld:b.10.73

1130. There's this fellow and he's got a budgie and it's in it's cage and it's swinging about and it looks right lonely, and anyway this fellow feels sorry for it, so he goes right, I'll go buy it another bird. And he goes and buys another budgie,. And then at night he hears a right awful scream and he comes down in the morning and the budgie he bought yesterday is dead and it's neck is hanging out of the cage like that (hung head to side twisted, tongue out) And he goes right, I'm going to buy a parrot this time. Anyway, he buys a parrot and at 10.00 at night he hears another terrible scream, and when he comes in the morning the parrots dead with it's neck in the cage like that. Anyway, this time he goes right I'm going to fix this budgie once and for all and he buys an eagle. Anyway, at 12.00 at midnight, he hears another terrible scream, and he goes down in morning and there's this eagle, like dead with it's neck like that and he goes right, I'm ging to buy a vulture. And anyway, he buys this vulture and sticks him in the cage, and it's necks is already like that see cause the cage is too small for it. Anyway, that night about 3.00 he hears a right terrible scream, you know right aggh, you know, oooh, anyway, he comes down in morning, the vultures dead, it's neck strangled, twisted in a knot, anyway, budgies got no feathers on, and the fellow goes, 'what happened?' anyway budgies goes, 'I had to take me coat off after that one.'

(budgie = small bird)
Ld:b.12.73 (Eng:b.13.74)

1131. My joke is similar to Jeremy's, it's about a budgie. He goes into a pet shop and buys a brand new budgie, it's only just been born. And he didn't know a thing about pets and he asked the man in the pet shop, what shall I do, first of all, to keep my budgie happy? So he says, well, I'd buy a cage. So he buys a cage, so he buys it the cage, and then, a few weeks pass, and the budgie still not happy so he goes back to the vet and says, I bought him a brand new cage and he's still not happy so he says, well, buy him a swing, that will keep him occupied for a few hours. So he buys him this brand new swing, and a few weeks pass and he's not happy at all. So he goes back to the vets and he's beginning to think this budgie is a bit of a waste of money and he says I bought a swing and a cage and it's still not happy, so he says, well why don't you buy him a mirror, he'll be hours looking in the mirror at himself. So he says alright, how much is the mirror? He said, it's a pound. So I'll take the mirror, So he takes the mirror. After a few weeks he's still not happy and he's really getting mad at this and he goes back to the vet and says look, my budgie still not happy, I bought him a mirror, a swing, a cage, and what else should I buy, he's still not happy. So he says, well, you ought to buy, say, yes, a friend. So he said alright, I buy a friend. So he buys this friend, it's costing him 4 pounds, it's costing him a fortune buying this stuff to keep his budgie happy. And after a few weeks his budgie dies. And he's really upset after spending all this money and he goes back to the vet and he said I spent a lot of money on my budgie and it wasn't happy and it died an unhappy life. And so he say, well did you buy everything to keep it happy. So he said ya, so he said did you buy a cage? So he said yes. Did you buy a mirror? So he said yes. Did you buy a swing? So he said yes. Did you buy it a mate? So he said yes. So did you buy it food? and he said oh.

Ld:b.13.73 (Eng:b.13.74)

1132. A kid walked into a pet shop and bought a bird. He went home and the next day he goes to the store and say, 'Mither, can I have some bird seed?' (said with lisp, and deep voice). He says no, not until you say it right. The kid walks out and comes back the next day. He says, 'Mither can I have some bird seed?' The mans says no, not until you say it right. This goes on for a week, and then the boy comes in and says, 'Mither, you wanna buy a dead bird?'

NJ:b.7.64

1133. There's this lady, and she has a black parrot, and a white parrot. And the white parrot is a very good one, it can speak. So can the black one. But the white one is right polite, and so she takes it to church. And black is always swearing, and being naughty, beating up the white one. And so, one day this black one gets sick of it, so it jumps into a tin of white paint, and it shoves the white one in a tin of soot. And the next day she comes to take it to church. And the vicar says, now we will sing Hymn 42, Stand Up for Jesus, so they stand up and start singing, and the parrot shouts, aye, sit down sit down, for Christ's sake, the people at the back can't see.

Ld:b.13.74

1134. Once upon a time there was a parrot. All it could say was who is it? So one day the old woman went out and the pamuen (postman) came and knocked on the door and who is it? The pamet (postman), and on like that and till he did ded (dead) and the old woman came back and said who is the pamet?

L:b.11.74

1135. There was a wizard and he had a parrot and everytime the wizard did a trick the parrot would say 'up his sleave' 'up his sleave'. One day the wizard and his parrot were on a ship and it sank. The parrots last words were, I give up, where's the boat?

L:g.10.74

1136. This is the story of the parrot and the captain. Okay, once there was a pirate captain and his parrot. And one of his crew got stuck up in the mast. And then so, the captain said, get him down. The parrot remembers that. Then, an enemy ship comes and the pirate says, fire at will, and the parrot remembers that. And they miss. Then a big ship comes and the pirate says fire at will and they hit the ship and the captain goes, hit a big one that time, and the parrot remembers that. Then, they go to church the next day. And then the preacher says, oh lord up in heaven, and the parrot goes, get him down. And the preacher says, if you don't shut up I'll throw this book at you. He says, fire at will. Then, so the parrot ducks, and then it hit the fat lady behind him and so hit a big one that time.

SD:b.10.75

1137. A man went into a pet shop and asked for 10 hamsters. The shopkeeper gave him 10 hamsters, said that they would last for at least a year. But in 10 days they had all died so the man went into the petshop again, and the told the shopkeeper that all the hamsters had died. The shopkeeper said I can't give your money back but if you chop them up till they are jam and put them on brown bread they taste lovely. So the man made them into jam and put them on brown bread, but they tasted horrid. He went to the shopkeeper and told him how horrid it was. The shopkeeper said I can't give you your money back but if you spread it over your garden, daffodils will grow. So he spread it over his garden daffodils, but in the morning there were tulips over his garden. He went to the shopkeeper and told him what had happened. The shopkeeper said well tulips do come from hamsterdam. (Amsterdam)

Ld:g.10.73 (Eng:b.10.74, g.10.74)

1138. There's this cow in one field and this bull another field, the bull jumps over this wall and it says Hiya, I'm Billy Bigballs, and everyday he does this and the farmer gets a bick sick of it, and he builds a 20 foot wall and he jumps over it and says Hi, I'm Billy Bigballs. And so he builds a 50 foot wall and he jumps over wall and says Hi, I'm Billy Bigballs, so this fellow gets right mad and he puts a 70 foot wall with barb wire on top and bull jumps over and says Hi, I'm Billy.

Ld:b.12.73

1139. There was these 2 fishes, and they were just swimming and do you know like little bubbles comes out, they're usually round. Well the other fish, they were squared and he goes, ooh, it must be something I ate.

Ld:g.12.73

1140. This old man with his fish and the fish said oh oh oh. This old man said I did not know that a fish used to laugh so, that the fishee fish said oh oh oh, who did not know that a fishee did not know how to talk and to make me laugh.

Ld:b.8.73

1141. There was these 2 frogs, there was 2 frogs, and they decided to go and visit each other and they met each other on top of a hill. And you know frogs have eyes on the back of their heads, and so, they stood straight up and he goes, I'll see if I can see what's it's like in your country and in mine. So he looked up that way, you know, and he sees his own country, and (thought he was seeing the other's) he goes, ah, it's no use in going, it's just like ours.

Ld.g.12.73

1142.   One day, this family of bears went out. And they came home
         and Daddy Bear said, who's been drinking my Scotch
         Whiskey? And Aunty Bear said I haven't. And Mother Bear
         said, who's been taking my sleeping pills? And Aunty Bear
         said I haven't. And Baby Bear said, who's been playing my
         Franky Bone record, and Aunty Bear said I haven't. And
         Mickey Mouse comes out the corner and says, 'hic, snore,
         give me the moonlight.'

         L:b.11.75 (Eng.b.10.73)

1143.   One day father bear, mother bear, and baby bear were eating
         some porriage when a spider fell in baby bears porriage and
         ate all baby bears porriage and said yum yum bubble gum,
         that was tart.

         L:b.9.74

1144.   There's this hyena and a monkey in the jungle and they're
         talking together, and the hyena goes to the monkey,
         everytime I go through that little shade of bushes over there,
         the rubber trees and shades and bushes and everytime I go
         through there, just as I get through when a big lion jumps out
         and keeps on hitting me and hitting me, until he goes away.
         And he goes, why does he do it? And he goes, I don't know
         but keeps on doing it just to me, when everyone else goes past.
         And he goes, well I'll come with you this time and I'll stick up
         for you. And they walk along, and just as they getting to the
         shade of bushes a lion jumps out on them, on this hyena, and
         the monkey gets up a tree, and he's looking down, and he's
         getting bashed in and anyway he comes down and the hyena,
         laid down like that (expression with tongue out, roll eyes,
         look sick) and he's going, and he says, why didn't you come
         and help me? And the monkey goes I thought you were
         winning, you were laughing so much I thought you were
         winning.

         Ld:b.12.73

1145.   There's these 2 policewomen, and they got a call on the radio
         that there is a gorilla on the loose. And the zookeeper said,
         don't worry because it's real tame, so just open the door and

he'll go right in. So they find the gorilla, they open door, and he goes right in. And then they got another call for burglary and they didn't want to take the gorilla to the burglary, so they flag down a car and tell the guy to take the gorilla to the zoo. So the guy says oh sure, I'll take him to a zoo. So the next day they get a call from the zoo, and they said that where's their gorilla, you know, so they go out looking for the guy and they find the guy with the gorilla still in the car and they flag him down and they say, what happened, we told you to take the gorilla to the zoo. And then the guys says we, I did, we had so much fun at the zoo we're going to Sea World today.

(Sea World = marine amusement park)
SD:b.11.75

XXV. UNINTELLIGIBLE JOKES

1146. Ken dod die did he no doggy.

L:g.9.74

1147. This man, and this man, and this man said, and and this man went to school, and this man went to school and there's this school teacher and he said, and he said here's some lessons. So this boy was in a joke and he came out and said a joke, and he says boom boom boom boom.

Ld:g.6.73

BIBLIOGRAPHY

Abrahams, Roger D. "The Bigger They Are the Harder They Fall," *Tennessee Folklore Society Bulletin*, XXIX, 1963, 94–102.
— "Ghastly Commands: The Cruel Joke Revisited," *Midwest Folklore*, XI, 1961, 235–46.
Barrick, Mac E., "The Shaggy Elephant Riddle," *Southern Folklore Quarterly*, XXVIII, 1964, 266–90.
Botkin, B. A., *A Treasury of American Anecdotes*, New York: Random House, 1957, 321 pp.
— *Sidewalks of America*, N.Y.: Bobbs-Merrill Co. 1954, p. 515–17.
Browne, Ray B. "Parodies, Prayers and Scriptures," *Journal of American Folklore*, vol. 72, 1959, p. 94. (*Cf.*: Montèiro.)
Brunvand, Jan Harold, "A Classification for Shaggy Dog Stories," *Journal of American Folklore*, vol. 76, 1963, 42–68.
— "The Study of Contemporary Folklore: Jokes," *Fabula: Journal of Folktale Studies*, 13. Band, Heft 1/2, 1972, 1–19.
Cansler, Loman D. "Midwestern and British Children's Lore Compared," *Western Folklore*, XXVII, 1968, 1–18.
Cray, Ed, & Marilyn Eisenberg Herzog, "The Absurd Elephant: A recent Riddle Fad," *Western Folklore*, XXVI, 1967, 27–36.
Dundes, Alan, "Anthropology 159," *Fybate Lecture Notes*, Berkeley, Calif. 1972, 87 pp.
— "The Elephant Joking Questions," *Tennessee Folklore Society Bulletin*, XXIX, 1963, 40–42.
— "Folk Ideas as Units of Worldview," *Journal of American Folklore*, vol. 83, 1970, 93–103.
— "A Study of Ethnic Slurs: The Jew and the Polack in the United States," *Journal of American Folklore*, vol. 83, 1970, 186–203.
— *The Study of Folklore*, Englewood Cliffs, N.J.: Prentice-Hall, 1965, p. 43–51.

— "Thinking Ahead: A Folkloristic Reflection of the Future Orientation in American Worldview," *Anthropological Quarterly,* vol. 43, 1969, 53–72.

— & Roger D. Abrahams, "On Elephantasy and Elephanticide," *Psychoanalytic Review,* vol. 56, 1969, 225–41.

— & Robert A. Georges, "Some Minor Genres of Obscene Folklore," *Journal of American Folklore,* vol. 75, 1962, 221–26.

— & Joseph C. Hickerson, "Mother Goose Vice Verse," *Journal of American Folklore,* vol. 75, 1962, 249–59.

Eastman, Max, *The Enjoyment of Laughter,* N.Y.: Halcyon House, 1936, p. 156–62.

— *The Sense of Humor,* N.Y.: Charles Scribner, 1922, p. 190–205.

Legman, G. *The Horn Book,* New Hyde Park, N.Y.: University Books, 1964, 567 pp.

— *No Laughing Matter* (Rationale of the Dirty Joke: Second Series), N.Y.: Breaking Point, Inc. 1975, 992 pp.

— *Rationale of the Dirty Joke: First Series,* N.Y.: Grove Press & Basic Books, 1968, 811 pp.

Loomis, C. Grant, "Mary Had a little Parody: A Rhyme of Childhood in Tradition," *Western Folklore,* XVII, 1958, 45–51.

— "Traditional American Wordplay," *Western Folklore,* IX, 1950, 147–52.

Martin, A. S. *On Parodies,* N.Y.: Henry Holt, 1896, p. 89–107.

Monteiro, George, "Parodies of Scripture, Prayer and Hymn," *Journal of American Folklore,* vol. 77, 1964, 45–52.

Musick, Ruth Ann, & Vance Randolph, "Children's Rhymes from Missouri," *Journal of American Folklore,* vol. 63, 1950, 425–37.

Opie, Iona & Peter, *The Lore and Language of Schoolchildren,* Oxford: Clarendon Press, 1959, 418 pp.

Poore, Charles, "Ardent Plea for the Art of Parody," *New York Times Magazine,* March 9, 1958, p. 33.

Simmons, Donald C. "Anti Italian-American Riddles in New England," *Journal of American Folklore,* vol. 79, 1966, 475–78.

Sutton-Smith, Brian, "Shut Up and Keep Digging: The Cruel Joke Series," *Midwest Folklore,* X, 1960, 11–22.

Very, Francis, "Parody and Nicknames among American Youth," *Journal of American Folklore,* vol. 75, 1962, 262–63.

Welsch, Roger L. "American Numskull Tales: The Polack Joke," *Western Folklore,* XXVI, 1967, 183–86.

Wilde, Larry, *The Official Jewish Joke Book; The Official Irish Joke Book,* N.Y.: Pinnacle Books, 1974.

— *The Official Polish Joke Book; The Official Italian Joke Book,* N.Y.: Pinnacle Books, 1973.

Wolfenstein, Martha, *Children's Humor: A Psychological Analysis,* Glencoe, Ill.: The Free Press, 1954, 224 pp.

NOTES

1. A. Dundes and R. D. Abrahams, "On Elephantasy and Elephanticide", *Psychoanalytic Review,* vol. 56, 1969, 225–239.

2. For other articles on elephant jokes see: a) R. D. Abrahams, *Tennessee Folklore Society Bulletin,* XXIX, 1963, 94–102; b) Mac E. Barrick, *Southern Folklore Quarterly,* XXVIII, 1964, 226–290; c) Ed Cray and Marilyn Eisenberg Herzog, *Western Folklore,* vol. 26, 1967, 183–186; d) A. Dundes, *Tennessee Folklore Society Bulletin,* XXIX, 1963, 40–42 (e) A. Dundes, and R. D. Abrahams, *Psychoanalytic Review,* vol. 56, 1969, 225–241.

3. For other articles on cruel jokes see: a) R. D. Abrahams, *Midwest Folklore.* XI, 1961, 235–246; b) B. Sutton-Smith, *Midwest Folklore,* X, 1960, 11–22.

4. A. Dundes, "A Study of Ethnic Slurs: The Jew and the Polack in the United States", *Journal of American Folklore,* vol. 83, 1970, 186–203.

5. For other articles on Italian and Polack jokes see: a) A. Dundes, *Journal of American Folklore,* vol. 83, 1970, 186–203; b) D. C. Simmons, *Journal of American Folklore,* vol. 79, 1966, 475–478; c) R. L. Welsch, *Western Folklore,* vol. 26, 1967, 27–36.

6. Martha Wolfenstein, *Children's Humor,* (Glencoe, Ill.: The Free Press, 1954) p. 132–133.

7. *Ibid,* p. 132–133.

8. G. Legman, *Rationale of the Dirty Joke,* (New York: Grove Press, 1968) p. 106.

9. *Ibid,* p. 106.

10. Wolfenstein, *op. cit.,* p. 85.

11. *Ibid,* p. 94.

12. San Diego *Evening Tribune,* Feb. 1, 1974.

13. Legman, *op. cit.,* p. 189–190.

14. One facet of Sigmund Freud's psychoanalytic theory, which states that the birth trauma is the prototype of all later anxieties.

15. A. Dundes, "A Study of Ethnic Slurs: The Jew and the Polack in the United States", *Journal of American Folklore,* vol. 83, 1970, p. 180.

16. *Ibid,* p. 202.

17. Iona and Peter Opie, *The Lore and Language of Schoolchildren,* (Oxford: Clarendon Press, 1959) p. 89–90.

18. Jan H. Brunvand, "The Study of Contemporary Folklore: Jokes," *Fabula: Journal of Folktale Studies,* 13. Band, Heft 1/2, 1972, p. 6.

19. Martha Wolfenstein, *Children's Humor* (Glencoe, Ill.: Free Press, 1954) p. 160–61.

20. A. Dundes and R. D. Abrahams, "On Elephantasy and Elephanticide," *Psychoanalytic Review,* vol. 56, 1969, p. 228.

22. G. Legman, *Rationale of the Dirty Joke: First Series* (N.Y.: Grove Press, 1968) p. 13–14.

23. Dundes and Abrahams, *op. cit.,* p. 228.

GLOSSARY

1. Tommy Cooper – funny comedian, wears a Turkish fez hat. Used to have his own television show, now on others' t.v. shows. His catch-phrase is 'Just like that.'

2. Larry Grayson – comedian, has his own t.v. show called "Shut that Door." Acts like a queer. Catch-phrase is 'Shut that door!'

3. Georgie Best – football player on Manchester United. Very good-looking; girls all swoon over him. Owns boutiques (clothes), has lots of money rolling in; didn't bother about football, didn't go to practices, disappeared right after games, didn't need the money. Got banned from the team; everyone sick of him and his doings. If not at game, usually with a girl. Turned up and asked to be let back on team; was let back, but some people mad about that.

4. Chuck Berry – pop singer, rock and roll, "Johnny Be Good," "My Dingaling."

5. Gary Glitter – pop star, really flashy clothes, wriggles hips somewhat like Elvis Presley.

6. Cliff Richards – pop singer.

7. Arsenal – football team.

8. Jokers Wild – t.v. show, comedians vary; each one tells a few jokes and then someone else is on.

9. Comedians – t.v. show, comedians vary; each one tells a few jokes and then someone else is on.

10. This Is Your Life – t.v. show: go up to celebrities while they are working, or ask them to a mock reception. Present them with a book and say, 'This is your life.' Book has photos, and biography of the person. The show has this person on, with the presentation of the book, and on the show they have people the person hasn't seen for years, relatives, old teachers, etc.

11. Doctor Who – science-fiction t.v. show. Doctor Who has a time-machine, called the Tardess; looks like a telephone kiosk or booth; goes forward or backward in time, and meets

monsters. Daleks are the main type of monster he meets, and they have a long prong in front and a funny machine-like voice that says 'Exterminate.' Kids used to go around with arm stiff in front of them being Daleks.

12. Coronation Street — t.v. show; on it a couple, Hilda and Stanley Ogden, who always complain and talk about other people.

13. Sago — similar to tapioca, rice-pudding.

14. Weetabix the Builder — breakfast cereal; it is advertised as the Builder. Comes in packet with two rectangular-shaped biscuits.

15. Tunes — methalade candy for stuffed nose; ad is 'Tunes help you breathe more easily.'

16. Marks and Spencer's — Marks and Sparks — a large department store selling mainly clothes, but also food, etc.

17. Marmite — yeast extract, spread on toast.

18. Wellingtons — black shiny boots, waterproof, usually worn by Irish.

19. Nkgnoks — chocolate candy or sweets.

20. Golden wonder crisp — potato chip.

21. sweet — candy.

22. treacle pudding — pudding made from treacle, dark or light syrup, usually dark, like molasses.

23. biscuits — cookies.

24. butty — sandwich.

25. gooseberry — green berry, tart-sour, used for desserts; furry when fresh.

26. Golliwog — trademark of Robertson's marmalade: black dolly, striped pants, red shirtwaist, black hair.

27. E-type — posh car; it's the actual sports model of the Jaguar: long, sleek, thin, like a Lotus (E-type Jag).

28. jumper — sweater, pullover; usually a man's sweater.

29. vest — underwear, man's T-shirt, girl's vest; pants — underpants.

30. bog-roll — toilet paper; bog — toilet.

31. pitch — a football field.

32. bollucks — 'balls,' testicles.

33. willy — 'cock,' penis.

34. bird, *or* chick — a girl, usually good-looking.

35. navvy – short for navigator; a worker on the road, usually Irish.
36. pouff – a homosexual.
37. prefect – There are usually a large group of them in a school (American: monitors). They are older kids, who are in charge of discipline, mainly at dinnertime, classroom, breaks and playground. Can't punish the kids themselves, but can send them to a teacher, or send them back to walk, instead of running.
38. zebra crossing – cross-walk for pedestrians at corners.
39. ladder in their tights – a run in their stockings.
40. camp – dressed effeminately or flamboyantly; sometimes a hint of homosexuality.
41. to waffle or rabbit – to B.S., talk a lot in papers or in conversations but not say anything; padding.
42. oh crikey – popular phrase, like 'oh golly.'

ACKNOWLEDGEMENT

Grateful thanks are due to all the schools who participated in this study, especially to the headmasters, headmistresses, and teachers who cooperated so fully, and gave up valuable classtime and made many suggestions and comments. Special thanks to Tony Green, and above all thanks to all the children who contributed their jokes and special humour.

The research carried out by the author was done at first at the University of Leeds in partial fulfilment of the Master of Arts degree in the department of Folk Life Studies.